Strategic Writing

Strategic Writing

The Writing Process and Beyond in the Secondary English Classroom

Deborah Dean
Brigham Young University

Castleton State College

Calvin Coolidge Library

National Council of Teachers of English
1111 W. Kenyon Road, Urbana, Illinois 61801-1096

Staff Editor: Bonny Graham

Manuscript Editor: Karen Bojda

Interior Design: Doug Burnett

Cover Design: Pat Mayer

NCTE Stock Number: 47542

Library of Congress Cataloging-in-Publication Data

Dean, Deborah, 1952-
Strategic writing : the writing process and beyond in the secondary English classroom / Deborah Dean.
    p. cm.
Includes bibliographical references and index.
ISBN 0-8141-4754-2 (pbk.)
1. English language—Rhetoric—Study and teaching. 2. Report writing—
    Study and teaching (Higher) I. Title.
PE1404.D3866 2006
808'.0420712—dc22
       2005030338

Contents

Acknowledgments

I need to start my acknowledgments with Susan Stone, Don Forney, and Carl Spears. Sue hired me for my first teaching job, and the three of them mentored me through those first years of teaching. I had good preparation from my university training, but a beginning teacher couldn't have had better examples of what good teaching should be than what they showed me.

Going back into a secondary classroom after a few years' break made me remember how much my students affect me, how much their learning and success matter to me, but mostly, how much they make me grow. I want to thank all my students, from seventh grade through graduate level, even though most will never read this. Each of you, in some way, taught me something and made me rethink what I did as a teacher and writer and was therefore a part of my development. I can't name you all, but I appreciate what you've taught me and what you still teach me as I remember your faces, your struggles, and your triumphs. I especially acknowledge the students whose work is included here. It was a joy to get in contact with some of you years after you were in my class, to find out where you are now (wow!), and to discover your willingness to share what you wrote as junior high or high school students.

I want to thank the Provo High administration and faculty, and Karen Brown in particular, for letting me teach there. The students I taught at PHS had unique needs that refined my thinking and teaching; that experience and those students have been an invaluable addition to my growth as a writing teacher—and they figure prominently in this book.

A special thank-you goes to teachers who have worked with me over the last few years and have tried out some of my ideas in their own classes. (What a lot of confidence you have in someone who is still learning!) A special thanks to the teachers who've shared their results with me for this book: Anna McNeel, Brittney Toone, Cecily Yeager, Cynthia Logsdon, Dawan Coombs, and Julie Larsen.

I appreciate my current colleagues' support during the final stages of this book. Bill Strong's words and encouragement have meant a great deal. Dixie Archibald found references I thought were lost for all time—thank you. Thanks to Chris Crowe, especially, for pushing me (even though I didn't always show appreciation for your using David like that) and for reading drafts and giving me very useful feedback, even when you had plenty of your own work to do.

Thanks also to Kurt Austin, my editor at NCTE. I had questions (plenty of them) and you had answers. What a nice equation.

Finally, none of this would be possible without my family's support. My children's graduation pictures show me standing next to them with student papers in my arms. I attended their band concerts and listened while I read student writing. They let me squeeze work in with their lives. What good kids! And they still ask how the book's going, even if they secretly wish I'd written something with more mystery or thrill.

Most of all, thanks to David, whose belief in me makes all the difference every day.

Introduction: Where We've Been and Where We're Going

Someone asked me about writing this book.

"What's it about?"

"Teaching writing."

"Oh." Then nothing. I could tell what he was thinking: *That sounds boring. Why can't you write something people will want to read—like a murder mystery or something?* After a long pause, he asked, "So how will it be different from what's out there?"

Good question.

My idea of being a teacher of writing has changed (I hope in positive ways) since I began teaching. I've had so many ideas that didn't work the way I thought they would, ideas that others described at conferences or in publications that sounded so effective but didn't accomplish what I wanted to accomplish or didn't work the way they were supposed to. I have felt like a mountain climber, finding handholds and footholds from time to time, slipping a little, climbing little by little. I'm not at the top, but I've found some vistas, some places to rest and contemplate before I climb again. During these reflective times, I've decided on certain principles that guide the next phase of the climb. These are the principles behind the teaching practices that led to this book, what make it different, I guess.

I want to use the writing process as a set of tools instead of the track my course runs on, a way of thinking about what writers do instead of a series of assignments students associate with school writing, a way of thinking that might make school writing valuable to all the writing students might do in a lifetime. But that's what I think all teachers of writing want from a program. How is this book different?

First, it presents process as a strategy. I acknowledge that not all writing needs the whole writing process—certainly some school writing does not. Journals and reader responses don't necessarily require revision or prewriting. Some writing is meant to show that students have done the reading or know the facts. Some writing is meant to promote learning. Does that writing always require the entire process? Because of the way I use the writing process in my classroom, my students should begin to see that elements of the process are actually strategies for improving thinking, expression, and communication, not just requirements for completion of a project.

I know that the opposite idea is out there—I have asked my university students about it. The majority of them tell me that they have "roughed up" drafts just to meet the requirement of multiple drafts, although some admitted to turning in two copies of the same paper and simply labeling one as a "rough draft." Since they received credit—and most of them made good grades—the idea of process was not strategic: It was busy work. So besides using the process as a strategy, I also *talk about it* as a strategy so that my students will see what we do as more than a sequence of "activities."

The writing process encourages more prewriting than earlier writing models and many forms of prewriting: freewriting, webs, cubing, clustering, heuristics. Many times, however, that prewriting simply provides a method of selecting or focusing on a topic. Less often is prewriting used as a way to come to know, to encourage curiosity, to learn to question, or to explore thinking from reading. Often the prewriting strategy doesn't really do what writers need it to do for them; it's just the strategy that the teacher requires. My use of process as a strategy encourages a thoughtful consideration and conscious use of prewriting techniques as strategic tools that encourage inquiry as well as topic selection and focus.

Considering process as strategy, I use writing more frequently to promote learning, not just to show learning. Thus, students question, explore, and develop thinking through a number of avenues prior to producing written texts that will be used to evaluate their thinking and writing. Inquiry matters.

Because I consider the writing process as strategy, my approach is also different in that the assignments are a means to an end, not simply ends in themselves. They are ways to practice strategies and to consider processes and differences in products and how different products change the processes for creating them. Although I expect students to produce quality products with substantive thinking, the emphasis is on strategies and how being strategic can improve our writing processes as well as our products.

Because I want students to practice the strategies, the assignments need to be interesting and unusual. Students won't get practice with strategies if they don't complete the assignments—and many of the students I've taught have been so unsuccessful with more traditional assignments that I lose them before I even begin if I don't do something different. Because I take a strategic approach, though, students are able to transfer the strategies they practice in interesting (they say "different") writing assignments to other, more traditional, writing. I know because I eventually assign a few more traditional assignments and have students apply the strategies to those, just to make sure. To begin, though, I ask them to write in ways that are interesting and different; that's part of the rationale behind some of the more unusual strategy practice ideas in this book.

Additionally, I want assignments to encourage students to write in a variety of genres for a variety of situations, to become sensitive to context as part of the thinking related to a specific writing task. Many times this means making more explicit the connections between reading and writing as students see how texts they read respond to considerations of purpose, audience, and genre—and that's an important part of this book. These connections should help students consider rhetorical choices authors make and how student writers might use similar choices when they compose. That's strategic.

And considering writers' choices requires more class talk, so sometimes classes aren't as quiet as writing classes might normally be. (Many students learn that talking is an effective strategy for them at all stages of the writing process.) Exploring the way writing fits into and impacts on social situations requires discussion, negotiation, and collaboration. To develop sensitivity to the ways texts work in different contexts and to consider their own procedures and processes, students need to explore others' responses to their thinking and writing. And that involves talk.

Since classrooms can't address all the possible writing contexts students will encounter, I want an approach to classroom practice that will create strategic writers who can adapt their writing to a variety of needs and situations. This does not mean I simply get a list of strategies from the back of a book like a vocabulary list and go through them in lessons one by one. To become strategic writers, students need each writing assignment to provide a way to practice strategies for process and strategies for product. (They overlap; in working on a writing task, students can't help working on both.) In the same way that we teach and practice and use reading strategies to improve reading processes and products (comprehension), we can consider assignments as places to use writing strategies. As teachers, we can think of what strategies each assignment calls for and encourage students to think consciously of those strategies and of other circumstances in which those strategies could be effective so that the students become writers who make writerly choices.

All of which leads to the last major difference of this book: that I try to make conscious use of all levels of knowledge: declarative, procedural, and conditional. The declarative explains and directs, while the procedural gives students practice with the strategies. The conditional helps students reflect on their use of strategies, come to know themselves better as writers, and consider how they might extend their strategy use beyond a particular assignment. These levels of knowledge take more time, but they're worth it.

Although I provide some ideas for practicing strategies and using levels of knowledge, this book is really just a starting place. It's not meant to spell out everything a teacher should or could do. I hope it works in the same way as the strategy practices I describe do for students: I hope it gives you a way to work through declarative, procedural, and conditional knowledge about teaching writing so that you can translate the ideas into assignments that work for the individual students and the needs you face in your own classroom. I hope this book invites teachers to engage their students in writing that is interesting and challenging. I hope, finally, that by beginning with this text and its ideas—and extending them in response to individual classrooms' needs—teachers can build a writing program that develops strategic writers, ones who have developed tools that allow them to respond effectively to a wider variety of writing situations than we can possibly address in school: a world of writing.

———

I'd like to add a few comments about reading and using this book. First, about the writing process as I use it: The chapters describe process as inquiry, drafting, and finishing. This is a broad generalization about the writing process that is necessary for organizing a book about it. In reality, as described in Chapter 2, the aspects of the process overlap. And for the sake of the book, drafting incorporates initial writing, what would normally be considered prewriting, as well as writing drafts. I hope this is evident as you work through Chapters 3, 4, and 5.

Next, about the organization of the chapters: Each chapter begins with a personal story related to the subject of the chapter because writing (and teaching!) is personal and because stories are a powerful way to make connections to concepts. I try to make those connections for my students with my own stories and encourage other teachers to do the same. If we talk about ourselves as writers, tell our own writing stories, I hope our students will too. And telling their own stories about writing will, I believe, develop in them a sense that they are writers.

The chapters are organized with the conceptual information first and the practical applications second so that readers can use the book in the way that best suits them: reading concepts only or applications only or in either direction. With each strategy practice, I include declarative, procedural, and conditional knowledge briefs to emphasize one of the key points of the book: that students need to work through all the levels of knowledge to gain from the strategies.

Near the end of each chapter, I include a fully developed lesson plan that gives teaching ideas for all the stages of the writing process and sample student work in response to the lesson. Finally, each chapter concludes with my reflection and places to go for more information on the ideas in the chapter. It's my wish that not only will we help students practice habits of reflection as writers in order to develop conditional knowledge but that as teachers we will also be more reflective about our teaching practices. My reflection, I hope, will spark that in readers. Readers can refer to the additional resources to act upon possible issues raised in those reflections.

1 Becoming Strategic

There is no master list of . . . strategies.
James Collins

*W*hen *I was a young teen, skateboards became the "in" thing for my neighborhood. I watched the friends who got the first ones, watched them race down the hills of the subdivision shrieking and laughing, and I wanted that freedom, that speed, that wind in my face. I saved up enough money and bought myself one—chartreuse green.*

The first time I tried to ride my skateboard, I crashed and scraped my knees and feet. Back then we rode barefoot to get a grip on the board—this was, after all, the olden days when skateboards first came out and weren't so fancy as they are today. No helmets or knee pads. No trick boards. The idea was to get a good long ride.

I tried again and again, without success. I always crashed. My friends told me better places to stand on the board and how to shift my weight. I tried their suggestions and a few of the strategies I had thought up at night, just before sleep, as I was thinking about trying again the next day. Eventually, I was able to ride down the hill, all the way, without crashing. It was just what I'd imagined (except for the serious vibrations caused by metal wheels on rough pavement). It was speed and wind and freedom—and it only took a week or so and a bunch of skin and blood to figure it out. It was wonderful!

Most of us are strategic beings by nature. When we want something enough, we find ways to accomplish our goal. What we do in the process is consider, try, and discard ideas—strategies—until we find what brings success. Current publications about reading are replete with examples of reading strategies, practices that help readers improve their literacy skills by emulating the things that better readers do as they read. Such an approach to reading builds on the idea of our being strategic, especially with complex processes, of making strategies conscious tools to be used when they are suitable. When I read articles about being a strategic reader, I substitute the word *writing* for *reading,* and the ideas still fit. The same rationale for being a strategic reader applies to being a strategic writer.

Strategies are tools. As with reading strategies, writing strategies are practices that experienced writers use to accomplish their varying purposes in writing. One of the primary strategies teachers today have at their fingertips is the writing process—but it isn't often used strategically.

Some of us probably still remember the really old days: days when teachers gave a writing assignment during Monday's class—the weekly theme—and we wrote it at home, alone, and turned it in on Friday. We wrote by hand, in ink, and recopied when we recognized mistakes. The papers were returned, generally on Monday, with our grade indicated by a red letter on the top. Sometimes we received two grades, content over mechanics, but the scores were generally unaccompanied by any comments (although the paper may have had errors in punctuation, spelling, or grammar corrected), and we looked at the grade and then put the paper away as we listened to the teacher make a few comments and give us the current week's topic. We were on a treadmill. What happened between Monday and Friday was up to us, as long as a clean, error-free paper was turned in at the end of the week. It seems now like an old black-and-white movie.

The Writing Process Movement

Research into writing helped change that picture. Composition scholars such as Janet Emig and Donald Graves, looking at what writers do as they write, began to note that writing was a recursive process, that most writers went through a number of stages as they wrote, and that these stages could be generically labeled to help beginners adopt a process that should enable them to write more effectively, more like experienced writers. In the writing process, as it came to be known, these stages were identified generally as prewriting, drafting, and revising. Within each of these general stages were a number of subprocesses (Flower and Hayes identified several in their research), but the main idea was that following this general process would improve writing. Peter Elbow's *Writing without Teachers* influenced a generation of teachers by promoting this perspective. From this beginning, the concept of writing as process took on a number of other features and aspects in classrooms across the country, carrying with it all sorts of assumptions and political issues.

The writing process movement focused attention on a number of concerns in positive ways. First, attention to process encouraged teachers to spend time on different aspects of that process, particularly prewriting. Now, before beginning to write, students brainstormed, used heuristics, created webs, and followed a number of other patterns designed to help them select, focus, and develop topics. Revision also received some attention from the writing process movement; teachers now had students help each other by making suggestions for improvement in their writing before they handed it in.

Another consequence of focusing on the process was that students, with their individual processes and ideas, gained importance and prominence. More emphasis was placed on writing for and about self, and more assignments linked student writing to student experience. This attention to students, in turn, shifted emphasis to different elements of writing. Although spelling, grammar, and punctuation might be important (at some later stage), they didn't matter so much as ideas and self-exploration. Even more important was voice. The process was about the individual—and the individual was represented best by voice and unique ideas.

Because attention focused on writers as real people with individual voices, more assignments addressed audiences outside of the teacher as a way to encourage authentic writing. Peers became one audience, partly through increased use of peer review. More opportunities for "publishing" were also considered as students wrote for school and class publications as well as for audiences in the community.

Eventually, though, deficiencies in the way this movement translated into practice became apparent. Despite the original intent that process be recursive, in the classroom, process began to look a lot like the old black-and-white movie, only with more detail: Monday was prewriting, Tuesday was drafting, Wednesday was revision, Thursday was editing, and Friday was publishing. A new pattern had taken the place of the old—and, in some ways, it isn't surprising. What happens to the individual writing process when it goes to school? It generally gets put into a pattern that fits school more than the individual.

In many classrooms, observers noted that the process began to take the place of a quality product; papers that showed evidence of all the steps of the process were automatically given top grades. (After all, the premise was that process would improve writing, so it must follow that papers following the process were better.) Talk of quality, of what makes effective or ineffective writing, was absent from many classrooms (Baines et al.).

Additionally, for many teachers, the content of writing was primarily personal experience. With younger students, that meant that substantive writing was sometimes significantly lacking because experience was limited. Although the writing process movement encouraged the implementation of more prewriting strategies, inquiry was really a matter of exploring what an individual already knew, not learning *about* something new. More and more writing became self-revelation, with some students even imagining life experiences to establish the effect they felt was the desired product in such classes (DeJoy).

Finally, the way many secondary teachers used the writing process in the classroom seemed to neglect the social component of writing, despite peer revision. More current research has investigated the complex social aspects of writing neglected by an emphasis on the individual: that writing, like oral language, is discourse, a communicative act that must consider the writer and the audience as well as the circumstances for the discourse. (A look at Carolyn Miller's writings, along with those of Bill Cope and Mary Kalantzis and of Aviva Freedman and Peter Medway, would be a good start to understanding the social perspective of composing.) But many classrooms focused so much on the individual aspect of the process that the social aspect was largely ignored. Process was a sequence of activities, and as I had my students walk through that process, it just seemed longer than the old way. I caught myself wondering if the process shouldn't change writing in some elemental way, not just stretch out the same old thing. Shouldn't the writing process be a strategy?

Recently a college student came up to me after a presentation and asked why his teachers had never presented the idea of the writing process as strategy: "All I thought was that I had to do a draft before the final, but it was just what they said to do. No one ever explained that there was a reason for doing the other things teachers asked us to do."

I wondered if some of my students might think the same thing: Despite my efforts to use process as a strategy, might they see it only as a sequence of activities leading to a product that was a dead end? I replied that teachers might have actually tried to teach this but maybe just didn't get the message across. I hope that's the case, at least. I hope it's not that we've missed the point of a writing process.

Developing Strategies

What I *think* the process should be in classrooms is a process of using strategies to accomplish a goal. And in order to be strategic, students need to stop thinking of prewriting, drafting, revising, and editing as products the teacher requires, as products they create after the paper is done in some cases—just to get the points the teacher would give for the "process." Instead, students need to be encouraged to think of the process as strategic. According to James Collins, "thinking strategically about writing means taking deliberate control over writing skills and processes" (vii). Control is a key concept to being strategic, and it implies conscious knowledge and use of tools throughout the writing process and from one written product to another.

When I first begin to talk to my students about being strategic writers, I ask them what writing strategies they already have in place. Their responses show, first, an unclear idea of what writing strategies are and, second, a limited repertoire. "I work hard," writes one student, and I wonder if he could learn to work smarter with strategies. "Rhyming," writes another. As a strategy? "I write about what I'm interested in," writes a third. When I prompt them, I have some say they use spell-checkers or ask their parents or friends to read their papers. That is about the extent of what I can draw from them, even with prompting. I am sure that students probably have more strategies in place than this; however, since conscious application is key to control of the tools for writing effectively, not knowing what strategies they already have means they have little or no control over actually using such strategies successfully.

Levels of knowledge are an important aspect of being strategic, of gaining control over writing. Declarative knowledge is knowledge *about* something. Knowing the way my friends stood on their skateboards as they shot down the hill or knowing that sentences have subjects and predicates or that paragraphs usually focus on one central idea—these are declarative. Procedural knowledge is knowledge of *how to do* something. Knowing how to stand on the board myself and shift my weight, or knowing how to start a sentence with a capital letter and end with punctuation and how to summarize the ideas of a paragraph into a topic sentence are procedural. And conditional knowledge is knowledge about *when:* knowing when to shift my weight to avoid potholes or turn a corner, or knowing when to use a fragment for effect and when it's best not to do so or when to put the topic sentence at the beginning of a paragraph and when to put it later.

Strategic teachers know the difference among these three kinds of knowledge—and they know that to help students become strategic, they have to work at all levels. Hillocks's research (*Ways*) suggests that many teachers spend the most time at the declarative level, talking to students about topic sentences and what constitutes an effective thesis, for example. Even though almost all teachers evaluate students on the products they hand in as a result of procedural knowledge, few spend time at the procedural level letting students write and evaluate the effectiveness of different kinds of topic sentences and thesis statements, practicing until they develop a sense of these conventions (Hillocks,

Ways 28). And fewer still move into the conditional knowledge level of having students notice the effect of paragraphs that have implied topic sentences or thesis statements delayed until the middle or the end of an essay.

As Collins summarizes the types of knowledge, "declarative knowledge gives us information, procedural knowledge gives us strategies for using information to accomplish objectives, and conditional knowledge gives us deliberate intention and design in using strategies" (53). Moving students from declarative into procedural and conditional knowing provides them control as writers, and it is strategic. And it requires instruction and practice and reflection; as Nokes and Dole note, "because strategy use is often demanding, students are not likely to engage in a strategy unless they are convinced that it will help them succeed" (167). It's my job as the teacher to convince them—and I can only do that by moving beyond declarative knowledge and into procedural and conditional knowledge.

Strategic instruction, then, cannot be about rules or about teachers talking to students or even about students writing on their own. It is much more about teachers' thinking about students and their writing needs, about allowing time for students to learn and try strategies— ones teachers hope will be beneficial and ones students discover individually with teachers' help—and about reflecting on those strategies either in talk or in writing. Good strategic teaching is more about possibilities and practice and thoughtfulness than it is about a list of activities or teacher talk.

Jim Burke, in his summary of effective literacy instruction, notes that "children do not develop composing strategies from red ink corrections (*nor from just writing*)" (199, emphasis added). We've all heard the first part of his statement; few have considered the second: Just doing something doesn't automatically make us better at it, especially if we do whatever it is under duress or unwillingly or without concern for effectiveness, the way too many students approach writing. I just think of my own children when it's their turn to do the dishes or when they are told to clean their rooms. Though they may have done both chores many times, simple repetition doesn't always make them better at either of them. Repetition combined with instruction or direction or modeling or scaffolding can help, though. And that's what teaching strategic writing should encourage—not just assigning writing but practicing it with strategies and then considering the effectiveness of those strategies. It means teaching writing rather than simply causing it.

To teach strategic writing, teachers need to think strategically. That means being reflective, considering what outcomes teachers want from each activity and how to make those outcomes meaningful in students' lives beyond the immediate assignment. In other words, *using* strategies isn't enough. Teachers have to think of them, and teach students to think of them, as strategies, as tools that can help them accomplish their goals as writers. Activities fill time, and they give us part of what we need to do to accomplish a task. These same activities can become strategies with a different perspective, with a new way of handling them.

So being strategic with regard to process doesn't necessarily mean stopping what we've done before. Instead, it means being more thoughtful about what we've done before and taking a different perspective on it. The processes that help us narrow or focus a topic or come up with a question we want to research—these must be considered as strategies, as tools. What does brainstorming really do for a writer? When might it be an effective tool? When might another tool be a better strategy to accomplish the writer's goals? These are questions both teachers and students need to ask themselves in order to become strategic about process.

The number of strategies has no bounds; it is limited only by what works. I know publishing writers who constantly find new strategies for new problems that arise in new writing situations. If they don't currently have a strategy to solve the writing problem facing them, they talk to other writers or think about the problem or play around with possible strategies until they find what helps them resolve the problem. That is being strategic. That is the perspective we need to teach our students. Certainly we need to teach them some strategies, some specific ways to solve challenges in writing, but we also need to teach them to become strategic themselves by looking for strategic solutions to writing problems and by being flexible in using different strategies to accomplish different writing goals.

Different Strategies

As I've considered my students and their needs, trying to develop ways to look at strategies consciously with them, I've thought that strategies exist for both process and product, both for accomplishing the writing task and for succeeding at the end product. At the same time, I don't believe that the categories are discrete; instead, they are a convenient categorization for talking about what writers do and can do to improve their writing. For the sake of this book and ease of discussion, I have divided strategies into three areas that roughly correspond to the writing process: inquiry, drafting, and product.

Most writing uses a combination of these strategies. So when I am preparing to teach a writing assignment, I stop in my planning and make myself a list. What strategies can I have students practice for each stage of this assignment that will help them both to be successful with this assignment and to practice strategies for other writing? I consider what students need to know or know how to do with inquiry, drafting, and product to be successful—and then I consider strategies they can practice to address each of those needs. So, for example, with the Writing about a Person assignment I describe at the end of Chapter 6, I know that students will need to understand the model before doing research so that during research they will not waste time gathering information that wouldn't be useful. Because of this consideration, I planned a reading strategy with models. I also know that students will need to keep track of the information they find during research, so I planned a note-taking strategy for them to use. I work through each assignment this way, making a list of the specific needs and the strategies that will address them—and then I have my teaching plan of strategies.

Strategies for Inquiry

In Chapter 2, I make a longer case for the need for inquiry in teaching writing to students, but as an introduction to the idea here, I consider what George Hillocks notes about inquiry: "If thoughtful inquiry does not lie at the heart of writing, then our students become little more than amanuenses. They cannot be writers unless they are first thinkers" (*Teaching* 214). Inquiry strategies are those that help students find, focus, *and* develop ideas. They help students think about their topics. They include strategies that help students generate possible topics through brainstorming or remember ideas through freewriting. They might include strategies that help students narrow a topic, such as questioning, or ones that help them explore a topic, such as webbing. Certainly inquiry strategies should include all kinds of ways to come to know more, as I describe in Chapter 2. The Collage Write described in the application section of this chapter is one strategy I have students practice as a way to generate ideas through inquiry.

Strategies for Drafting

There is not one correct way to write. There is not one product that will receive an A in every writing situation a student will face in school or in life—although I have had a teacher tell me he tried that in college, turning in the same paper over and over again. He was disappointed that it didn't get an A in subsequent uses. I was disappointed that he thought it would or could. His story suggests a mind-set, a belief in one right way to write and therefore in one right way to teach writing. A strategic perspective recognizes that texts respond to contexts, to audiences, to purposes.

Because, as Richard Larson notes and as many teachers can attest, "writers by and large do not know enough about how texts work" ("Revision" 99), student writers need to learn strategies for understanding how texts work and strategies that help them replicate aspects of texts in different contexts. Students need strategies for reading texts, contexts, audiences, and purposes. These strategies I call strategies for drafting, and they help students adapt as writers, a key aim of teaching writing. Strategies for drafting include all aspects of writing between inquiry and revision: planning, reading sample texts to get ideas for drafting, thinking, organizing—*and* putting ideas on paper.

In an attempt to get students thinking about their own drafting strategies, I pose a question to my preservice teachers about what they do when they face writing in a genre with which they are unfamiliar. One student, Julie, responded with this story: She'd had a summer job at a local business. The owner of the business asked her to write letters to overdue accounts to endeavor to get payment from them. She recalled that she thought about the task for a while, even attempting to write some letters. Finally, aware that her attempts might not be effective, she asked if the office had copies of such types of letters from the past. Someone found several. Julie read them, noting their features—the language, the tone, the structure—and then was able to successfully write her own letters. When I share Julie's story, I ask if others have had similar experiences. Many have. I explain that they have developed drafting strategies, an ability to understand from models how text types work in different contexts. They also have developed the ability to imitate what they discover through reading multiple texts.

Both the ability to discover textual characteristics and the ability to imitate them are drafting strategies. In a world that can ask our students to write more types of text than we could possibly teach them in school, they are better served by being taught adaptive strategies than by learning the few specific genres we have time to teach. To that end, then, we are more likely to achieve success if we engage students in writing that interests them, writing that they will participate in, and writing a variety of genres, so that they can practice inquiry, drafting, and product strategies that will give them more options. The practice

Annotating Texts in the application section of this chapter is one strategy for helping students learn to read a text like a writer, looking for what it does so they can imitate it if they need to. Chapters 3, 4, and 5 develop drafting strategies further.

Strategies for Product

Strategies for product help students revise and clean up writing to address concerns about audience. These strategies include understanding revision for global concerns by learning ways to re-see a text. They also include effective use of peer evaluations and understanding revision for local concerns, including editing texts in readiness for publication. These strategies help students understand the difference between revising and editing. Strategies for product can include anything that helps students develop sensitivity to text so that they can use the choices more experienced writers use to serve their own purposes as writers. Chapter 6 explains more strategies for product. In the application section of this chapter I describe an ongoing strategy practice, Writer's Logs, designed to help raise students' awareness of choices that they as writers can consider during revision.

Reflection

For writing-process activities to become strategic, students—like teachers—have to develop a habit of mind. They need to be pushed a little to think about what they do *as* strategies, to develop conditional knowledge. Mostly students are in the habit of just doing what the teacher says because he or she says it or because their grades will reflect it if they don't. Not only to make the strategies conscious but also to try to move them from procedural knowledge to conditional knowledge, I ask students to reflect.

As Carl Nagin notes in *Because Writing Matters,* "to develop as writers, students also need the opportunity to articulate their own awareness and understanding of their processes in learning to write. Research has shown the importance of such metacognitive thinking in becoming a better writer" (82). So moving strategies from declarative into procedural knowledge, moving from explaining to practicing, although valuable, isn't enough to help students improve in the long term. They also need to have conditional knowledge so that they self-regulate—control!—their own processes as they write. And reflection is the key difference in a strategic approach because it causes students to see assignments as strategy practices, not ends in themselves, and the writing process as adaptive, not simply as a sequence of assignments completed and forgotten.

Kathleen Yancey makes the connection between competence and reflection when she recognizes reflection as "growth of consciousness" and cites Sharon Pianko: "The ability to reflect on what is being written seems to be the essence of the difference between able and not so able writers from their initial writing experience onward" (4). I want my students to become able writers, so reflection is a necessity. But this way of thinking has to be learned; students don't do it without help and practice. As John Dewey notes: "While we cannot learn or be taught to think, we do have to learn how to think well, especially how to acquire the general habit of reflecting" (34). This is what I hope my repeated use of reflective questioning helps students develop. It's a slow process, though, and sometimes it's more successful than at other times.

Because I want my students to develop reflective habits—and because it isn't easy for some students to do without repeated practice—they write reflections all through the class. Sometimes I have students reflect in a letter in their portfolios, using questions Kathleen Yancey suggests, about how they anticipate that I, as their teacher, will read their papers. What will I think works, and what I will wonder about? Do they agree with my anticipated reactions? What are they proud of? What follows is part of Saramarie's letter in response to these prompts that accompanied her reversal paper (an assignment described in Chapter 4) on what it's really like to jump off a moving train.

> I really like this paper because it finally got my experience down on paper. I have been telling the story of my train jumping for a year now, and so it was fun to write it down. I am also pleased with the supporting material I included. I do worry that maybe my story is still a little bit too long. I tried to condense it in places, but it still takes a while to get to the action. It was also kind of fun to use some of the sentence constructions we learned in class.
>
> I hope you will laugh at my paper and like it. You may think that I needed to present more of a common view, and have more of an introduction, but I have to say that I like it how it is.

Although these letters help students reflect on their processes and my reading, at other times when a writing assignment is turned in, I have students respond in class to shorter reflective questions unique to the writing we've just completed and the particular strategies we practiced. The questions are adaptations of the following general patterns:

1. What strategies did you use on this writing assignment that worked well for you? Consider strategies of inquiry, drafting, and product in your answer.

2. Why do you think they worked well? In other words, what did each strategy do for you that improved your ability to write or your writing?

3. Under what conditions might you use these strategies again?

In reflecting on an assignment that uses a collage as a strategy for developing an idea, described in the application section of this chapter, Larry responded to these questions this way: "The collage really absorbed me. Once I got out of that mindset, I was surprised to see what I thought about writing. The collage was also a great outline for the writing." In reflecting on the same assignment, Sid wrote this: "It made it [writing] a little easier. I was able to think a little more about it since I had to find pictures describing how I felt. If I see a picture of what I'm feeling, I can better understand it and write about that subject easier than if I was just given a subject." These reflections help the students consider how a strategy helps them so that they are more likely to use it when it is needed in the future.

At the end of each quarter, after students have written short reflections for all but their informal writing, I ask students for a longer reflective piece. I give a prompt like the following:

Reflective Writing for First Quarter

- Using a metaphor to develop an idea
- Using art to generate ideas
- Using drawing to clarify or organize ideas
- Reading a product through says-does [described in Chapter 3] to get ideas for content or organization
- Using questioning to develop ideas
- Questioning purpose, tone, and audience in a model to get ideas for voice, content, or organization
- Talking to develop an idea
- Answering questions to develop an idea
- Brainstorming to get an idea
- Using the six traits [described in Chapter 3] to get ideas for inquiry, drafting, or product
- Researching to develop content

- Imitating a model's voice and word choice
- Counting words in sentences to revise for sentence fluency
- Using sentence types to establish a tone
- Using peer reviewers to get ideas for revision
- Drafting in class
- Developing vocabulary skills
- Practicing sentence-level skills: combining, moving, adding

The list above contains many of the strategies we have practiced this quarter. You may be able to add some that I have not included or that you discovered on your own. (That would be wonderful!) As we have discussed, strategies are like tools. You need certain ones for different jobs—and you need to have some in your toolbox that you don't use often but that are helpful for those less frequent jobs you have to do.

For this reflective writing, consider which strategies you have found most helpful and why. Consider conditions under which you might use those strategies in future writing situations. Be thoughtful, clear, and thorough. I will evaluate this writing on the qualities just mentioned. You can use this paper to plan, to make marks or notes, for whatever you need. When you are finished, attach this paper to the back of your writing and hand it in.

With one class, a writing remediation course for students needing to make up credit or prepare to retake the state writing test, when I explained the expectations for this in-class writing, Larry, a student who had cooperated willingly all quarter with the shorter reflective pieces, snorted.

"What was that?" I asked, inquiring about the snort.

"This is just busy work," he replied.

I was shocked. We had written reflectively before this, and now I was getting this reaction? I didn't know where it came from, but I took a few minutes to remind him and the rest of the class that we needed to *think about* the strategies as well as use them in order to make them useful tools. The incident reminds me that it's not an easy task to push students to consider what they do, what works, and why. Still, there are more often some bright spots. Here is what Isac wrote, who at the beginning of the quarter had listed "rhyming" as his only strategy:

Using Art to Generate Ideas: This strategy helped because when
I look at art or pictures in newspapers and magazines, it gets me

thinking why this person took the picture. What was the person or animal thinking in the picture? That is two papers right there. In the future I could see myself using this strategy a lot. I could use this strategy for any type of paper, I think. By looking at pictures, I can think a whole lot better because I ask myself questions and eventually I want some answers.

Using a Model to Develop Ideas. This strategy is my personal favorite. I think there is no better way to write a paper. If you read a paper before you start yours, not only does it have you thinking of topics that you want to write about but in the paper it shows you several different ways to construct that paper. I think in the future I will not write another paper unless I get to see a model of every paper I have to write.

At the end of another quarter with different strategies practiced, Larry (the snorter) wrote the following in his reflection:

Interviewing for topic ideas is a brilliant strategy. Interviewing people gives me as a writer a better understanding of my audience. . . . Asking potential readers what they think of ideas can redirect writing. As I found in my name write, asking those with a similar background (in this case, same name) changed my direction from factual to personal. Interviewing also helps determine reader's knowledge, and questions about the subject. This proved valuable in my brochure writing. Being a topic I enjoyed, I could've gone on any of a thousand tangents. Knowing what was wanted helped me direct my knowledge.

Reflection can work. If we work at it and have our students work through declarative and procedural aspects of strategies, the conditional aspect—reflection—can help them become strategic writers and gain control over their writing.

Applications

Strategy Practice: Collage Write

Declarative knowledge: We can expand ideas for writing through a variety of strategies, including metaphorical thinking.
Procedural knowledge: First write what you already know or think about the topic; then find pictures that connect to your idea. Finally, use the visual metaphors to expand your thinking in your writing.
Conditional knowledge: Under what other conditions could visual images create metaphors that might help me expand my thinking or take a new perspective? In what other writing situations would this help me? How might I use this strategy without creating the collage?

Early in my writing course, I ask students to write in response to this prompt: "To me, writing is . . ." They usually write for about three minutes at most and then stop. I want to introduce them to the concept of metaphor as a writing strategy, but they are stumped by the idea. They say writing is boring or hard. I press them to consider things that writing is like, but they don't produce much more writing. So I pull out my box of magazines and ask students to make a collage of pictures that represent what writing is to them. We spend some time in class on two separate days. When the collage is done, I give them an assignment: Using the collage, finish the statement "To me, writing is . . ." I ask them to develop the ideas from the collage, not simply list them, as a way to expand and explain their ideas. All of them can write now—and write for more than a page about what writing is to them. Here is part of what Jack wrote in response to the prompt after he'd completed the collage:

> Writing to me is like the picture I chose of a football player carrying a football, because you can only go so far before you get stopped or make a touchdown. Writing is like carrying the ball and getting knocked down because when you are starting to write and you get writer's cramp or you just can't find the right word for how you're trying to explain something, it's frustrating, just like getting stuffed when you have the ball. Writing can also feel like making a touchdown. For example, when you have a good idea, you just keep on writing and going without stopping until you finish your story, or make the touchdown.

In the end-of-the-quarter reflection on strategies, eight weeks after the previous assignment, Jack wrote this:

> Using art to generate ideas was a good strategy I learned this term because I am a visual learner. It helps me see the idea instead of just sitting there and thinking about it. It was really easy for me to generate ideas on the assignment we did on "What Writing is to Me." I found myself using that strategy on another assignment I had in my other English class. It works very well for me.

Metaphors are a way to help extend thinking, but students sometimes find them challenging to create. Given our visual culture, the use of images to stimulate metaphorical thinking can be a helpful strategy for generating ideas on many topics, and it makes use of Howard Gardner's theory of multiple intelligences. As Gardner notes, students "learn, remember, perform, and understand in different ways" (11).

Strategy Practice: Annotating Texts

> *Declarative knowledge:* Texts function in unique ways that address their audiences, purposes, and contexts. We can identify the ways texts do that and consider them as options for our own writing.
>
> *Procedural knowledge:* Use questioning and note taking to analyze how a text works. Choose and imitate aspects to meet your own writing needs.
>
> *Conditional knowledge:* How might the questions we ask texts need to change to fit our needs or the various aspects of different texts? When would annotating a text be helpful to me as a writer?

In several occasional papers my class had written (an idea I borrowed from Bill Martin that helped my students think about writing as communicating with a peer audience), students raised issues related to current entertainment. Given their interest, I thought they might make good arguments about the effect of entertainment on society. I used this annotating strategy to help them discover options for drafting their arguments. After inquiry strategies—reading to develop lists of evidence and actively discussing ideas both pro and con—students are ready to begin planning a draft. First, though, I have students read a couple of short argument papers, which we discuss and annotate together. I pose questions such as the following:

1. Where is the author's position statement? Underline it. Write it in your own words in the margin.

2. Where are his or her reasons? Highlight them and number them. In the margin, make a note about what kind of evidence the writer uses to support each reason.

3. How does he or she arrange those reasons (if you can see a kind of logic to the arrangement)? Write a sentence or two at the bottom of the page about the rationale you think the writer uses to choose and arrange the reasons.

4. Where does the author consider alternative views or opposing perspectives? Put a star by these, and write a sentence about the effectiveness (or not!) of the placement.

When students begin drafting, they have a couple of models of arguments to use as guides to help them arrange their own ideas for an argument instead of relying on what I call the default strategy of a five-paragraph form. Most students prefer the options of models they have annotated—and they have learned a strategy for helping them examine other texts for options they can use during drafting. In fact, later in the course, as students were beginning drafting in class (a practice I insist upon to get them started), Isac was just sitting for a long time. I approached him and asked him if there was a problem.

"Should I write this as a five-paragraph essay or what?" he asked. His problem wasn't ideas but structure.

I replied that a five-paragraph essay was an option—what in class I had called a default strategy, one to use if you have no other viable options—but I reminded him that he might have some models in his folder that could also suggest possible organizational strategies to him. After a moment of thought, he asked, "The one about the golfer?"

"Sure, that's one." He dug around in his backpack (not in his folder where it should have been), pulled out a wrinkled handout annotated from class, and smoothed it out on his desk. After a few moments, he started to write. He had clear options now.

Strategy Practice: Writer's Log

> *Declarative knowledge:* We can build a sense of how to polish writing effectively by paying attention to what good writers do with language when they write.
>
> *Procedural knowledge:* Pay attention to effective sentences and passages. Analyze what a writer does and what the effect is. Consider how you might use the construction in your own writing to meet your own needs as a writer.
>
> *Conditional knowledge:* When I write, which one of the constructions that I've noticed might help me? How can I use the sense I am gaining of sentences to help me in my own writing? How has this log helped me as a writer?

The log is independent writing, which means students do it mostly outside of class. About every three weeks, they turn in fifteen entries from about ten pages of reading. When I introduce the log on the second day of class, most students laugh because it sounds like such a small amount of reading for an English class. Even after we do the first few logs in class, they still look at each other as though they're getting away with something and I haven't figured it out yet. After they've worked the first complete log, though, they don't laugh anymore. When I reminded one class that they had thought the assignment length was funny, one student responded, "It isn't the number of pages. It's the thinking you have to do. It's hard work."

I give them the following model, and, as I mentioned, we practice in class to get started.

Writing logs: You should read about ten (10) pages every three weeks from any source or combination of sources you want that are appropriate to respond to in school. The log is not about content, so you shouldn't write about what the reading *says*. Instead, you should write about the writing itself.

Directions: For each page you read, make up to two entries in your log, each one noting something specific the writer has done, why it works (or doesn't), and when you might want to use (or avoid) the same technique. If you want to make a copy of the page of text instead of copying the sentence, you can do that and attach it to your log with the examples marked. (I'll show you an example of this in class.) Otherwise, a log entry should look like this:

> *Source:* book, *Life the Movie,* by Neal Gabler, page 18
>
> *Passage:* "Entertainment—movies, rock music, pulp novels, comic books, television, computer games—sinks its talons into us and pulls us in, holding us captive, taking us deeper into the work itself and deeper into ourselves, or at least into our own emotions and senses, before releasing us."
>
> *What works:* I like the part inside the dashes, how Gabler takes a broad word, "entertainment," and then inside the dashes lists a whole bunch of forms of entertainment, showing specific examples of what he means. It lets me know as a reader exactly what he means by the term—and I like how it sounds like a real person talking, taking a little side trip in the middle of a sentence.
>
> *Using it:* When I have a word that I might want people to know more about, I could put a list of examples inside dashes right after the word. I would just have to make sure they are all more specific examples.

Here is one log entry from Justine:

> *Source:* "The Ball" article from *Sports Illustrated* (we read in class) [Smith]
>
> *Passage:* "It looks like such a simple thing, the ball in the metal box."

What works: Holding back the subject that you're talking about calls attention to something before you say what it is.

Using it: I would use this when I am trying to get the audience's attention before I say what my main subject is.

By completing the log entries, students are building skills in reading texts from a different perspective: They are learning to think like writers. They are building independent product strategies.

Lesson Plan: Introducing Strategic Writing

Objective: Students will understand what it means to be strategic about writing.

1. Since the idea of being strategic in writing is usually a new one to my students, I introduce it first through shared experiences. Puzzles or games that ask students to find a way to complete a task more quickly or effectively are ways to provide this shared experience. One activity I use involves a square divided into thirty-six smaller squares (see Figure 1.1). I hand this out to students and ask them to count the total number of squares in the figure. After a few minutes, students say they have it figured out, and I ask them for that number. What they answer isn't as important as how they figure it.

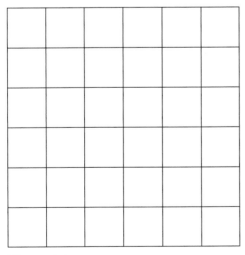

Figure 1.1

The first time I tried to count the squares, I drew around each square as I saw it. It took forever, and I still missed four. My husband used a different strategy and came up with a different number. We were both convinced we were right. Even if we had come up with the correct answer, though, my daughter had a better strategy, and her answer was both correct and fast. She simply counted the number of squares on each side of the figure and then squared that number and every number below it down to one. Thus, a square with six smaller squares on each side would add up to $36 + 25 + 16 + 9 + 4 + 1 = 91$ squares. The point, I tell students, is that I could (perhaps!) get the right answer any number of ways—the way I was figuring it or the way my husband figured it— but the way my daughter did it accomplished the task more accurately *and* quickly. I follow this activity with a discussion of tools: tools for building, for cooking, for gardening, for playing golf. We have a wide selection of tools to help us accomplish whatever task we need to accomplish. Strategies for writing are like tools to do other jobs. My daughter's strategy was a tool to help her accomplish her task more efficiently.

2. Next I ask students to consider ways they use strategies in their lives. They can give me many examples. The way they drive home is strategic because they consider traffic, stop signs, and other factors, including the shortest distance (although that isn't always the way they get home, because of other factors). They use strategies in all kinds of games and sports. They use strategies to get out of chores at home, to figure out the best way to get their math homework done in German class without the teacher's catching on, to figure the best way to convince their dad to let them take his car to the dance. Collins notes that even copying is a strategy many students use as a default (116). When they don't know how to do something one way or don't have the time or inclination to do it that way, they find another, one they think will give them success.

Some of my junior high students use a default strategy when they don't know how to conclude a piece of writing: They just write "The End." In much the same way, when I'm hanging a picture, if I can't find the hammer, I might use any weighty instrument (such as the bottom of a saucepan) to pound in the nail. These actions are strategies—not always effective ones, but strategies nonetheless. The point I try to get across to students is to consider themselves as strategy users already, so that they can make the connection with strategies for writing. And I want them to think of how using productive strategies rather than less effective ones matters, too.

3. After students understand the concept of a strategy, I apply the idea to writing. I use a short clip from the film *Finding Forrester* as one way to do this. In this scene, Jamal is typing in Forrester's apartment as Forrester poses a question about starting sentences with the word *and*. Jamal responds with a series of reasons, all beginning with *and*, describing the conditions under which it would be appropriate to begin a sentence with a conjunction—and when not to. To me, his response reflects strategic thinking as it applies to writing, and this is what I want students to see.

I use this clip to have students begin thinking about writing as strategic, about using aspects of writing to accomplish a goal and considering audience and context and how these affect a writer's choices when he or she writes. That is key: for students to begin to see strategies as tools and as options they have at their disposal. They don't have to use every one every time they write, but they should regard them as a tool box, a set of golf clubs, a whole palette of paint colors. Whatever the metaphor, students need to see that strategies in writing are a collection that they can draw from to use in different ways and in different situations.

4. It is at this point that I pose the question I discussed early in this chapter, asking students to write what strategies they already have available to them. As I mentioned earlier, some students are able to think of more strategies than others. I ask them what they do when they have to write something for a school assignment. Many write that they wait until they can't wait any longer and then just throw something on paper. I ask them if this is a successful strategy for them. As I can expect, most tell me it is not. "Why do you keep using it?" I ask. They tell me they don't know another way—or don't care to use options that are available, such as starting earlier. At this point, students are usually ready to consider the ways that learning and practicing strategies might be a benefit to them. For their reflection practice, I ask them to freewrite about what they see as the potential for using strategies to write. It is a good place to start, and just where I want them to be.

———

10/31: Sometimes I wonder if what I'm trying to do really matters to my students—are they becoming more strategic as writers? Or am I just doing the same things as all the teachers who've come before me? Today, it seemed as though maybe something is getting through. We were reading a student sample of the reversal essay they are working on. As we read, Jack said, "That's a good strategy." I asked him what he was referring to. "This part, here. Where he asks two questions and then goes on to answer them. That's a good strategy because it made me want to know the answer, too, so I kept reading. I'm going to try that." Then he went back to his reading as though nothing momentous had happened. For me, though, it was a big deal. He was thinking about writing as strategy, about options writers use as strategies to create effects—and he was doing it when I wasn't even asking him to do it!

On the other hand, Alec is still not doing anything. The other day, during in-class writing, he was drawing a cartoon figure. I asked him what he was working on. He said it was a strategy. I asked him how it helped him write more effectively, and he said it was his writing mascot. "See? I put it under the paper I'm writing on and it inspires me." Sure. He was using the idea of strategy to avoid doing any writing! Using my own tool against me—and against himself, since he never wrote anything that day. What can I do to make a difference, to make more of a difference to these students who don't write and who don't want to write? How can I help them see strategies as ways to accomplish goals when they don't even set writing goals?

Additional Resources

Collins, James L. *Strategies for Struggling Writers.* New York: Guilford Press, 1998.

Hillocks, George, Jr. *Teaching Writing as Reflective Practice.* New York: Teacher's College Press, 1995.

Nagin, Carl, and National Writing Project. *Because Writing Matters: Improving Student Writing in Our Schools.* San Francisco: Jossey-Bass, 2003.

Nokes, Jeffery D., and Janice A. Dole. "Helping Adolescent Readers through Explicit Strategy Instruction." *Adolescent Literacy Research and Practice.* Ed. Tamara L. Jetton and Janice A. Dole. New York: Guilford Press, 2004. 162–82.

Yancey, Kathleen Blake. *Reflection in the Writing Classroom.* Logan: Utah State UP, 1998.

2 Strategies for Inquiry

I am not a genius. I am just passionately curious.
Albert Einstein

My maternal grandmother was only thirty-eight years old when I was born—and apparently that was too young in her mind to be labeled "grandma." We called her Mom instead. I had another grandma, my dad's mother, but it wasn't until I was six years old that I realized that Mom and Grandma were the same relationship to me. It was an exciting piece of information to learn. Through listening to adult conversations and observing the world around me, I had figured out something wonderful! When Mom came to visit us the next time, I raced outside, calling "Grandma, Grandma," my arms spread wide for the hug I expected. Instead, she climbed back in the car and sat there. I was bewildered. My knowledge excited me, but it obviously did not excite her.

Learning can be exciting; sharing that learning can be complicated. Most teachers have had the experience of reading student papers that are so unorganized as to be painful, so lacking in substance as to be mind-numbing. When I first started getting those papers, my inclination was to wonder about my students: What kinds of students were these? Were they not learning anything, or were they unable to communicate what they'd learned? But it didn't take long for me to begin to wonder about myself, about my teaching, and about my preparation of students for writing. James Reither could have been describing me at that early stage in my teaching:

> We proceed as if students come to us already widely-experienced, widely-read, well-informed beings who need only learn how to do the kinds of thinking that will enable them to probe their experience and knowledge to discover what Rohman calls the "writing ideas" (106) for their compositions. (288)

That's what I was doing as an inexperienced teacher: I was asking them to write from nothing, at worst—or, at best, assuming students would (somehow) know how to access the knowledge they needed to write effectively. George Hillocks notices the same deficiency, but he generalizes it (thank goodness) so I see that I'm not the only teacher at fault:

> The point is that in practically no place other than school and college writing classes is writing treated as something that can be

> accomplished with little or no inquiry. To satisfy this requirement
> of no inquiry, students are asked to write about topics of such a
> general nature that they can be expected to fulfill the assignment
> off the top of their heads. Such topics hardly ever allow for real
> meaning making. They encourage students to rely on texts that
> float in the community mind, much as waste paper blows about
> the windy streets of Chicago. (*Teaching* 15)

How often do I do this? How often do I assume that prewriting will not
only help my students decide on a topic for their writing but also help
them know enough to write competently about it? If we think about it,
when we read something, even about a topic that we know well, the
best pieces contain a surprise of some sort—an angle or details that we
hadn't known before. Tom Romano suggests that information and a
unique perspective are keys to voice (*Crafting* 21). This has been brought
to my attention several times. When I read interesting nonfiction, it is
usually interesting because the writer moves beyond common knowledge with enough information and a different perspective to have lots
of voice.

In the introduction to *Acts of Revision,* Wendy Bishop makes a similar point, noting that "writers consume more than they produce. Their
meals include words, images, landscapes, memories, books, thoughts,
emotions, and hours, among other things" (v). She cites Kristina Emick,
who discusses her inquiry into a topic most people would think they
know well enough: hangnails.

> I researched the OED [Oxford English Dictionary] to find out how
> the word *hangnail* developed, how it gets used in idioms, and
> how its meaning changed over time. I searched beauty books for
> information on what causes hangnails and how to take care of
> them. I researched newspapers to find out if hangnails had shown
> up in recent news (they had, and both instances ended up in the
> essay). (v–vi)

Emick's example typifies the kind of information gathering that leads
to interesting writing.

Teaching Inquiry

I teach a minilesson that I hope will help my students see the need for
inquiry on almost any topic. Although a teacher can do this activity with
any number of essays or children's informational picture books, I use a
well-written essay I found in the newspaper about ice cream sundaes.
It reminds me of sundaes I have known and loved, but it goes beyond
that. It informs me.

In class, I first ask my students to think about ice cream sundaes. I make sure they have all eaten them, asking them if they have minimal experience or more extended experiences with them. Generally, they have eaten numerous sundaes in their lives; most of them have made sundaes at least a few times. So I ask them to freewrite about ice cream sundaes for five to ten minutes. After they write, we talk about how our experience helps us generate ideas. Then I ask them to follow along as I read an essay on ice cream sundaes by Kay Rentschler.

When I finish, I ask my students if the essay is a good one. They agree that it is. Then I ask them to note any details that a regular person who has made and eaten sundaes in his or her life might not know. We find many, including the difference between caramel and butterscotch toppings (they begin with different kinds of sugars, for one thing) and the origin of sundaes (although the French invented parfaits, Americans created sundaes). Students note a number of other details that a writer probably would need research to know. Then we discuss how those details make a piece of writing better because they create a bit of surprise for the reader, even if the reader knows the topic fairly well. Of course, there's more to good writing than knowing a lot, and Rentschler's essay has wonderful word choice and fluid sentences to enhance the content. But the point is clear to my students: To write well, we usually have to do a little more than rely on what we already know.

As a teacher learning to teach writing, I began to see that just as my students eventually need strategies to help them shape text appropriately for different contexts, they first need strategies to help them learn how to come to know enough that they can write interestingly and knowledgeably about a topic—and I don't mean prewriting per se. Many prewriting strategies help students discover a topic: narrow it (focus) or explore what they already know. Few, it seems to me, really teach inquiry strategies. And the more I think about it, the more inquiry seems as though it should inform the writer during most of the writing process. I visualize it as in Figure 2.1. Inquiry both precedes drafting and encompasses it. Inquiry should inform writing even through most of revision—but I've been guilty of not helping my students see that in the past. Now I want them to see how important inquiry is to all aspects of the writing process.

When I first started to think about this idea, I considered all the ways we come to know what we know in life (even the process described in the narrative I began this chapter with). No matter what specifics are on the list, the ideas generally can be grouped into these categories—and they overlap somewhat:

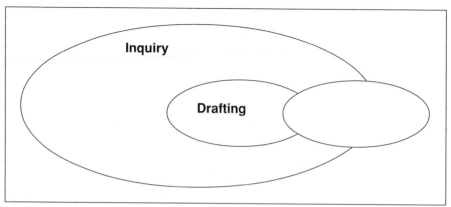

Figure 2.1. Inquiry should inform writing throughout the process.

- Experience
- Art/drawing
- Talking/listening
- Reading/viewing
- Writing

Within these broad categories, then, what strategies exist to help students? That answer is limited only by a teacher's imagination. But I find that these categories help me to generate ideas for inquiry strategies for any writing assignment. Table 2.1 shows some ideas to get started. In the rest of the chapter, I discuss each general area conceptually first and then give strategy practice ideas in the application section.

Table 2.1. Examples of Inquiry Strategies by Category

Experience	Art/ Drawing	Talking/ Listening	Reading/ Viewing	Writing
Field trips	Chart	Debate	Reading literature or nonfiction	Freewriting
Virtual field trips	Illustration	Talk show	Doing library research	List
Experiments	Collage	Drama	Reading for pleasure	Poetry
Enactments	Diagram	Discussion	Viewing a documentary	Journal
Manipulating objects	Metaphor	Speech	Surfing the Internet	Outline

Experience

Some knowledge comes from students' experiences, and we can draw on this for obvious writing situations such as personal narratives, short stories, or poetry. But other writing can be informed by experience as well. I-search papers, first described by Ken Macrorie, are research papers that use personal experience to select a topic of "need rather than simply interest" (129) and to ground the entire research and writing process: "to remind the reader and writer that there is an *I* doing the searching and writing" (127). Even arguments contain elements of personal experience from outside of the classroom. Teachers should help students understand how to draw on this lived experience, understand that they have learned things that can contribute to their writing, and also understand the limitations of personal experience.

I like to use a passage from Annie Dillard's *An American Childhood* to help students grasp this concept. In this excerpt (20–22), she remembers being a little girl and watching a "monster" come into her room each night. It was a bright entity that made a swooshing sound as it swept around her room, coming toward her and then evaporating suddenly in the corner before it got to her. At some point, she put what happened in her room each night together with what she had observed outside her room during the day and realized that the "thing" was nothing more than the lights of a passing car shining through her window. Her eloquent description of what she calls the coming together of the inner life and the outer life makes concrete the abstraction of how experience becomes knowledge. My students, once they see her point, can provide a number of examples in their own lives of such coming-to-know, much like my own experience with my grandmother. As teachers, we also need to consider how we can create such experiential coming-to-know inside the classroom—how to make experience an inquiry strategy for student learning and writing.

I imagine we have all seen or tried methods of experience-based learning, such as taking our students outside to record sensory details in the crisp, fall air. I had friends who told me they used ocean tapes to recreate an experience for their students so they could write poetry. My own experience with that strategy wasn't so successful. Here is what I wrote in my journal about it afterward:

> It was one of those gray days just before the buds burst on the trees. Winter had been our whole life, and spring was a figment of our imagination. My class was writing poetry. I decided to try what I had never tried before, although Katherine said it worked well in her class. We turned off the lights, writing by the light

from the windows, and I played ocean sounds. I told the students to get comfortable, relax, and write whatever came to mind—no requirements. We had about thirty minutes. The waves pushed against the shadowed walls of the room, and the seagulls swooped and called from the corners. Frothy water foamed at the edge of the carpet. Tides lapped at the legs of desks. Suddenly—the harsh sound of the bell cut through the rhythm of the waves. Class was over! I jumped from my doze, rushed to the light switch, and realized I had to awaken my class and send them on to math and science and history with red splotches on cheeks and foreheads. Hurry. Hurry. Don't tell anyone that we didn't write a thing. Instead, we took a vacation in the middle of a wintry school day.

Needless to say, I didn't try that experiential strategy again that day! But as teachers we should try to consider productive ways we can use appropriate classroom experience to help students come to know more about a topic and to learn that experience can be a strategy for knowing that will be useful in many writing situations. As I learned from my experience with the ocean tapes, it's important to plan thoroughly for these experiences. My timing, perhaps, wasn't the best for the selected experience—late winter wasn't the best time to turn off the lights and relax. Teachers need to consider multiple aspects of timing and context to ensure that experiential learning in the classroom produces effective inquiry to prepare students to write. Writing reviews of school plays or concerts, for example, would require students both to prepare for and then view the play or concert. Teachers would need to allow time for the preparation and viewing in order for the experience to provide all it could for writing.

One strategy practice for helping students see how experience can provide more information for writing is the still-life practice, an idea I borrowed from Charles Hakaim's article in *English Journal*, "A Most Rare Vision: Improvisations on 'A Midsummer Night's Dream.'" When we read the play in my ninth-grade language arts class, I want my students to understand the characters and the relationships among them. Following Hakaim's advice, I collect a few props, which are assigned to specific characters (the white scarf would mean the character is Hermia and the blue scarf, Helena, for example). Then students are put in groups and assigned certain points in the play. When we arrive at that point in our reading, the assigned group creates a living diorama so that the body language and positioning dramatically depict the relationships of the characters to each other at that particular moment. The students plan their positioning and then assume it; the rest of the class then analyzes and discusses what they represent and the way the text is represented by the portrayal.

I take pictures, which I place on the bulletin board in the order they occur in the play, thus providing us with a more permanent visual timeline of the relationships as they change through the play. Students experience—and better understand—what occurs with the characters and the plot. At the end of the play, when the students write a character analysis, many use the shifting relationships to help them explain the character they write about. Although Hakaim's idea and my application are both with the same Shakespearean play, the idea can apply to many pieces of literature.

For some students, acting out what they read is a strategy that makes their reading meaningful enough to them to write effectively about it, and many other dramatic strategies exist that can help students come to know literature enough to write more effectively about it. As teachers, we need to match the experience to the need for inquiry and frame it as a strategy.

Art/Drawing

A long history associates art with writing. Catherine Hobbs presents an interesting history from ancient Greece to the present, tracing the use of images from adding emotional appeal to a legal argument (from Quintilian) through the Renaissance tradition of combining words and pictures in emblem books (32) to modern technology that can incorporate text with graphics to create a number of effects. She concludes that

> the visual world is holistic. . . . [V]erbal language is linear. . . . Language decomposes holistic reality, allowing writers to convey what is really seen out there in the world into the mind, where we can once again recompose it to represent the holistic world. (38)

Because of the ease with which current technology can combine images with text, using each to enhance the other, we see a resurgence of the connection of words and images, not only in the increased number of picture books, both fiction and nonfiction, that appeal to older readers, but also in a variety of genres. Even traditional print genres—newspapers and magazines, such as *USA Today* and *Reader's Digest*—are using more graphics and other visual devices (color and font style or size) to enhance the messages of the text.

I have found it useful to connect graphics with all aspects of the writing process, but especially as a strategy to extend knowing. What I have noticed is that art, in any number of forms, can help students come to know more about their topic. In many ways, the images work as metaphors for students, creating avenues of thinking they might not have considered otherwise. In their book *Metaphorical Ways of Knowing: The Imaginative Nature of Thought and Expression,* Pugh, Hicks, and Davis cite Howard Peele: "Metaphors offer a ready perspective for comprehending something new. They are particularly useful at an early stage of learning: They provide a starting place; they make connections to that which is already well-understood; they suggest possibilities for further exploration" (11). This is exactly what we want for students from inquiry strategies.

In the application section of this chapter, I describe a strategy practice that uses abstractions to help students articulate their thinking. For some students, the opportunity to think in art is an important way to investigate their ideas before they begin writing. In strategies described in other chapters, students also use art during drafting to enlarge or articulate ideas.

Talking/Listening

In exemplifying how teachers can help students acquire procedural knowledge through what he calls *gateway activities,* George Hillocks describes students in small groups and in class discussions—talking. He notes, "Allowing for more interchange, the collaborative group has the advantage of more ideas and shared responsibility. Ideas from one person will stimulate the thinking of others" (*Teaching* 154). And Peter Elbow, addressing the concern students feel that they don't have anything to write, points out that "the cause is not insufficient input but insufficient output. Talking and writing put words and thoughts *into* students' heads" ("Writing First!" 10). Many of my students need to talk about their ideas in order to develop them. Sometimes I do, too.

Even though talking is noisy and time-consuming—and it can allow students to move off task—it still has benefits as an inquiry strategy that make it useful. In general, I use talk in the following ways during inquiry:

- To generate topic ideas
- To focus an idea through peer questioning
- To clarify a topic choice through discussion
- To determine audience interest in possible topics
- To determine audience questions about topic

Sometimes this talk is structured: Groups have specific tasks to accomplish in the allotted time and are accountable for a topic, focus, or list at the end of it. Sometimes my students have used talk while planning to write, when I have given them planning sheets and they need to ask others about their ideas. "What could be a place I'd look for my rule about not sitting too close to the TV?" was a question Isac asked his neighbors during one such planning time. What followed was an informal brainstorming session as several students started generating ideas, rejecting some, and elaborating others until Isac (amid a lot of laughter) had some idea of where to go with his topic.

When I first started teaching, I thought student talk meant I didn't have control over my class; I didn't value what it could contribute to student writing. I'm much more open to talk now, even though I know there are still times when talk isn't on-task or even helpful in the way I want it to be. I feel that the benefits that are gained for some students make it worthwhile even if other students don't use it the way I want. Still, since I structure some of the talk, I feel that much of the time it benefits students in their writing—and it teaches them a possible strategy for other contexts, for other times when talking about the writing task or subject might help them as writers.

Although much of the talking that works as inquiry is informal—questioning, brainstorming in small groups, discussion—I also plan more formal ways to help students use talk to develop ideas prior to writing; one of those uses the talk show format. I give topics to the "shows" so that the questions can be guided—and sometimes I let students suggest those topics, subject to my approval. So, for instance, with *To Kill a Mockingbird*, one talk show is titled "Growing Up in a Small Town in the South during the Depression." The panel consists of Jem, Scout, Miss Maudie, Miss Stephanie, and Aunt Alexandra. Another one is "Parent-Child Relationships and What Works," with Jem, Scout, Atticus, and Bob and Mayella Ewell.

Each panel has a moderator who works with the panel members to develop questions before the panel presents. The characters are expected to develop their own answers and stay true to the evidence in the novel. The class members act as audience and as judges to evaluate the accuracy of the responses, which are discussed after the panels perform. Some of these work better than others (as teachers might expect), but all of them give students a chance to use talk to help them consider aspects of plot and character that they might not articulate otherwise and then, when students write, to know enough about the literature to write more knowledgeably.

Reading/Viewing

Reading is probably one of the most important ways we come to know more, and many helpful books have been written about how to help our students read more effectively. All of the strategies those books suggest can help students read to know more and therefore can inform their writing. Interestingly, almost all of those strategies combine writing and talking with reading in order to help students understand, retain, and extend the knowledge they gain from reading. As examples, discussion, journals, KWL (what I *know,* what I *want* to know, what I *learned*), and literature circles all combine reading with another mode of learning.

Most of the time, these strategies are described as ways to improve reading comprehension. As one teacher notes, "Annotating helps readers reach a deeper level of engagement and promotes active reading. It makes the reader's 'dialogue with the text' (Probst) a visible record of the thoughts that emerge while making sense of the reading" (Porter-O'Donnell 82). I propose that this "visible record" not only can improve students' reading but also can provide students with the knowing they need to write effectively about their reading, if teachers extend it in that way. For the purpose of helping students write with more substantive knowledge, since there are so many other places teachers can find information about reading strategies, I focus here on specific note-taking and annotating strategies I use to help students move from their reading to their writing.

Note taking is a strategy that encourages a reader or listener to focus on and organize the meaning of a text. Sometimes, however, simple note taking may not be enough to accomplish the purposes of learning. Instead, beginning writers and learners may need additional help in learning how to make sense of the information they read. In that case, something like the double-column note-taking method is more effective. On one half of the page, writers take notes of the important ideas they read or hear. On the other side, they provide commentary about those ideas or facts: They comment, question, analyze, compare, connect, prioritize, or otherwise mess around with the material they've read. The messing around with text provides more of an avenue into writing about the learned information than simple note taking may (note taking that sometimes leads to plagiarized writing anyway). Big People, described in the application section of this chapter, is a collaborative information-gathering strategy that provides students with practice in preparing to write about characters in literature. Although I describe its use in a specific way, teachers can adapt the idea to provide students with a strategy that applies to other reading situations as well.

Writing

Writing itself can provide strategies for helping students come to know, either by exploring what they already know, by developing depth or synthesis, or by guiding students to know more. Langer and Applebee, in a study of how teachers use writing in classrooms, generalize three ways writing is used to promote new learning:

1. To draw on relevant knowledge and experience in preparation for new activities

2. To consolidate and review new information and experiences

3. To reformulate and extend knowledge (41)

Listing and freewriting can help students prepare to learn new information as well as to articulate what they have learned. Note taking and summarizing can help students remember and make sense of their learning. Dialogue journals and poetry can help students reframe learning to reinforce it or find new areas for inquiry. All such writing can help students make connections that they might not otherwise make without the impetus of writing for a sustained period of time. In this way, then, students use writing as a way to learn.

I introduce my students to the idea of writing to learn by explaining what it is *and* what it is not. It is, as Charles Duke notes, writing which "leads to clearer thinking and understanding" (1). It is sometimes informal and may involve more than one person. It is *not* writing that will be judged or assessed in the same way that writing for other purposes might be. A sentence from *Writers Inc.* explains it well: "When you write to learn, you are *not* trying to show how well you write or how much you already know about a topic; you are writing to learn more" (Sebranek, Kemper, and Meyer 397). This is key to understanding writing to learn—it can't be used for evaluating skills and knowledge it is not designed to measure.

With that in mind, many writing-to-learn strategies are open to use, and a number of them are found in textbooks and journals. Choosing among them should be based on the writer's purposes and needs. Students need to know that some kinds of writing will help them generalize while others will help them find detail or support. Some help them refocus, and others help them see whether they understand or not. Over the years, I've compiled the following list of possible ways to use writing to come to know:

- Learning logs
- Written debates or dialogues

- Exit slip or admit slip—a short summary of what you know or think you know about topic
- First-thoughts freewrite
- Written directions
- Instant version—a short version of a paper you are working on
- Nutshelling—a one-sentence explanation of the importance or relevance of something learned
- Stop-n-write—at any point in a reading assignment
- Summarizing
- Unsent letters
- Listing
- Cubing—a view of a topic from multiple perspectives
- Clustering
- KWL—what I know, what I want to know, what I learned
- Bio-poems

I am sure the list can be extended, and any of these strategies could be useful to student writers, depending on their needs and purposes, and could be practiced a number of times throughout a course. Two keys are essential, though: Students need to see that this writing is not an end in itself but an avenue to learning, and they need to understand how to use these types of writing strategically in their writing processes. One strategy described in the application section of this chapter is a specific writing-to-learn strategy that can also become the frame for a complete assignment: the A–Z List. It uses a writing frame to help students generate ideas. The other strategy practice described in the application section is a poetic form, the two-voice poem, that also uses a frame to help students both generate ideas and discover where there are holes in their current knowledge that need to be addressed through further inquiry.

Those mind-numbing papers I mentioned at the start of this chapter would have had more chance of being interesting if I'd provided more inquiry strategies and opportunities for my students. I've learned, like Yvonne Siu-Runyan, that "students get in trouble when they write about a topic for which they have little information. . . . The topic doesn't develop and the writing lacks fluency and details" (171). Inquiry is essential to good writing. And teachers need to make it an essential aspect of *all* writing that students do, not just research paper writing. As George Hillocks notes,

> Inquiry has been excluded from writing courses except for the "research paper," which, in many high schools at least, is really only an exercise in copying from library sources, not inquiry at all in the sense I intend here. Yet in my meta-analysis of research on teaching writing, approaches that involved students in active, original inquiry, even on a small scale, had far and away the most powerful effects on student writing. (*Teaching* 95)

Certainly we teachers will not want to neglect what research shows can be a powerful tool for student writers, but we also need to provide students with strategies to conduct that inquiry.

Applications

Strategy Practice: Abstractions

Declarative knowledge: Color and shape can help writers articulate their thinking and make connections between what is known and what is new.
Procedural knowledge: After reading or discussion on a topic, create a symbolic representation of a general idea, and then use that abstraction to inform writing on the topic.
Conditional knowledge: How did making the abstraction help me write about my ideas? How might this strategy work to help me with my thinking prior to writing other assignments?

To introduce the thematic idea of alienation prior to a unit in tenth grade on modern literature, I have students read and listen to some short sample pieces of literature of the period. After we read each piece, students list the emotions the writing evokes in them. When we've finished the reading, I ask them to review their lists and discuss them, and I introduce the concept of alienation as it connects to the emotions they've noted. Then I ask them to consider all the emotions and represent them visually (and abstractly—this isn't a drawing) with construction paper on a five-by-seven-inch card. Their representation is not limited to two dimensions. After students create the visuals, they write an explanation of their visual and how it relates to alienation. I always receive more thoughtful answers because the art stretches students' thinking, resulting in more depth.

In response to this strategy, Kristana cut an oval hole in her card. Around the hole, from the back she attached irregularly torn pieces of red construction paper, like rough fingers pointing into the absence. A yellow square was attached to the top right corner of the card, extending beyond it. An irregularly shaped black spot was attached in the top left corner, and sharp, narrow triangles of peach pointed into and away from it. Two green zigzags were placed between the black and yellow. This is what she wrote in response to the visual as her explanation of alienation (the highlights are mine):

> The cutout oval represents a sense of *loneliness*—the *hollow, empty* emotion. Red, fingerlike tears reach through the circle to represent *frustration, confusion, and reaching* for answers.
>
> The orange slivers point toward the corner for *reflections, introspection, and insight* that pierces the shapeless, black *gloom and confusion*. The green zigzag is life and curiosity, *the continuance of thought*. The yellow square is *solidarity and hope*, interrupted by *questions and contradictions*.

By looking at the italicized words, I can see that Kristana is synthesizing the texts and creating a definition of alienation in all its aspects. The graphic helps her put the abstract idea into words. I've sometimes asked students to use this same strategy when they are blocked on other kinds of writing: create an image and then write. Once I prompted an eleventh-grade student with this strategy when she was trying to write an essay on theme in *King Lear*. It helped.

Strategy Practice: Big People

Declarative knowledge: We can read texts for specific information that helps us develop more informed writing; others can help us find this information.
Procedural knowledge: Read text. Reread it with a purpose. Take notes that relate specifically to the writing task. Use the notes to write.
Conditional knowledge: How did this strategy help me write my character analysis? How did it help me with the content for my paper? This time, I worked with a group to find the information I needed, and we used large pieces of butcher paper to record that information. How could I use this strategy without those aspects to help me write a paper in another class? What if the topic isn't about character? How could I make this strategy work for other writing?

When my students write about character, one of the hardest things for them to do is to collect evidence from the literature on which to draw to defend their conclusions. I use Big People as a note-taking strategy that helps them through this inquiry stage. I begin by bringing in large pieces of butcher paper, about six feet or so in length. I put students into groups and assign each group one major character from the novel. With markers, they draw a person's shape (life-sized or larger) on the butcher paper and then take notes about the person inside the character outline. As a group, they review the character traits they remember from our reading of the novel. These they list, with spaces between, on the paper. Then they go through the book looking for specific incidents that exemplify the character traits they have noted. These are written as notes with the page numbers next to them. As an example, for Atticus from *To Kill a Mockingbird*, one consistent character trait students note is courage, and an incident and page number in support of that trait might be "not afraid of Mrs. Dubose, page 100." Students list at least four traits and at least three pieces of evidence for each trait.

After several classes of students have collected their evidence in this way, most of the book and many character traits are reviewed. When it's time to begin drafting a paper on character, I hang all the Big People posters around the room, surrounding us as we write. Students are free to choose any character they want to write about, not just the one they took notes for. As they draft, they are free to collect page numbers and evidence from the posters around the room. The page numbers help them if they need to look at details or use a quotation. This task helps them consider the use of evidence to support character traits in their analysis. In general, the knowledge students need to accomplish the writing task is addressed, and they are ready and able to write about characters from this inquiry.

Strategy Practice: A–Z List

Declarative knowledge: Heuristics can help us generate ideas or find holes in our knowledge that require further inquiry.

Procedural knowledge: Use a common heuristic such as numbers or letters to generate ideas on your topic. Determine where else you need to conduct inquiry.

Conditional knowledge: How did this strategy help me to know more about my topic? What did it add to my content knowledge? How did it help my writing process? How could this strategy be useful in other writing situations, even if I'm not writing an ABC book or report?

Joe Antinarella and Ken Salbu describe a heuristic they call the A-to-Z list. The alphabet list can be applied to any topic the students are studying and pushes students to think about or find some aspect of the topic for each letter of the alphabet, thus expanding an idea or generating more aspects of a topic. This strategy could be useful when students are in the early or middle stage of inquiry, writing about a piece of literature or a nonfiction topic, since it structures their brainstorming. Students can then choose to focus their writing on one of the ideas they've generated with the completed list. Some students, after choosing that focus, could use the strategy again to guide inquiry into the topic: focusing it or deepening it perhaps. Finding topics to fit the letters they originally couldn't fill might be an expanding strategy that students can apply many times in their writing life.

I have used this approach with responses to literature, although my students then use the A–Z List to create an ABC book, with a letter per page, each one with a paragraph and an illustration. After I shared the idea with one of my student teachers, Brittany Toone, she tried it with her seventh graders who were doing research projects. They not only used the alphabet to expand their research, but some also used it as a format for their final writing. Here is the introduction, the ABC list, and one paragraph from Arwen's project:

Introduction:

> In this ABC book I will help you choose and raise the puppy of your choice plus give you several helpful hints about showing, breeding, and training your dog as well. Getting a new pet is a big responsibility and hopefully this book will help you consider all the possibilities.

ABC list:

A—AKC	N—Neutering
B—Breeders	O—Obedience
C—Crate training	P—Puppies
D—Dos and Don'ts	Q—Quiet Time
E—Exercise	R—Recreation
F—Food	S—Safety
G—Grooming	T—Time
H—Health	U—Utility and Show Dogs
I—Interesting facts	V—Veterinarian
J—Jealousy	W—What kind of dog is right for you?
K—Kennels	X—eXtras
L—Leash training	Y—Yelling
M—Mating	Z—Zilch

Example paragraph:

E is for exercise. All dogs need to have a chance to go outside and go to the bathroom, stretch, etc. Depending on the breed, though, some dogs will need more or less exercise than others. Working dogs, hounds, and pretty much any dog that isn't very lethargic need to go on a walk at least once a day or more. Non-sporting dogs (especially Bulldogs, I know, I raise them.) don't need to go on walks or play fetch and stuff as often as, say, Labradors. How often you will be able to exercise with your dog must be carefully considered in choosing your breed.

Strategy Practice: Poems for Two Voices

Declarative knowledge: Writing about a topic from different perspectives can help writers explore the topic and learn more about what they know and what they still need to learn.
Procedural knowledge: Read some sample poems from Paul Fleischman's *Joyful Noise* and generate a list of ideas about how the poems are structured and how they accomplish their purposes. Then, based on a selected topic, write a poem for two (or more) voices. Use the ideas from your poem to help develop your paper on the topic.
Conditional knowledge: What did this strategy help me discover about my topic? How did it help me when I wrote my paper? In what other writing situations might this strategy help me during inquiry or drafting?

I have used this idea with older students to help them find areas they still need to develop during the drafting of an informative essay, but Laura Apol and Jodi Harris describe their use of two-voice poems as the product of a research unit with fifth graders in an article in *Language Arts*. The poetic form encourages students to look at two (or more) sides of a topic, as each voice represents perspectives on the topic.

The advantage of a two-voice poem over another writing-to-learn strategy, the T-chart, is that the poem's form encourages students to recognize relationships between perspectives instead of just listing them. This strategy is helpful for many kinds of writing but is especially useful when students need to write persuasively, when they need to acknowledge differing perspectives on a topic. Many of my students comment that they have to think about the topic differently because of this writing-to-learn strategy, and most find that the poem's form pushes them to consider ideas that they hadn't thought of before or to recognize an area of the topic they have not developed sufficiently. This exploration often leads to more research (or at least thinking) before drafting begins. Here is Megan's poem for two voices on the topic of New Jersey, a state where she'd lived:

I know a lot about New Jersey	I know a lot about New Jersey
It's the	It's the
Armpit of America	
	Garden State
It all seems so	It all seems so
	Fragrant
Stinky	
	Flowering
Barren	
	Warm
Freezing	
	Friendly
Mean	
	Life-giving
Murderous	
	Heaven-sent
Hellish.	
In the morning I wake up to	In the morning I wake up to
	Children playing baseball and
	eating ice cream,
Policemen with search-lights	
set on high beam	
	Neighbors with smiles on
	strolling around,
And bodies from shootings	
lying on the ground.	
The people are	The people are
	Wealthy, affluent, with
	goals and ambition
Just trying to stay for one	
year out of prison	
	Always rushing around to
	The next business meeting
Waiting, quietly wondering	
if today they'll be eating.	
The streets have their	The streets have their
	Lamp-posts and bushes
	all laid out with care
Trash heaps and joints	
Strewn about here and there	
I live in the North	I live in the South
And here I will stay	And here I will stay
'Cause this armpit's my home	Because this garden's my home
And I like it that way.	And I like it that way.

I ask my preservice teachers to try this strategy during their inquiry for the reversal paper (described in Chapter 4), and then I ask them to think reflectively about it and tell me what it did for their thinking and when it might be a valuable strategy for students. This is how Berkley responded:

> I think the poem for two voices is a great strategy for teachers to use in the prewriting stage. First of all, I think students would have a lot of fun writing it. It would raise their level of interest in what they're writing (hopefully). Also, this is a great way to brainstorm. To write the poem, students must have a good understanding of the topic. They also must choose what stance they are going to take with it. Another reason why this is a good strategy is because it causes the students to look at the issue from two different perspectives. They must think differently than they normally do.

Once students start thinking of writing as a way *into* writing (some see it just as *more* writing at first and need to be convinced), then they can really start to be strategic as they use different kinds of writing to accomplish their specific goals.

Lesson Plan: I-Search a Word

The plan that follows is an adaptation of one published in *English Journal* by Gaylyn Karle Anderson. It provides opportunities for practicing a variety of inquiry strategies during the process of creating an interesting, informative paper. In my planning, I consider what my students need to know or know how to do to be successful on this assignment. Some their major needs are these:

- A general concept of words and how they come to mean something
- An understanding of how to gather information about a topic (in this case, a word) and where to go for that information
- Knowledge of how to group different ideas effectively
- An understanding of the difference between narrative and informative writing

To help students be successful with this writing, I use the following strategies.

Teacher Plan for Inquiry Strategies

1. I begin by generating interest in the idea of words and how their meanings are fluid by having students answer some questions and then compare their answers. Questions include some like the following:

a. At what age is a person *old?* Is it the same age or a different age as *ancient?* If not, when is that?

b. How many people in this class have *blonde* hair?

c. If an island is *tropical,* what is its average temperature?

d. Label each of the following as a *city* (C), *town* (T), or *suburb* (S). (Here I list several communities in our area.)

e. If a bank robber was described by the witnesses as a man of *average* height and weight, what would he weigh? How tall would he be?

As a class we go over students' responses, sometimes listing them on the board so that students can see the wide variety of responses given to questions that they might have thought would have similar answers. From this activity, students conclude that many words have flexible meanings.

2. Next I introduce the idea of word histories by giving students some examples of words that have changed or shifted meaning through time. *Folly* now means an act of foolishness, but in the past it has meant wickedness, lewdness, and madness. It's definitely become less serious through time. The word *candor* is another example (the following is from the online version of *Oxford English Dictionary,* although many word-history books exist to help teachers as well):

a. It meant purity and integrity in 1610—but that meaning became obsolete around 1725.

b. Another definition developed around 1637, when the word was used to mean impartiality or freedom from bias.

c. A third definition was used from about 1653 to 1802, when the word meant freedom from malice, or kindliness.

d. Our current definition, "freedom from reserve in one's statements; openness; frankness" developed around 1769.

e. Related to this word is the word *candidate,* which developed originally from the same base, meaning whiteness. In ancient Rome, candidates for office wore white togas to symbolize their worthiness as candidates. This is a little different from today's use, and my students find this word especially interesting in election years.

By sharing a few word histories that are of interest to students, teachers can help them see that words change through time, that definitions are not static. The assignment will help students see that words can also shift in meaning as they are used by different individuals in varying contexts.

3. Next I tell the students that they are going to choose a word to research and share with the class. I tell them that I know it sounds weird—students in the past have told me that—but it does help them practice lots of inquiry strategies, generate writing, and learn something about words in the process. I have a list of words for them to choose from, abstractions for the most part (some from Anderson's article and some I've added), words that I know will be found in a variety of sources and that have the best potential for interesting word stories. I provide one list for students to sign up on so that they don't duplicate words. A sample list is as follows:

courage	love	hate	knowledge
pride	jealousy	foolish	wisdom
beauty	sweet	envy	bitter
unique	gentle	kindness	confident
compassion	crazy	energy	vengeance
charm	smart	silly	jolly
funny	generous	charitable	heroic
benevolent	sincere	patient	solemn
tragedy	sentimental	responsible	safe
dangerous	respect	reckless	strong
wonderful	ingenious	clever	dull
mean	fabulous		

4. After students have selected a word, I have them freewrite on what they already know about the word and what they think they might find, as Anderson suggests. Then I give them the assignment sheet to get them ready for the inquiry that will follow. Some adjustments might need to be made for the library facilities that are available in each school. My requirements are slightly modified from Anderson's.

I-Search a Word

As we have already discovered, some words don't mean the same thing to everyone—and words don't always mean the same thing through time, either. It's one of the aspects of language that make it interesting and complex. As an introduction to the way we will learn about language, writing, and speaking in this course, you will research a word that may have a variety of meanings and uses, and you will report on what you find to your teacher in a paper and to your

---

continued on next page

classmates in a speech. The writing for this paper will not be like most papers. It will partly be a story of your search and partly a report of your findings. But don't worry: When it comes time to draft, I will give you some ideas to help you.

For the inquiry part of this assignment, you will need to look up your word in a variety of contexts, listed below. As you do, be sure to keep notes of your findings and of your sources (the back of this sheet is a good place since you might be able to keep track of this bright paper!). Remember that you want to find ideas that will surprise and interest the reader, so be on the lookout for those.

Required:

1. Look up your word in an unabridged dictionary. Write down all the definitions. If that dictionary doesn't tell the history and origin of the word, you may have to look for your word in the *Oxford English Dictionary*. Find the origin of your word and some interesting history.

2. Look up your word in a thesaurus. Copy synonyms and the bold-faced words. If you have trouble finding your word in other places, you might try one or two of these words as substitutes.

3. Look up your word in a magazine search. Find a magazine article that uses your word. Write a summary of the article and write the exact sentence where your word is found. Answer this question in your notes: What aspect of the definition does it seem as though the author is using in this source?

Choice: Do *any two* of the following, *as a minimum*. (You can always do more; that would give you more information to use in your paper!) After each search, answer this question: How does it seem that this source is using my word?

1. Find your word in a concordance of the Bible or another religious book. Find a verse that contains your word and look it up. Copy your verse and the verses before and after it. Be sure to write the citation.

2. Look up your word in the *Concordance to Shakespeare*. Find a passage with your word in it and look it up. (Our library has several volumes you could use.) Copy the passage that contains your word and whatever comes before and after it. Include in your references the play's name and the speaker's name along with the act, scene, and line.

3. Find your word in a book of quotations. Copy a quotation that uses your word in an interesting way, and include the name of the author and date of the quotation.

> 4. Look up your word in one of the indexes to poetry that our library owns. Using one of the poetry anthologies in our library, find and copy a poem that contains your word.
>
> On _____ you will turn in your final draft of your paper, along with your notes, previous drafts, bibliography, and peer response sheet. On that day, you will also give a presentation to the class about your word. Your presentation will include a visual which we will work on in class.

5. I provide students with time in the school library (for those who can't go otherwise). I make sure our time is used wisely by establishing first where in the library students can find the different kinds of information they need. Since my library never has enough computers, dictionaries, or other sources for the whole class to use at once, I divide students up alphabetically and assign certain students to use certain sources first and then rotate them as possible (since some work faster than others). I alert the librarian to our project so that he or she can be prepared for the kind of inquiry my students are doing.

6. I also use synectics (described in the lesson plan in Chapter 4) as an additional inquiry strategy for this paper. Not only does it help students with their concept of the word, but it also can work as an introduction if nothing else works for them or their word.

7. After students have completed the library inquiry and synectics, they make a collage about their word in class. By now they know a little more about their word, and the collage encourages additional metaphorical processing that helps students clarify their thinking prior to drafting. Every time I've done this, I've also noticed that students talk about their words while they create the collages, even asking other students to keep an eye out for some specific image. This builds social relationships that are good for a writing class at the same time as it gives those students who need to talk out their thinking an opportunity to do so. Additionally, when they give their presentations, most students find the collage to be a good prop: The attention of the class is focused on the art instead of so much on them.

Teacher Plan for Drafting Strategies

1. When students are ready to begin drafting, I provide some general guidelines for this paper. Because it probably isn't like any other paper

they have written, most students don't have a good idea how to organize the information they've collected. I give them the following plan as a rough idea, again adapted from Anderson's suggestions:

    a. In the first paragraph, introduce and develop audience interest in the word by telling the most interesting thing you found about it or a story about why you picked the word you did, or you may use the paragraph you wrote for the synectics strategy practice.

    b. In the second paragraph, tell the story of your search for information. Don't tell about every little detail ("then I walked over to the computer area"), but focus on the main ideas of your search, any problems you encountered, and how you overcame them. This should be a place to talk about your processes of inquiry and to think about what you do and how you do it.

    c. For the body of the paper, use as many paragraphs as you need. Group your ideas in ways that make sense to you. In these paragraphs you should summarize your information, give your interpretation of the evidence, and respond personally to what you found. Did the word's meaning or use change in different settings? If so, how?

    d. In your conclusion, provide your overall response to the word. What does it tell you about the use of language in general? You can use one of the strategies we'll talk about in class [and described later in this section] to help you conclude: summary, bookend, project/predict.

2. Since grouping of ideas is challenging, I give a minilesson on grouping ideas to help students see what I mean about how to organize the body paragraphs. I bring a box of about twenty-five items from around my house: a tape measure, buttons, an extension cord, a spool of thread, pencils, a thumbtack, a cookie, and so on. We clear out the middle of the room where I dump out the box. Then I ask for a volunteer to group the items into four piles, with no fewer than two items in any one pile. The student will need to have a reason for the grouping, and the rest of us try to figure it out as he or she works. After doing this a couple of times so that students can see different rationales for grouping the items in different ways, I have them go back to their desks and see if they can find reasons for grouping their findings certain ways. For many students, this activity helps with the abstract concept of grouping ideas in paragraphs.

3. When students have general ideas about grouping, I have them use outlining as a strategy for making sure they have a logical flow to their ideas. I use a sample paper I wrote to walk students through my think-

ing and grouping. I show them the outline of my ideas and how I've arranged them. We discuss possible rationales for grouping other than a default grouping by source or chronology: ideas related to the origin of the word, ideas related to a particular meaning or sense of the word, ideas related to the causes of change in the word's use. I don't worry about complex outlines—this works more like a list for most of them—but it is a strategy some find useful in other writing later on. I suggest that they use one Roman numeral for each paragraph. If the paragraph is going to use information from one source only, the outline should tell the approach to the word that will be addressed. If the paragraph will use information from more than one source, the outline should tell the purpose of the paragraph. Here is my sample outline:

> I. Introduction—movie idea and original meaning linked
> II. Narrative of search
> III. Meanings—definition and synonyms
> IV. History
> V. Meaning *painful* or *cruel*—Shakespeare and magazine
> VI. Poem—why people become bitter
> VII. Conclusion—reflection

5. A minilesson on conclusions is helpful for some classes. I talk about possible ways to end, sometimes giving an alternative to the way I ended my model paper. I try to collect examples of each of these to help clarify them. I give students the following options, although they can use something else instead if it works for their paper. These are strategies that might work, but as writers the students have to decide for themselves which strategy to use.

> a. Summary: This is saying the main ideas of your paper again in different words. This is a good reminder if the reader might have forgotten the ideas presented, but if your paper is short, it might not be a good strategy as it seems to suggest that the reader isn't smart enough to remember some ideas for a few minutes.
>
> b. Bookends: This is having a catch at the beginning of the paper that you return to at the end. It's a good way to make a paper, especially a shorter one, feel connected all the way through, but it does depend on having something catchy at the beginning.
>
> c. Project/predict: In this kind of conclusion, you project into the future: What might happen in the future with this word? What prediction can you make about the way this word might change

or be used from now on? If the ideas in the paper relate to change, this is a good way to be creative and reflect the ideas of the paper, but if the prediction or projection isn't related to any evidence in the paper, the reader might wonder if the author is just being silly or can't think of any other way to end the paper. The prediction has to make sense.

6. By now, students should be ready to draft. I provide some class time for this so that I know they are started before they get home and forget what we talked about in class. With some classes, I ask for specific paragraphs—the narrative, for example—to be done before they leave. In other classes, I allow students to work on whatever part they want, as long as they work.

Teacher Plan for Product Strategies

1. We do guided peer evaluative readings. When students are finished evaluating one another's papers, they bring the completed evaluations to me for a quick check. If the evaluative reading is thorough, I initial the form and the student receives credit. This is the prompt I use:

Author _____ Editor _____ Teacher's initials___

Editor: Read the paper all the way through first. Then answer each question below and follow the directions given.

1. Check off all the parts of the assignment that are included in the paper:

   __ introduction   __ story of search   __ synonyms

   __ definition   __ history of word   __ poem

   __ Shakespeare   __ magazine   __ Bible

   __ quotation

2. Rate the introduction on how interesting it is, with 5 the most interesting:

   5 4 3 2 1

   What question(s) do you have about the word? Remember that a good introduction should interest the reader, so you should have some question that would make you want to read on.

3. Is the search too long? Does it tell too much that doesn't matter? __ Y __ N

   Does it tell problems the writer encountered? __ Y __ N

Does it tell how problems were resolved? __ Y __ N

Is it told like a story with specific details? __ Y __ N

What was interesting about the search?

What was boring?

4. For each of the body paragraphs, do the following:

    a. If the sentences don't contribute to the main idea, put a ? by the paragraph. (Remember our practice!)

    b. Put an E by sentences that give examples or evidence from the inquiry. Put a C by sentences that explain or give a comment about the example or evidence.

Which body paragraph was the most interesting? Why?

5. What strategy did the author use to conclude? How did it work? What could make it better?

Take this sheet with the draft to have the teacher initial it. Then return both to the author.

Author: Read over the editor's comments. How good a job did he or she do (10 is best)? ____

What three *specific* things are you going to do in your revision to improve the *content* of your paper (not spelling or grammar!)?

1.

2.

3.

2. When students turn in their papers, they respond to reflection questions: What particular inquiry and drafting strategies did I use that were helpful to me? How did they help me? In what future writing experiences could these strategies help me with my learning and my writing, and how?

Here is Kim's response to this assignment:

Funny You Should Use That Word . . .

How many times have you asked, or heard others ask, "Do you mean funny-ha-ha or funny-peculiar?" Into which of these categories does the "funny" in "funny-money" fit? Funny farm? Curiously, even with a word as common as "funny," we need context to determine its meaning in any particular instance. If you were to ask a native English speaker what funny meant, you might get answers as diverse as "It's strange— really weird" to "You know—funny—it makes you laugh." Sometimes we can look at how a word evolved to explain its diverse meanings, but the history of the word in this case might even lead to more ambiguity, rather than less.

I look up at the clock and sigh. This word is harder to research than I thought it would be. It is so common that there is hardly anything I can find about it. At least dictionaries *have* to define what other books refuse to define. I am interested in what I have found thus far. Funny used to mean a small boat, not unlike a dinghy. So, was there any connection between that use and the connection of the words today? If someone is dingy (crazy), they may be sent to the funny farm (mental hospital). Coincidence? Probably. I run another search, once again coming up with poetry that uses the word, but may not even be humorous or thought provoking. Nobody has to look up what "funny" means— there is generally no need to study the word, so nobody bothers to write about it. It is too prevalent in society to need any kind of explanation. Sometimes the things that surround us are the hardest to define. Try describing light to someone who is blind sometime. You are likely to give up in frustration, all the time knowing perfectly well what light is. Glancing again at the clock, I email myself the references I have found before I pick up my bag and walk out of the library.

When we say, "That's funny," what do we mean? George Bernard Shaw uses the word as it is probably most commonly used: "Life does not cease to be funny when people die any more than it ceases to be serious when people laugh." Here, funny means humorous, laughable, amusing, involving comedy. However, if one applied that definition to Isaac Asimov's quote, s/he would surely miss his meaning. He said, "The most exciting phrase to hear in science, the one that heralds new discoveries, is not 'Eureka!' (I found it!) but 'That's funny. . . .'" Suddenly, funny is something strange, peculiar, or unexpected.

Historically, the definitions of funny differ even more than they do now. Funny was a small pleasure boat in the late 1700s and early 1800s, according to the Oxford English Dictionary. Going back even farther, "funny" was once a verb meaning "to become stiff with cold, to be benumbed" from the early 1700s till the mid-1800s. In the 1750s, funny meant tipsy. In the 1850s we have evidence of the "funnies" as we use the term today—for comics. Although some loose connections can be established, like a person becoming numb because they were out in a boat on the cold sea, or because they had been drinking too much, these meanings seem to have very little to do with one another. As we look at the earlier meanings, it is more comprehensible that Shakespeare did not use this word in all of his writings. Nor is it surprising that we cannot find reference to it in the Bible.

The contemporary definitions, however, may be more closely linked than they appear to be upon casual inspection. Many of the poems and quotes I found had to do with the idiosyncrasies that life presents. The world is filled with the peculiar, the unexpected. This is a primary element in humor. Humor often involves unexpected events or items, or unexpected vision about everyday encounters. Humor is peculiar.

Humor is an essential, as well as inevitable, element in any society. In "Burden of Spoof," we read that humor is an effective way to reach students in a classroom. Here, a teacher uses spoofs on government internet sites to show how unreliable the internet can be. The point is that one must have concrete, not just electronic, evidence for one's claims. Humor is a common denominator, and it can bring students to a new understanding without the usual protests.

On the other hand, Oliver Wendell Holmes argues that humor is dangerous when not carefully monitored. In "The Height of the Ridiculous," he presents a scenario in which unrestrained wit is the cause of physical harm to his servant. His tone is facetious.

To see the world around us clearly, particularly the elements that are the most obvious, we must sometimes step back and examine our assumptions. As George Bernard Shaw said, "When a thing is funny, search it for a hidden truth." By so doing, we will understand with less confusion or miscommunication that which we "know." We may end up understanding what is meant in an older text by, "We used a funny to get us to the mainland." This can also help us to become better communicators as we recognize the need to clarify even the ideas that seem to be self-explanatory. In this way, we might be able to sidestep a few of the inevitable accidents of life. After all, Eeyore observed, "They're funny things, Accidents. You never have them till you're having them."

References

Oxford English Dictionary, Second Edition, 1989. http://dictionary.oed.com
www.quotationspage.com

School Library Journal. "Burden of Spoof." New York; October 2000.
www.thesaurus.com

Granger's World of Poetry

1/11: Today students wrote reflective pieces about their overall favorite strategies. Several named inquiry strategies as important to them as writers. Justine wrote this: "Talking in class was another one that helps. Some teachers just hand you a sheet with the requirements and then they're done. [ARGH—sometimes I do this!] It really helps to brainstorm ideas as a group." I guess responses like this one make me rethink what I do for inquiry strategies. Do I use them enough? Do I make sure I have time to practice strategies that might be helpful for all the learners in my class? Do I make the purpose of the inquiry—especially when it's not traditional—clear enough that it becomes strategic for my students? I can do better, or at least I can be more consistent.

Additional Resources

Angelillo, Janet. *Writing about Reading: From Book Talk to Literary Essays, Grades 3–8.* Portsmouth, NH: Heinemann, 2003.

Langer, Judith A., and Arthur N. Applebee. *How Writing Shapes Thinking: A Study of Teaching and Learning.* Urbana, IL: NCTE, 1987.

Pugh, Sharon L., Jean Wolph Hicks, and Marcia Davis. *Metaphorical Ways of Knowing: The Imaginative Nature of Thought and Expression.* Urbana, IL: NCTE, 1997.

3 Strategies for Drafting: Investigating Genre

Once students learn what it is to engage deeply and write well in any particular circumstance, they have a sense of the possibilities of literate participation in any discursive arena.

Charles Bazerman

When I first considered moving from public school to the university, I responded to an advertisement I had seen in a professional journal. A representative from the university phoned me a few days later. We had a short conversation, and he asked me to send him a vita. I agreed, although since my work had been in public schools (and not in academia), I wasn't sure, exactly, what a vita was. I figured the Latin meant "life," so he must want my life story. I knew enough about audience to consider that the university would be mostly interested in my professional and educational life, but I still wrote a narrative that began, "I was born in Anchorage, Alaska, . . ." and sent it off.

A few days later, I received a call from the same representative. He had received what I had written. He said it was a very "nontraditional" vita. Would I like to see his as a sample and perhaps send in a more traditional one? I said I would. When I received his vita, I was horrified to see how far off I had been! I didn't know the genre at all. I used his as a model and successfully wrote my own, albeit much shorter, vita.

Despite my vita mishap, I was lucky. I had had the advantage of some instruction in writing and some careful teachers who helped me understand that writing different genres requires different characteristics in the writing—and I had a considerate reader on the other end of my writing. I have shared this story several times since it happened, and I have heard many people tell me how they have missed opportunities because they did not understand the genre they were expected to respond in. One man was not admitted to graduate school because (he found out later) he had misjudged the genres involved in his application. As a teacher in public schools, I share this story with my students to help them understand the potential power available to them through writing—and through paying attention to the expectations of written discourse that each community holds.

Genre

By definition, genre is discourse that arises out of recurring communicative acts in certain social situations. Memos in the workplace are such a genre. My vita is such a genre. Understanding genre requires some understanding of the social context it arises from as well as an ability to read a text with certain considerations of the social nature of its context in mind. As Irene Clark notes, current considerations of genre move beyond the form: "[G]enres also help shape and maintain the ways we act within particular situations—helping us as both readers and writers to function within those situations while also shaping the ways we come to know them" (243). In the strictest sense, some theorists claim, genre is understood only from being part of the community that uses the genre. Because of that, these theorists (Dobrin, for example) suggest, writing in school can only teach school writing, nothing that really transfers beyond school.

I don't fully agree. I believe that teachers can teach students strategies in school that will help them write beyond school: strategies that help students look at how texts work in relation to their context and strategies that practice achieving those effects of texts. Petraglia, citing speech communication scholarship, notes that "the ideal rhetorical training will have at its core the development of a sensitivity to the rhetorical possibilities available to students and will provide some guidance as to how they may determine to select among those possibilities" ("Life" 62). This, to me, is the general idea underlying a strategic approach to genre. Without reducing genre to only forms—*and that is essential to avoid product-only teaching*—genre can be considered from outside its context if students develop sensitivity to how structure reflects purpose, audience, language, tone, and content.

One way I introduce this concept of genre to students is with a book, *Dragonology: The Complete Book of Dragons,* "edited" by Dugald Steer. The book purports to be a complete record of what is known about dragons, with the stated intent to pass this knowledge on to others as the author's "final accomplishment as a dragonmaster." Since dragons obviously don't exist, I ask students to consider the kinds of texts this book uses to *act* as though they do. The author takes advantage of genre expectations in the reader, using texts that carry validity in their nature: maps, classification charts, encyclopedia entries, life-cycle diagrams, directions for hatching and caring for dragons, and detailed figures of scales (with samples), eyes, and claws, to name just a few.

I ask what the author might have intended by using these text types, and students can see that he's trying to make something seem more real—true!—than it is. We talk about why we think charts or graphs affect us this way. Students find the book fascinating, and it works well to introduce them to the concept of genre as more than form, of genres carrying messages beyond the form.

An approach to teaching genre from the perspective of sensitivity to texts, then, means teaching students to question texts: what they do and why they do it and how they accomplish their purposes. Although he is directing his comments to teachers at the college level, Anis Bawarshi makes a compelling case for the practices I present in the rest of the chapter:

> Rather than teaching students some vague and perhaps question-able notion of what "good" writing is, a notion that most likely cannot stand up to disciplinary standards or scrutiny, we gain more by teaching students how to adapt as writers, socially and rhetorically, from one genred site of action to the next. (156)

In teaching, then, we help students develop this ability to adapt by providing them with strategies that allow them to interpret and then claim as their own, at least in some small degree, ways of responding appropriately in different writing situations. The wider variety of genres students have exposure to and practice with, the more they will build awareness of the subtle ways texts work to accomplish their purposes, and the more able they will be to write in a variety of genres.

One way to help students consider what they already know about genres and how they differ is to practice several and then reflect on the differences students can see beyond form. This practice can help students understand that the "usual" expectations of any genre are only the beginning of composing and not the end. Although many sources can effectively initiate discussion about writing, perspectives, and genres, one good practice text is a wordless picture book titled *You Can't Take a Balloon into the Metropolitan Museum* by Jacqueline Preiss Weitzman. The book portrays the story of a girl visiting the Met and being told by the guard at the entrance that she cannot bring her balloon with her into the museum. He indicates that he'll care for the balloon until her return but inadvertently loses it when a bird pulls the string from a handrail. The rest of the book is a delightful parallel story of the adventures of the guard following the balloon through the city, mirroring the surprisingly similar tale of the girl's journey through the museum (complete with miniature reproductions of famous works of art).

An obvious application of this picture book is to have students write the story. It can be interesting for student writers to compare their stories afterward and reflect on the differences they found in their stories and how these differences show individual perceptions and styles within the genre. But what if students go beyond the expectations of a narrative? What if students' stories include a journal entry the girl might have written in response to one of the paintings? What if the stories include a series of pager messages the guard sends the grandmother as he chases the balloon through the city and she shepherds her granddaughter through the museum? What if students write the stories in groups, and some are responsible for short, reportlike paragraphs on the artwork or artist being shown, in much the same way that The Magic School Bus series (Scholastic Press) combines fiction and nonfiction? Practicing a variety of genres can help students recognize both the possibilities and limitations of different genres.

Two former students, Cecily Yeager and Cynthia Logsdon, now seventh-grade teachers, took this idea to heart and used *An Island Scrapbook: Dawn to Dusk on a Barrier Island* by Virginia Wright-Frierson as a model to teach their students how to write several functional genres (as required by the state core curriculum). The picture book tells the story of a day on a barrier island but includes sketches, diagrams, lists, and other genres as supplemental texts that complement the storyline. Cecily and Cynthia asked their students to choose a place they liked and write a story of a day in that place. They taught features of required functional genres such as personal letters, rules, instructions, and short reports, but they encouraged students also to use other genres, such as packing lists, recipes, maps, wanted posters, daily schedules, store receipts, and poems. Using a grant they had been awarded, the teachers purchased bound empty books for students to use. The results were amazing as students wrote in a variety of genres to tell their stories about their favorite places.

Here are Danielle's directions as an example of one genre in her book:

> How to pet a sting ray safely:
>   Have you ever wanted to pet a sting ray, and not get zapped or bitten?
> Well, if you follow these simple steps it is possible.
>   1. Go to an aquarium (that lets you pet sting rays).
>   2. Get down on your knees around the pool.
>   3. Wait until a sting ray comes by you.
>   4. Reach over with *one* hand and pet it on the back.
>   5. Make sure one hand is holding on to the edge.
>   6. Only pet the sting ray on the back.

7. Don't go too close to the tail or mouth.
8. If you happen to fall in, just simply get out. The sting ray *WILL NOT* come after you.

Hopefully with these steps you will be able to pet sting rays safely. Good luck.

And here is Ashlee's researched short report:

Hermit Crabs can be found in tide pools and at the bottom of the ocean sand. Hermit Crabs are nocturnal, which means they come awake during the night. They like to bury themselves in the sand during the daytime. If they get too much sunlight, they will dry out and die. Hermit Crabs shed their skin in a method called molting. Younger Hermit Crabs molt more often than the older crabs. They use pressured water to break off their exoskeleton. Often times someone will pick up a shell and they do not even consider that it could contain a Hermit Crab inside. IF that should occur, then they are sure in for a surprise when they get home!

Explicit instruction and practice in multiple genres such as these seventh graders had can help students develop sensitivity to the different ways genres work and the work different genres do. As Amy Devitt acknowledges, "historical evidence suggests that people use familiar genres to act within new situations. . . . Individuals can only draw from genres they know, however. The more genres they know, the more potential antecedents they have for addressing new situations" (204). We teachers can't teach students every genre they will need to know in their lives, so we teach the ones we have the time and resources for, and we teach them strategically so that students develop genre awareness. By teaching students to embellish their stories with a variety of functional genres, Cecily and Cynthia help their students develop this awareness of the ways different genres work to accomplish different tasks for different situations.

A genre approach, then, includes strategies for analyzing and questioning texts. This idea is not new, although the idea of it being used as a strategy may be. Stuart Greene has written of a strategy he calls *mining texts*, one similar to what others call *reading like a writer*. Greene asks students to question texts about their content, structure, and language and to use the questions to discover the ways texts work. Drafting strategies like Greene's text mining teach students how to question texts in order to figure out what a text is doing as well as what it is saying. Reading texts this way, as William Strong notes, helps "students gravitate toward effective writing over time and begin to appropriate the characteristics of quality texts" (160–61).

Understanding Texts

Even in school classrooms, despite the lack of authentic social context, we can help students learn about genre with certain kinds of assignments. When I teach my students to write letters to the editor of the newspaper, for example, we begin by looking at the newspaper as a whole, at the different parts and what they are designed to accomplish. The strategies we use include observing, questioning, and comparing (Dean "Going Public"). Through these strategies, we can interpret the purpose of each text and how the choices the authors make help to accomplish those purposes for certain contexts. So, for example, news articles generally have a unique organizational structure, placing most important information first, while feature articles often begin with an interesting fact or anecdote to draw the reader into the writing. The purposes and anticipated readers have a lot to do with the different decisions about organization and introductory techniques, even content. These explorations help students understand audience and purpose as aspects of writing different genres.

Another way I help students use observing, questioning, and comparing to teach genre as a strategy is when I assign them to write a group book modeled after The Magic School Bus series. These texts combine narrative with exposition, and students need to recognize and imitate the different types of text. Using questioning strategies, students investigate the text to find out what kind of content best fits each text type and what purposes are best achieved by each.

I have used the assignment as a conclusion for a unit on the history of English, but I have also used it as a way to understand the setting of a novel; students research the time period and then write the book as though our class went back to that time. In this assignment, I establish categories of information for students to choose from in their research to ensure that students get a rounded perspective. They must remember what they know about textual characteristics, however, in order to put the appropriate information in the different genres. They can incorporate some researched information in the story of our class's visit to that time, such as poodle skirts and ponytails in our visit to the Disneyland of the fifties. Other, more factual information finds its place in the short expository pieces on each page that match what's occurring in the story: the opening of Disneyland in 1955, along with other Disney achievements of the time—television shows and movies.

Another practice for students to develop genre understanding is the interview. In the application section of this chapter, I describe an interview strategy practice that allows students to design the interview, not just report one, although that is good practice as well.

Reading as Strategy*

One way we can learn genre outside a particular social context is through reading models, as described earlier. However, using models in the classroom is not without its problems. In many cases, the inappropriate use of models has led to a focus on form and product and a subsequent lack of concern with ideas and process. Hillocks is referring to this presentational style of teaching in his admonitions against the use of models (*Research* 117, 247). However, models do have a long and valued history in a different sense, in a sense that connects reading and writing in the strategic ways we're discussing.

In a classical education, students learned to think and write—learned grammar and vocabulary, even—by copying, memorizing, and speaking the words of the masters who'd come before them. Part of the underlying idea was that such immersion in the style, ideas, logic, and language of the masters would find its way into the minds of the students, providing a good model for the time when their own experience was developed enough to need expression in original writing. Although times have changed, the use of models to assist learning in some fields is still evident.

Students will imitate the genres they are familiar with. I've seen it too many times as a teacher to ignore the connection. How many times do pieces of "persuasive" writing sound like shopping channel commercials? (Students don't really *read* persuasion, but they hear it on television as a text.) How many times are analysis essays really plot summaries in weak disguise? Students fall back on the models they know—for genre, for tone, for organization. To refuse to use models seems to me a rejection of the powerful relationship that exists between reading and writing.

Although research suggests that the use of models does not by itself automatically improve student writing, some evidence suggests that models can be a beneficial strategy. The conclusions of Charney and Carlson and of Smagorinsky show that combining the use of models with other methods of writing instruction helps students write more

----

* Portions of this discussion about models were previously published (Dean "Partnering").

effectively. Both studies also recognize that the *way* models are used in the classroom is key, that *active analysis* as opposed to simply reading a text is essential to understanding the characteristics of the model text and seeing it as more than a formula, seeing it as an array of choices. And when Hillocks describes the environmental mode of instruction, the instructional method that his research found to be three to four times as effective as either the natural or presentational modes, he notes that it is characterized by "high levels of student interaction concerning particular problems parallel to those they encounter in certain kinds of writing" (*Research* 247). This is precisely the process being described here. This is what moves such interaction into the realm of strategy.

One way I have used models actively involves highlighting. After we read a movie review (I choose one that evaluates a movie most students have seen), I ask students to use a highlighter to mark the sentences that tell the author's general opinion of the movie, the overall evaluation of it. Next, using a different colored highlighter, they mark the sentences that summarize the movie. Finally, I have them use another colored highlighter to mark the sentences that analyze the movie, that tell how the movie worked or how the actors acted. This can be tricky, but if I begin with a review that I've made sure is pretty clear, most students can do it. It is good if they notice evaluative statements mixed with analysis, since it helps them see that the purpose of the review is to evaluate a movie or book. The analysis works in the service of that purpose, providing a way for the reader to determine whether the writer can be believed or not.

I usually have students do the highlighting strategy with at least two or three reviews to allow them to see some variety and to give the discussion that follows a solid foundation. Students look at their highlighted reviews and draw some conclusions about where summary elements might be placed in a review. How much of the review is taken up with summary? Where is analysis, and how much of the review does it make up? Where is the overall opinion of the movie, and can it be in more than one place? If it is, is it stated exactly the same way or differently each time? Through this practice, students are able to understand how to construct and balance their own reviews, thus helping them solve potential problems through the use of reading models. And they are given a strategy that works with a number of genres: Research papers have quotes and commentary, and personal essays have narrative and reflection.

Teachers need to be strategic in their selection of models and when they use them as well as how they use them. Models should promote analysis and effective writing, be engaging in content, and be accessible and appropriate for students. One of my biggest challenges has been overcoming inappropriately chosen models. Once I used a model from a class text: "Why I Am an Agnostic" by Clarence Darrow. I wanted to use it to show how an author writes with and against the grain, but students in one high school class were so inflamed by the ideas that I could never get to the writing as a model. I learned to consider my models more carefully.

Greene summarizes the effective use of models: "The goals of teaching students to mine texts are, first, to encourage students to develop a sense of the options they have as writers and, second, to enable them to articulate their reasons for making the choices they do in different situations" (42). The way for teachers to use models is thus first to choose the models purposefully, then to help students learn to read them like writers, leading them to explore the choices writers make, and finally to help them see these choices as options for their own writing. In the application section of this chapter, I describe two strategy practices for helping students question texts to discover the options they offer writers: Says-Does and Six Traits. Both of these strategies should help students avoid the misuse of models as forms. Instead, these questioning strategies, and others teachers might think of, can help students consider models as sources of options that they can try in their own writing. By learning to read models this way, students develop the ability to adopt the genres they need for the situations they find themselves in instead of having to rely on forms that may restrict them or (as I did) using the wrong genre for the occasion.

Applications

Strategy Practice: Interview

Declarative knowledge: Some information is best given directly from the source. In these cases, interviews (or reports of them) serve to provide both information and insight into the subject.

Procedural knowledge: Develop questions for the interview subject. Gather needed information. Report the information in a dialogue format that imitates speech (including fragments and speech expressions).

Conditional knowledge: What strategies did I use that helped me understand the genre of the interview? How might I use those strategies to understand and write a different genre?

Leigh Ann Tyson's book *An Interview with Harry the Tarantula* is a good model for students who are practicing the interview genre. As the title states, Tyson uses an interview format to present information about tarantulas. The interview is presented as a radio show, with the announcer Katy Did posing questions and eliciting information from the guest, Harry Spyder, a tarantula from California.

After we read the interview together, students list information they learned about tarantulas. We discuss the characteristics they notice about the genre; the form is most noticeable, and I ask them to consider why a writer might use this genre to present information. They usually say because it seems more personal than reporting the information. This understanding is important later when they need to avoid reportlike language in writing their own papers. I have students look for at least one interview of someone they are interested in on the Internet (many are available) because I want them to start to notice genre characteristics beyond the form. After reading a couple, they usually see that an event triggers the interview. Something happened to the interviewee. In good interviews, the questioning of the subject about the event leads to the audience's learning more about the subject rather than just about the event.

After examining and questioning several interviews, I introduce the assignment and ask students to begin considering possible topics. I have a friend who teaches second grade, so I propose that my students write their interviews like the one in *Harry the Tarantula*—informational, not necessarily of a human subject, and on a topic of interest to second graders—so that we can share their final papers with that class. The interview inquiry sheet that follows moves them through selecting a topic and generating questions about it:

Interview Inquiry

Choosing a Topic

1. What topics are you interested in knowing more about that might be of interest to second graders?

2. Choose one from your list above and write it here. Tell why you selected it.

Beginning Inquiry

1. Write a list of questions you have about your topic right now.

2. Talk to at least three other people, and ask them what questions they have about your topic. Write the questions they have that are different from yours here, along with their names.

When you are conducting your inquiry, consider these questions and write the answers to them on the back of this paper. And if you find anything else interesting that you didn't have a question about before (and it is better if you do!), write that information on the back of this paper, too. Be sure to keep track of the sources (books, articles, Web sites, and people) that you use to answer your questions. Find those interesting details you didn't know you would learn!

After inquiry (research and note taking), students consider what event could have instigated the interview. Then I provide a minilesson on open and closed questions, taking students once more to the models so that they can see the way different types of questions are used to elicit information from the interviewee. Students develop more questions about the interesting details they have discovered. In this way, they design both general-interest questions and more specific ones.

In writing their answers, students review the models again to discover the strategies Tyson and the other interviewers use to set up the frame of the interview. During drafting, we also review the models to see how they imitate speech and reflect the personality of the subject being interviewed. From Harry, we note the following: informal expressions ("Oh sure"), fragments ("Mostly crickets."), hedges ("I think . . ."), expressions and tone that reflect personality ("Ha! Good luck making a meal out of me."), and sounds unique to speaking situations ("Burp. Excuse me."). Katrice's response to this assignment, below, shows that she understands the general nature of the genre. She is able to devise questions that elicit information at the same time that she shows humor and personality in presenting that information.

Close Call with Predators

Hey there, and welcome to the #1 Show in Africa. We're your hosts, Chimp and Zee, and right now we are here with Carmine Flamingo who just had a close call with a python. But before we go any further, we have met up with Carmine at the scene to ask her a few questions.

Chimp: We are standing right now at the attempted murder scene in the heart of Africa at Lake Nakuru. So Carmine, what were you doing right before the attack?

Carmine: I was feeling a little chilly, so I lifted my leg up and tucked it up inside of my feathers to keep warm and then nestled my head into my mom and fell asleep.

Zee: Tell me, Carmine, did you ever see the python coming?

Carmine: No, but I'm pretty sure everyone else did because when I woke up everybody was gathered off the shore line and onto the land, squawking about.

Chimp: Did go completely bananas when the python tried to make you his lunch?

Carmine: Well, certainly. Wouldn't you? I saw my whole life flash before my eyes, which isn't very long since I am only five. Our usual life span is about 44 years in captivity; it's a lot safer in the zoo, you know.

Chimp: I see. So tell us, Carmine, how did you manage to

Zee: escape the python's mighty squeeze?

Carmine: Well, at first I froze, trying to think of what to do. Then I naturally just started squawking and flailing my wings about. Then I puffed out my chest, forcing the python into deeper water until I was up to my tail feathers. I then dove under the water and surfaced around the snake and glided safely back to shore.

Chimp: Did you ever suspect that this would happen to you?

Carmine: I knew it was a possibility, but you always just suspect that it will happen to someone else.

Zee: I've heard that flamingos cluster in groups of about a million. Have you been able to spot your mom yet?

Carmine: No, not yet. It's kind of hard trying to spot her . . . you can't tell those guys apart.

Chimp: Ha! Ha! You have quite a sense of humor about yourself.

Zee: So Carmine, what does your name mean? Do you know?

Carmine: I was named after the color of my bill. Of course we flamingos have very special and delicate features, soft pink feathers, carmine red bills with black tips, and stand at approximately 40 inches in height with vibrant orange eyes. No other bird can mock our rare features.

Chimp: Well, Carmine. Thanks

Zee: for your time

Chimp and Zee: This is Chimp and Zee on another special edition of "Close Call with Predators."

On the day the interviews are due, we present them orally in class to allow students to experience the oral nature of the genre. Then we give them to the second-grade teacher to share with her students. It would be instructional, in terms of conditional knowledge, to have students write their research in the form of a report, either before or after they've written the interview. Then they could compare and contrast the two genres and what they allow writers to do in terms of purpose. Do both allow writers to reflect what they know? Does one or the other restrict the amount or type of information? If so, what options does that give writers about choosing a genre to fit a specific purpose? Given the differences, what purposes could writers have for choosing one way of reporting information over the other?

Strategy Practice: Says-Does

> *Declarative knowledge:* We can ask specific questions about texts to help us get ideas for our own writing: ideas for content, organization, and voice.
> *Procedural knowledge:* Read a text first to understand what it means. Then question what it says and what it does in order to determine how it achieves meaning. Choose from among the ideas that are gathered from your questions to generate your own text.
> *Conditional knowledge:* From the options I found in the model, which did I choose to use? Why did I choose the ones I did and not others? How could I use the says-does strategy for other writing I do?

Instead of using models as formulas, I want my students to think of them as presenting options that are available to them as writers. One way I do this is exemplified in the first writing assignment of our course, an assignment that asks students to introduce themselves to me. I use as the model an excerpt from *The House on Mango Street* by Sandra Cisneros called "My Name" (10–11). This text is popular with teachers because of its interesting writing, and students like it too because of its ideas.

We begin by reading the excerpt together and then discussing what it reveals about the author. In this discussion, I encourage students to make text-to-self connections with the ideas Cisneros expresses. They might think of how they have felt alienated or different; some talk about the image of the line "She looked out the window her whole life, the way so many women sit their sadness on an elbow" and how it reminds them of someone emotionally even if it doesn't remind them of that person literally. This discussion allows us to respond to the text first as readers before we turn our attention to the text as writers to see what options it can teach us that good writers use.

To investigate the text, I use a questioning strategy called "Says-Does," which is not unique to me. Somewhere in the distant past a colleague shared this name, though I had already been using the idea. It's an effective strategy for teaching students how to read a text like a writer. I use it myself, especially when I'm trying to write in a genre I've not written in before.

Whatever text it is used with should be chunked into workable pieces. With "My Name," we begin with the first paragraph and summarize what it *says*. Students note that it shows both positive and negative feelings that Esperanza has about her name. We continue this process, paragraph by paragraph, with students individually answering the question "What does this paragraph say?" before we answer it as a class. This discussion provides students with options for ideas to include in their own writing: the origins of their names, stories about people they are named after, other names they would choose to have and why, other names they've been given or called by at home or at school. Again, these aspects of what the text says are presented as options to help students develop content, to have something to say, but they are still options. Jill chose one of those options to begin her response, and it's evident that just giving students options for approaching a topic can encourage some powerful writing:

> My name doesn't really mean anything. Just a few short sounds smushed together to form a one syllable nothing. It doesn't stand out in a crowd, like so many other female names. It slumps its shoulders and shirks to the back of the line, patiently waiting its turn while so many others cut in front. If you look back far enough you'll find out that in some sordid way it means child of Jupiter, the Roman god equivalent of Zeus. The ancient pagan gods did so much philandering that this distinction means next to nothing. Jupiter, just after another cheap thrill, corners a river nymph in the forest and months later a child is born to a world where she is half god and half common, to a world where she is useless because she is not a whole of anything, just pieces of nothing. Just another bastard child of a father who couldn't care less.

The next part of the strategy is to ask what each paragraph or section does. Beyond what it says or what information it communicates, how does each paragraph add to the whole, or what purpose does each paragraph serve? We realize that the first paragraph intrigues us, partly because, despite the title, it doesn't tell us the speaker's name. Again, we work paragraph by paragraph, first as individuals and then as a class, through the short essay. We see that Cisneros organizes her ideas by beginning with what Esperanza's name means to her, then going beyond herself to what it means in her family and to how her name is said at school, before finally coming back to her own wish for a different name. She writes about Esperanza's dissatisfaction first and ends with her dream. Again, these are options students can choose to use or not. Larry uses Cisneros's strategy of delaying information to create interest by not saying his name in the first paragraph:

In Latin, my name means laurel-crowned. In Old English it means bright fame. It means light, and promise. It is like an Olympic flame. Glory, honor and hope. It is the name my father carries, and his father before. Now I carry the name, not only as a record of my life, but an ongoing testament to their bright fame.

In discovering what the text does, students are also discovering how it does it, how language and sentence fluency help to create the effects they feel. Despite my nervousness as a teacher to encourage the use of fragments, I let students use whatever choices Cisneros uses (without naming the constructions) if they can make them work the way she did. They notice the listing, the metaphors, the imagery, the "short" sentences. They can try them all, and many do, successfully. Following is Justine's whole paper. It's evident which options from our discussion she chose to use and where she went with what she needed to communicate her message. That's essential to me, as it shows that students are thinking strategically—not looking at the models as forms that must be strictly followed. In this strategy practice, the model's choices offer students a chance to write effectively but also to reveal their feelings in a subtle way—as Cisneros does. It's clear in this writing, for example, that Justine is still working around the idea of self-identity that Cisneros addresses as a subtext in her essay.

It comes from a 1980 song. Just a random name Pat Benatar sang about that struck gold. There is no definition and no meaning, nothing. It is a name that nobody can seem to spell or say correctly. They make it sound really complex, like a name that nobody has heard of. Instead it isn't complex. In fact it's very simple and unique. My mother says that it is a good thing that nobody has the same name as me; it's supposed to make me feel different than everyone else. But I don't want to be different.

My mom was seven months pregnant and still had no idea what to name me. She had thought of all sorts of common girl names. As soon as some rock and roll blonde singer came on the television of her favorite soap opera and started singing, my mother caught interest. She heard the song in the car, on the tv, even in concert. It was the hip new song at that time that everyone caught interest in. Now all those people are in their forties and have forgot all about it. For some reason my mother stuck to the rock and roll blonde and named me after it.

Justine. Yes, the same name of the girl that inspired the singer to write and sing about her. Now I am all grown up and don't resemble any of the same qualities that Justine had. The song says that she was an ambitious young girl that had lots of dreams and goals. She lost her dreams by getting married and moving off to a small town, making her living by being a housewife that fed the kids and cleaned the house. I don't want to be the same young girl that waits all day, waiting for her office-working husband to come home.

   I would like to change my name, something like Jacklyn or Allison something that sounds familiar to people, a name that is not different and not an outcast from everyone else. I still want a unique name that fits the little pink-dress-wearing girl that I am deep down inside. The girl that nobody says I should show anymore now that I am all grown up and I have responsibilities to fulfill, not the dreams that they think I should become, but what I want.

Since I've used the says-does strategy with my students, I've become aware of others who also use it. Bean, Chappell, and Gillam use it for summary writing or to begin a rhetorical analysis. The authors provide a list of verbs from which students can draw to consider what a portion of text does. Since the "does" part of the strategy is sometimes hard for students to articulate, especially at the junior-high level, I think using the list of verbs to give some ideas would be helpful. Some of the verbs Bean et al. list are these: adds, asks, compares, continues, contrasts, demonstrates, describes, elaborates, explains, extends, illustrates, informs, predicts, proposes, questions, reflects, repeats, summarizes, supports (55–56). Teachers and students can consider additional verbs that describe what writers might do when they write to help students discover their own options.

Strategy Practice: Six Traits

Declarative knowledge: By using the traits common to all writing, we can question a text to discover how it works and what options are available to us as writers.

Procedural knowledge: Use the traits individually to question a model text. Use ideas before inquiry, use organization and voice before drafting, and use sentence fluency, word choice, and conventions before revision. Consider each time the options you discover that might help you in your own writing.

Conditional knowledge: Which options did I use from the model? Why did I use them? Although I may never have to do this kind of writing again, how can the six-trait questioning strategy help me in other kinds of writing?

The six-trait model* (Spandel, *Creating*) uses the traits of ideas, organization, voice, sentence fluency, word choice, and conventions as a model for assessment—and also as a vocabulary for talking about writing before assessing it. For me, it also provides a perfect heuristic for reading texts like a writer, for helping students investigate a text and see what it has to offer them. I have used it with an assignment modeled after a picture book, *My House Has Stars* by Megan McDonald (Dean, "Framing").

I begin by introducing students to the text. I read the framing aspects of the book: the introduction, some of the pages (each one describes a "house" in a different place in the world), and then the conclusion. We discuss what the book is trying to do and how it does it overall. Then I ask students to read individual pages in small groups and build a list of the kinds of ideas the author uses in her descriptions. Although there are patterns to the ideas—ideas that are found in all pages, such as descriptions of the surrounding area and indications of the kinds of activity in which the people who live there engage—there are also variations. One page describes some cultural artifacts that are unique to the belief system of the place. Some pages describe who made the house or specific songs the inhabitants hear there. Since there is variation as well as pattern, I like students to read several pages as they build their lists of ideas.

From the small groups' lists, we build a class list, which becomes important because it will guide students' research during inquiry. In choosing a place to write about, I suggest that students pick a country of their heritage, but I also allow them to pick a place they are interested in. By allowing a wider choice, students are more engaged in the writing, but some problems also arise that wouldn't otherwise. For instance, some students like to write about a place they've visited for vacation or a place they ski or have a cabin. These choices sometimes create problems in that students think they know everything there is to know about the place and therefore see no need for further inquiry, a requirement for the assignment. We sometimes have to go outside the list of ideas the class generated to help these students find information they don't already know—and that an audience wouldn't know—so that the final piece is informative as well as interesting.

---

* Based on the six-trait model developed by Northwest Regional Educational Laboratory.

When students have completed their research, we return to the models to pose questions about organization and voice. Questioning about these traits helps students focus their investigation on the options that will benefit them most as writers at each stage of the process. Students notice the way McDonald groups her ideas and how she begins with details that are close and continues with more distant ones before connecting to the sky and stars at the end of every description. Although the book is written in a child's voice, my students notice that the voice is informed and engaged. I give them the option of imitating the voice of the book (a child's voice), but most choose to write in their own natural voices—and that's also an option that we can discuss as strategic: What difference in effect does that choice make, and why would it or wouldn't it work?

After drafting, we look again at the models, questioning them about the traits of sentence fluency and word choice. Students' discoveries provide me with a chance to help them see how these two traits are separate but also work together to enhance voice. We can talk about the variety in length of sentences and how the model texts resemble speech more than the informative texts students are used to reading. I direct them back to their drafts to work on revising for these traits, guided by the choices in the models.

Many students choose to imitate the format of the model text in their final draft; McDonald superimposes the text on a world map where the place being described is circled. This assignment for research-based writing is especially engaging and helpful, in my experience, for students who are reluctant writers. Here is Isac's example, which uses some of the options we discussed for each trait:

> My house has many rooms. Each room is separate. It is built above water and is resting on stilts. This is nice because when the air blows through, over the water, it cools the house. It is square with a cone-shaped roof, which is made of palm leaves. We use breezeways to get from room to room, or to shore and back.
>
> My grandmother, who lives in the farthest room, tells us stories about the Tupapau, an evil-minded spirit who came back from the dead to torment the living. If you drive after dark around the island, you'll notice that many houses keep a light on all night. This is to keep Tupapau away.
>
> My house has lots of water, water that reflects the stars. In the reflection I can also see the o'te'a'tane dancing on the shore, scattering and then arranging themselves, like the stars above them, above me.
>
> My house has stars.

The six traits help students read texts for strategies they can use as writers, and once students learn how to use them, they can help themselves learn options for a variety of genres they might need to write.

Lesson Plan: How-To Writing

In my planning, I consider what my students need to know or know how to do before they began drafting this assignment. Some major things they need are these:

- An understanding of how processes are explained—what process writing looks like or what it can look like
- An understanding of why this genre needs clear details, consideration of the audience's needs, clear organization, and effective transitions
- An understanding of how differing purposes change the voice and choice of details
- Comprehension of why knowing the process well is important to a good explanation

To help students be successful with this writing, I use the following strategies.

Teacher Plan for Inquiry Strategies

1. I introduce the genre simply with this handout:

How-To Writing

How-to writing gives instructions. It tells someone how to be something or do something. Because it has a unique purpose, it also has unique structure and tone. Notice what those might be in this how-to writing from Vicki Spandel:

How to Be a Shark

Never *blink.*
Never *cry.*
Scare the pants off everybody.
Leave home as soon as you can pack.
Avoid restaurants.
Look even more dangerous than you are—it could land you a screen test.
If you have to act up, *do* it around goldfish.
Make a ton of money off the tooth fairy.
Retire in Hawaii where they appreciate you.

---

continued on next page

Ms. Spandel made at least one characteristic noticeable by italicizing certain words. What else can you notice about this genre's tone? Another version of how-to writing is from a book titled *How to Lose All Your Friends* by Nancy Carlson.

As I read the book, you will see that Nancy Carlson's how-to shares some of the characteristics of Ms. Spandel's, but it also has some variations. While I read, list the similarities and differences here:

SAME   DIFFERENT

I try to guide students to see the use of imperatives in this genre, the (mostly) logical order of ideas, and the generally impersonal tone (although this ranges along a continuum).

2. Next, to help students understand the complexity and numerous options writers have in explaining processes, we look at a variety of more developed texts. I like the humorous essay by Russell Baker, "Slice of Life," that is in our textbook. Other how-to models could include directions for putting a table together; I have one from assembling just such a piece of furniture myself and use it in class. I find models on the Internet as well as in other places. (One short column I found in *Sports Illustrated* was "How to Beef Up and Be a Bully" by Ian Thomson.) The book *The Worst-Case Scenario Survival Handbook, Student Edition* (Piven and Borgenicht) provides a number of models of how-to writing. I decide which might be most helpful for students to read. By looking at several models, students begin to envision what this kind of writing can do. I select the models with the age of the students in mind, as some models use the how-to genre to make social commentary. If students can appreciate this use, I like them to see the option of social commentary as a potential purpose of this kind of writing. It's a creative use of genre. Questioning the models, the purposes, and the choices the writers made to accomplish those purposes is one of the ways students begin to build a picture of the genre.

3. A way to address the need for clear details involves a classroom activity using gumdrops that I first learned from *Ideas Plus* (McComiskey). I arrange my students so that their desks are back to back in pairs. Each student receives seven gumdrops and six toothpicks. (Getting them to leave them alone until we are ready to begin can be tricky.) All students facing the front of the classroom create a three-dimensional figure us-

ing the items they've been given. The partners keep their backs to this work, and no talking goes on. After about ten minutes or when all are done, the person who created the figure tells the partner how to create the same design. Students are to keep their backs to each other during the whole experience. I tell students that the second person can only ask for directions to be repeated and cannot ask clarifying questions. When everyone's finished, we all get up and walk around looking at the designs.

Some partnerships succeed and some fail. That, however, doesn't matter so much as the next part, or rather the part after students get to eat their gumdrops. We clean up and get back into order, and then I ask what this activity teaches. Of course, they make the connection to the need for clarity, but I push them to think of what this actually entails. Usually, they can come up with considering the needs of the audience, using precise words—and we talk about how words can be taken more than one way—and the necessity of breaking the process down into very small steps. We even notice that the original orientation of the items is important to the whole process.

4. As a strategy for understanding how different purposes require different writing choices, we look again at the models, this time with a different purpose and in more depth. We want to look at the writing with "mining" in mind—how do the choices affect the purpose, and what are those choices? I provide students with a worksheet for each model, which they use to take notes as we practice questioning:

[Title of Piece]
  Audience(s):

  Purpose(s):

  What does the author do in the text to accomplish these purposes for this audience?

As an example, I will walk through the questioning using Baker's essay. We have read it already, so I ask students what they remember about it. They usually say it is about carving a turkey and that it is funny. I ask them why it is funny. They indicate several points, and we start to categorize what makes this process description funny. Students note the contrast of the tone with the steps in the process: Part of the process he describes requires spilling gravy on the guests to buy the carver time. The turkey burns the carver and rolls around the table, yet all these events are told in a matter-of-fact tone, much like the tone of the directions for putting a table together. But here we see what can happen if the process goes awry—and we experience it when we actually follow simple directions.

Students should recognize that exaggeration is a part of the humor: "If using the alternate ax method, this operation should be performed on a cement walk outside the house in order to preserve the table" (Baker 219). Part of the humor is created overall by the sense that no one really wants to complete this process. This understanding is created by the carver's expressed preference for watching a football game instead of carving a turkey. And, finally, part of the humor is created because some aspects of this process have been experienced—perhaps in serious instead of humorous ways—in most people's homes. Here we see everything go wrong that can go wrong, but we identify with the humor because we've usually seen at least one of these unfortunate occurrences ourselves. For each aspect of humor that students find, I ask them specifically what Baker has done to create it; from that we can build a list of techniques that students might choose from if they decide to write a humorous how-to paper.

Finally, I ask students how this essay uses the characteristics we can see in a piece of serious how-to writing. First, Baker starts the essay by reminding us that this is a process; his first line is, "How to carve a turkey" (218). Then he provides steps with imperatives at the start: "Assemble," "Begin," Exercise," "Take." He explains some of the steps as well as possible hazards or mistakes the reader might make, just as other how-to pieces do. It is in these alternatives and problems that much of the humor exists. This questioning strategy should be used with other models to expand the range of options students have when they write.

5. At this point, I give students the assignment that follows:

How-To Writing
All around us we see people making use of instructions or directions—how to lose weight, how to succeed in business, how to get the girl or the guy, how to play this game or install that program. This

type of writing (this genre!) is so prevalent, in fact, that some writers use it to create humor, to say the opposite of what they say on the surface, to comment on social behavior. Despite the differing purposes for using this genre, perhaps in spite of them, the genre in all its purposes shares certain traits and accomplishes certain purposes.

Now you're going to write instructions! Explain how to do something or how something works—or use the characteristics of a how-to paper to create humor or social commentary. Vent about something people do that bugs you or comment on interesting human behavior. This paper allows you to do those things.

6. Students brainstorm to make a list of possible topics to write about, topics they can be successful with. I pose questions they can consider for possibilities: What do you know how to do well? What have you done many times? I encourage them to think of situations that occur in their lives every day: they do homework, drive, socialize, eat. For each, they can think of processes; some of these are also appropriate for writing social commentary. I have students consider practices or behaviors they find humorous or puzzling. I suggest they think of actions no one would ever want to do (lose a job through your own fault, lose a girl-friend or boyfriend). I encourage students to contribute specifics as we go along so that we can have a list of ideas from which everyone can draw. Then I ask students to star the topic they are most interested in and answer these questions:

- What audience do you want to address?
- What audience characteristics do you need to plan for?
- What purpose(s) do you want to achieve?
- What will you do in the text to accomplish your purpose for this audience? What strategies did the authors we read use that you could use too?

Teacher Plan for Drafting Strategies

1. When students have picked a topic and have some idea of the purpose and approach they are going to take, I give a minilesson on imperatives to help students understand the nature of these sentences and the ways they can be used effectively. We've already discussed them when we looked at the models, but now I have them practice writing them (leaving out grammatical explanations). I want them to understand that imperatives don't have to start with the verb, that some are

buried after introductory clauses or phrases. Here's what I give them; we go over their responses as a class so that I can help them see options for their own writing.

Put a check by the sentences that are imperatives. If the sentence is a fragment, write it as a complete imperative sentence.

1. Show us the pictures from the party
2. A jigsaw puzzle with hundreds of pieces
3. Whistling in the dark
4. Be sure to lock the door when you leave
5. Cared for the wounded fox
6. Please don't open my mail
7. Before you begin, write the first letters in a row
8. Collecting all the albums ever made by Whitney Houston
9. After wrapping the towel around your hand several times, grab the turkey
10. Agreed to the plan

---

2. With the idea of imperatives in mind, students create a list of steps in the process they have chosen. We refer to the models and note that not every sentence in this writing is an imperative (too strong), but the major steps (and some minor ones) are imperatives, so that is the form their list is to take. I urge them to visualize the process, making sure to list as many of the important steps as possible. I show them my own list (below) and help them see that I might add more items to the list or group some of these together into substeps as I write.

How to Liven Up a Play or Cultural Event

- Leave your cell phone on.
- Talk to your neighbor.
- Act like you're at a football game.
- Eat food.
- Take any seat you want even though the printed ticket says you have another one.
- Come in late.

> - Make loud comments about the play or performance or what you think will happen next.
> - Put your feet on the seat in front of you.
> - Wear a tall hat.
> - Disrupt those around you through inappropriate social behaviors. In other words, pass gas, belch, snore, or sniff loudly.

After students have a list, they show it to three people to see if those people see gaps or more steps to add. The students then choose to take the advice or not.

3. Students use their list of imperatives to begin drafting, again referring to previous discussions and the models to see how each step is developed according to the writer's purpose. Again, I use my own draft to give students some idea of what I think as I write, how I use the things I have experienced, and how some ideas pop into my head just because I am thinking of the strategies the authors used, posing questions: What if something goes wrong? What could happen if . . . ? What could be worse than this?

> Come in late. This is bound to create bad feelings among other members of the audience. Once the play or concert has started, the lights will be dimmed. In the dark, you will have trouble finding your seat so you will have to stumble over people and climb over them just to find out you read the signs wrong and this isn't your seat anyway. On your way back out, be sure and fall into at least one lap. That always enhances people's enjoyment of the play.
> Eventually, just take any seat you want, even if it's not the one you paid for. If the real ticket owner comes in later, that just works to your benefit. He will have to climb around in the dark, and you and he will have to have a conversation about whose seat it is. You will both have to stand up, blocking others' views of the performance, and you will have to search your pockets for your stub and talk about the situation, which will be even more of a disruption. You can tell him you had to take his seat because you gave yours away to an elderly woman who couldn't walk this far and see if he has compassion and will go take someone else's seat. If you have a very compassionate audience, you could ruin the whole performance by making a number of people switch to the wrong seats and causing confusion the whole night.
> Be sure to leave your cell phone on. In fact, you might want to have the ringer set extra loud so you can hear it above the performance. If it rings, answer it. Take any calls that come, and carry

on the necessary conversation. Especially good are conversations that tell the caller what you are watching, in detail. But after you've exhausted that, talk about what the guy next door was wearing when he ran out after his barking dog last night or what the girl in your class said about the girl who stole her boyfriend away from her. Be sure to mention names and spend as much time as you want in these phone conversations. You could even send a picture of the performance and then one of your face while you gag yourself as commentary. All of this will help pass the time while you are there.

During drafting in class, my students often talk their ideas out with one another. Again, this is a strategy some students need to develop ideas.

Teacher Plan for Product Strategies

1. When students have a draft, we discuss introductions and conclusions. Again, I refer students to the models for options. Some essays have longer introductions that establish a context for the directions that follow. Others are brief and direct: "How to carve a turkey: Assemble the following tools . . ." (Baker 218). We discuss the ways different strategies work for different topics, how some need more of an introduction and why. We repeat the process by looking at effective ways to write conclusions before students revise these aspects of their drafts.

2. How-to writing requires effective use of transitions, so I provide a minilesson on this during the revision phase of our writing. We refer to the models to look at writers' options for guiding their readers through the processes described. Students learn that different processes (and different purposes) require different types of transitions: showing orientation through time or space or more abstract orientations such as order of importance. Students can revise their transitions by modeling them after selections whose purposes best fit their own.

3. For revision, students use questioning strategies similar to the ones we used for questioning the models. I encourage them to write questions where they arise, to suggest places where authors can take the idea beyond its current level, to see if the author's purpose is being achieved. This way, the strategy we used to begin this genre writing is also the one we use to end it.

4. Before final revisions, students use the grading criteria to conduct peer evaluative readings. They go through a peer's paper and comment on how the paper could meet the criteria in each area more effectively. Those criteria follow:

Name _____

How-To Writing

Ideas _____
- The ideas show process, humor, and/or social commentary (as a purpose).
- The steps are clear and elaborated, leaving no confusion in the mind of the reader.
- The ideas are shaped into directions for doing something, even if that something is negative or humorous.
- The ideas are unique, appropriate, and interesting for the audience.

Organization _____
- "Directions" follow something close to chronological order.
- Ideas are linked by a sense of connection and logical order (transitions!).
- An interesting introduction gives a sense of purpose or context to the ideas.
- An interesting conclusion provides a sense of closure.

Voice _____
- The tone of the paper is informative or funny and appropriate for the content and audience.
- The tone stays consistent throughout, with declaratives modifying the effect of imperatives.
- The reader feels a sense of engagement on the part of the writer.

Word Choice _____
- One vocabulary word is used effectively in the essay.
- The words are consistently precise and effective to create tone and clarify meaning.

Sentence Fluency _____
- Sentences vary in length to replicate speech patterns and increase fluency.
- Careful attention is paid to combining ideas accurately and effectively.
- Use of imperatives effectively creates the tone and style of the genre.

Conventions _____
- Spelling, grammar, and punctuation errors are minor.

TOTAL _____

5. When students turn in their work, they reflect on the strategies they used to write this paper: Which strategies did you use that you felt contributed most to your writing of this paper? (Consider strategies for both process and product.) How did they help you? How might those strategies help you in other writing for this class or outside this class?

Here's Justine's paper, written in response to this plan:

> Have you ever wondered what you could do to get out of a speeding ticket? How to persuade a cop to leave you with a warning? You can get a ticket without attempting to stop him, pay the fine, and you are done. Why not try to get out of that written cop commission? It can't hurt. Here is all that you need to know to get a cop's sympathy.
>
> When those bright lights flash behind you, your first step is to put on your seatbelt. This shows the cop your interest in the safety of yourself and others joining you on the street. It also saves you the price of the fine. If you have a radar detector, make sure it's hidden under the seat. Or you could just throw it away because it obviously didn't work anyway. When you come to a complete stop, make sure you don't rev your engine while he gets out of his car. This might excite him into thinking he's getting the opportunity of a live televised high speed chase. He'll be very disappointed if you were just testing out your engine. Don't try this escape route unless you plan on following through with it because, if he makes it to your window before you take off, your chances of making his paycheck greater just got larger.
>
> Invest in some churchy, spiritual music and have it close by in the time of need. As the cop hears this playing, it gives him a different feeling. Putting on some heavy metal music won't do you any good. This might scare the rookie cop or make the veteran even more angry because I'm sure he's heard that enough. While looking for your information, it helps to have the passenger seat cleaned off with only a mother-to-be book clearly visible to his or her eyes. This gives the police a sense of warm motherly feeling, and it will intimidate them into thinking at any minute you will be going into an emotional emergency if he gives you a ticket.
>
> Don't have your consumed alcoholic beverages anywhere in sight: that guarantees a ticket of all sorts and a search of your vehicle. Your goal is to get the cop's sympathy for the "pregnant" young lady so he will just give up on this catch and move on to the next, leaving you with a simple verbal warning. If all else fails and you just want to have some fun, here is what you can do. Pull out your little brother's play gun and politely ask the officer to compare it to his own. Be prepared for the incontrovertible consequences. This might either make him feel proud of his trusty weapon because it's bigger than yours or it might just get you a first class ticket. However, if you're lucky, a comfortable back seat in the reliable police car. Use your knowledge and perform it at the next

stop. No matter what the result turns out to be, at least you brought excitement to the boring ritual.

———

10/27: I was introducing the next assignment, subtly I thought. We just read an essay and talked about how it took a common view of a topic and then showed how that perception wasn't exactly accurate. I asked students to brainstorm what things they knew about that they could do that same thing with—show readers that they didn't know everything about that topic. I suggested general categories: activities, pets, groups, hobbies, etc. That was how I ended class, with the listing and no mention of an essay.

Of course, I wasn't as sneaky as I thought I'd been—I've had students tell me in the past that even if they are having fun, they know it will be building toward some writing assignment or another. So I shouldn't be surprised, I guess, that they don't fall for my subtlety. As Isac walked by me, he said, "I'm going to need some models, you know. I really think that's the best strategy, at least for me. I just want you to know I'll want some models before you have us write this essay." And then he walked on past me out the door.

I know I use models to help me shape my ideas in appropriate ways for different writing situations, and I want my students to have that same ability. Am I always effective? Do I always provide them with adequate strategies that help them access the models, not only for class but for life? I know that many of my colleagues say that lower-performing students should just have prescribed forms for writing, that the complex considerations that constitute genres are too much for them. It's tempting sometimes to go there, to reduce genre to forms when the students are struggling, when working with them seems like *so much* work. Still, the rewards of some of them getting it seem to make it worth it. I think. I hope.

Additional Resources

Bawarshi, Anis. *Genre and the Invention of the Writer.* Logan: Utah State UP, 2003.

Bazerman, Charles. "The Life of Genre, the Life in the Classroom." *Genre and Writing: Issues, Arguments, Alternatives.* Ed. Wendy Bishop and Hans Ostrom. Portsmouth, NH: Boynton/Cook, 1997. 19–26.

Chapman, Marilyn. "Situated, Social, Active: Rewriting Genre in the Elementary Classroom." *Written Communication* 16 (1999): 469–90.

Cope, Bill, and Mary Kalantzis. "Introduction: How a Genre Approach to Literacy Can Transform the Way Writing Is Taught." *The Powers of Literacy: A Genre Approach to Teaching Writing.* Pittsburgh: University of Pittsburgh Press, 1993. xx.

Devitt, Amy. *Writing Genres.* Carbondale: Southern Illinois UP, 2004.

Lattimer, Heather. *Thinking Through Genre: Units of Study in Reading and Writing Workshops 4–12.* Portland, ME: Stenhouse, 2003.

4 Strategies for Drafting: Considering Audience

But it is only through the text, through language, that writers embody or give life to their conception of the reader.

Lisa Ede and Andrea Lunsford

I went back to finish my bachelor's degree as a mother with children stretched between elementary school and junior high and my husband working out of the area. Needless to say, we were short on money and therefore driving older cars. One time, I loaded the children into our old van to drive eight hundred miles to spend a week we had off from school with my husband. After we arrived, I noticed that I could smell exhaust fumes in the car and went in to a shop to find out why. The shop's repairman told me I needed a whole new muffler and exhaust system, costing more money than I could afford. As we stood under the car and I thought about where the money would come from, the repairman told me (a selling point, perhaps?) that the system came with a lifetime warranty. I laughed. Rust was falling like dark snow around us as we spoke. I didn't care about lifetimes; I cared about the eight hundred miles I had to drive the next day with my children in the car. I got the system.

When I returned home, I found out that I hadn't really needed the whole system, that the repairman had taken advantage of me and my lack of knowledge about cars, a story I see reported in the news all the time now. I wanted to break something! Instead, I wrote a letter of complaint to the corporate headquarters of the shop. I was careful to consider the potential audience of my writing: the corporate office. I considered length and tone and content; I wanted to make sure that my letter might not be thrown out, because I could imagine a corporate office would receive numerous letters of complaint. I considered which points would be most persuasive in making my complaint and what I could do to build credibility in the eyes of my anticipated reader. I not only received a refund and a letter of apology but also credit for a future visit to one of their shops and an assurance that the business would improve its way of treating female customers.

I benefited in my car repair situation because I had had careful teachers of writing who had helped me understand the importance of considering audience when I wrote. Certainly, I considered audience very

consciously as I wrote that letter. Thinking about audience has an impact on ideas (which ones I choose and which I leave out), organization (what should come first, second, last), language (what words I use
and how I use them), even genre (whether I should use a memo or a
letter form). And effective writing for our students should be about
audience, too.

The concept of audience, however, has come under some scru-
tiny in the decades since I was taught the traditional rhetorical relationship: audience–writer–subject. More recently, the idea of audience has
come to hold a number of meanings: who the writer intends to read the
work, who the writer imagines might read the work, and who actually
does read it. When I was writing my letter of complaint, I imagined a
primary reader and another group of readers (since I also considered
that the letter might have to move through a sequence of readers' hands).
And I considered those readers' interests and concerns as I wrote and
revised. But I also had to think about my own concerns and larger concerns, too. Was I representing many women who might have been taken
advantage of as well as my own concerns? As Douglas Park notes, "'audience' is merely a rough way of pointing at the whole set of contexts"
related to a particular piece of writing (314). In other words, it's complicated.

Peter Elbow has suggested that sometimes an audience can stifle
writing, even block it ("Closing" 336). He doesn't advocate ignoring
audience forever, although that's how some have interpreted his words;
instead he advocates waiting to consider audience until later in the
writing process, until after ideas are on paper. Although I understand
his position, I think that considering audience, like considering genre
and purpose, can sometimes provoke writing rather than inhibit it.
Imagining a person or group or set of characteristics can often help to
generate writing that just looking at a blank page cannot. For instance,
many students have trouble filling a page with writing that has no clear
audience—the kind of writing that begins many English classes: "Write
a page about anything you want." I have myself balked at such a
prompt. But if I'm told to write to a particular group of people or person, I can often do it: Write a letter to Scout or Jem. Immediately, I begin to think of what I know about them from the novel and how I might
comment on an incident in the book or what I have done that might
connect to something they did in the book. Even a pretend audience
helps me begin to write—and I've seen it help my students, too.

Audience Considerations

Despite these complicating perspectives, the concept of audience is still very much a part of a strategic approach to teaching writing. We teachers still want students to be aware of what writers do to adapt writing for different audiences so that they will be better prepared for situations outside of our individual classes. As Ryder, Lei, and Roen assert, "Every form of writing is working to persuade other people to see the world as the writer does. . . . The more we can help our students to see this aspect of what they write, the more audience will become a factor that shapes [student writing]" (61).

Walter Ong has suggested that "the writer's audience is always a fiction" (55), that writers create an idea of the audience rather than write to a specific person. Certainly, this is true to an extent. Even when a letter is written to a specific person, the writer shapes text to his or her interpretation of that person or to a role that person plays instead of to the whole, real person. In an effort to make audience a more important factor to student writers, many current publications in secondary education promote the idea that students write only to "authentic" audiences, real people outside of the classroom (Meeks 77, for one example). Letters about Literature, a writing contest open to students from grades 4 to 12 sponsored by the Center for the Book of the Library of Congress, is one way teachers could provide students with audiences outside the classroom. In addition to the contest rules, the Web site (http://www.loc.gov/loc/cfbook/letters.html) provides effective lesson plans for helping students practice writing in a genre—letters—to an audience outside the classroom. Kids on the Net publishes student writing online (http://kotn.ntu.ac.uk/). Another site, http://www.publishingstudents.com, lists publications that publish student writing. These and a number of other sources can help students write for audiences outside the classroom.

Although I know from experience that finding audiences outside of the classroom adds a dimension to writing that is often missing in much school writing, I'm also certain that there are many times when teachers need to have students write pieces that are not easily addressed to audiences outside of the classroom. For example, as an English teacher, I often want to know that my students can think analytically about a piece of literature and express that thinking in well-developed prose. However, try as I might, I rarely find an audience outside of the classroom for such writing.

And I don't think that's all bad, either. I know that there's a derisive tone when people talk about writing for the teacher, but I agree with Pat Belanoff when she comments about grading (and therefore about being the primary audience of students' writing), "If I can help students understand how to get an A or B in my class, I will be helping them learn to figure out how to analyze and impress other audiences too, both in and out of school" (153). Certainly teachers will want students to have audiences outside of the classroom when they can, but when they can't, a teacher's grading criteria and stated expectations can also help shape an ability to write for an audience.

Since finding outside audiences isn't always possible, some teachers hope to teach the concept of audience by creating a hypothetical one, an idea which has its benefits and limitations as well. If the purpose of the assignment is to help students learn to provide cues for readers other than the teacher, such assignments can have value (as I hope to show later in this chapter). But if the idea of an imaginary audience is only to pretend a context, the limitations weaken the assignment—and the students' ability to learn about audience cues from it. For instance, when a state writing assessment frames a written response as a letter to the school board and the students know that piece of writing will never see a school board, will only be seen in fact by the scorers of the exam— what is the point? Students are not fooled by fake audiences when they know the writing is really being used for another reason: to measure their written language skills for state assessments. Joseph Petraglia suggests that such attempts contribute to a "reductive view" of writing instruction ("Writing" 92). I would add that they don't teach students what we want them to learn about audience either.

We further misconstrue audience for students when we ask them to write about literature to us (a way to encourage critical and creative thinking at best, a way to check if they read or listened in class at worst) and ask them to pretend the audience doesn't know anything about the literature. If we are the only audience and our purpose is assessment, don't we confuse audience considerations for students by then saying they should introduce the literature with the title and author and a summary of what it's about—write as if the audience knows nothing? Certainly we don't give students a chance to consider audience at all when we give such conflicting messages.

So what does all this mean for actually teaching audience? I suggest three points.

1. Teachers can provide students with opportunities to write for readers outside of the class as a way to broaden and improve a sense of audience for writing.

2. If the writing is not going outside of the classroom, but one of our goals for an assignment is to help students understand and practice "the signals provided by the writer for his audience" (Long, cited in Ede and Lunsford 78), teachers can take a strategic approach to audience by helping students become aware of (1) how writers create cues for the reader to indicate how to read a piece and (2) how writers adapt to some concept of audience as a way to shape writing.

3. Finally, we can become more honest about audience in our classroom. If writing is going to be graded by us (teachers), we need to acknowledge that we are *one* of the *readers* for the writing, even if we are not the *intended* audience. Our comments on student writing can go a long way in helping students understand how readers respond as well as how other intended audiences might respond.

Practicing Audience Moves

Ryder, Lei, and Roen present an interesting approach to helping students think about the role audience can play in writing by explaining three kinds of relationships writers have with readers (55). In the first, the writer is also the reader; the relationship is singular. Writing for this audience might include journals (in the true sense of the word—not class journals) or other writing that is intended just for the writer to work out thoughts on paper: notes or writing to learn. The second type of relationship is when the writer is addressing a specific person. Students who write only for the teacher perceive this kind of relationship, and personal letters may also be written from this perspective.

The authors describe the third kind of relationship as one where there are multiple audiences, sometimes with differing concerns and characteristics, what they call *triadic*. Writing with this relationship can require very complex audience considerations. Ryder et al. explain that "to some extent, the audience role in the triadic situation is one that writing teachers find most comfortable. Rather than have students speak to us directly, we prefer that they speak to another audience while we listen in" (55). This is often the case when teachers try to have students consider wider audiences than just the teacher. But in reality, we either set up a false audience role, which doesn't teach our students what they should know about audience, or we create a challenging situation that we should guide students through more carefully.

Teachers can consider this perspective of audience-author relationships—self, specific other, multiple others—in designing writing assignments. Do we give students opportunities to practice audience strategies from all perspectives, and do we ask students to reflect on the ways they shaped writing differently in each circumstance, to note the processes and thoughts that changed as the audience changed? These considerations are important in helping students learn how to adapt texts for different audiences.

In helping students develop the conscious attention to audience that might help them build adaptive writing skills, teachers can provide writing opportunities that shift audiences—both real and fictional—and thus help students develop stances that fit the needs of different contexts. In the application section of this chapter, the Personality File strategy asks students to take the perspective of a character writing to himself or herself for several journal entries and then to write a letter from that character to another character in the literature. The journal entries help students develop a sense of what writers do when they write only to and for themselves, and the letter helps them consider the shifts necessary when they have to write from that perspective to someone else. Additionally, students start to build an ability to perceive the characteristics of possible audiences by stepping into another's shoes.

Cuing Audiences

Current research and theory on audience has looked carefully at the way a writer cues the readers to let them know how the writer expects them to read a piece of writing. These cues may be instinctive for some students and for some writing situations. However, I also try to make such cues strategic by having students practice considering different aspects of audience in different assignments, making cuing more explicit.

One of the cues writers provide to identify audience is through what Ryder et al. call "naming moves" (57). These are the names and pronouns writers use to position themselves and readers. One assignment I use to help students consider and practice these kinds of cues is the Postcards strategy practice, described in the application section of this chapter. The book *Stringbean's Trip to the Shining Sea* (Williams and Williams) is a story told through a series of postcards to the family back home. Interestingly, the first page is a postcard to the book's readers that acknowledges that the audience is really not the persons to whom the cards are addressed. In a way, then, the book represents a complex consideration of audience—plural, written to one group but knowing that others will be the actual audience. The book provides a good opportunity for students to learn about writing to one audience while knowing another one will be the primary audience, much the way we ask them to do with writing that we grade but direct to be written with other audiences in mind.

Ryder et al. use the phrase *strategy moves* to describe the cues that address what the audience knows or doesn't know and what the audience cares about. I want students first to be aware of how these cues function in texts they read and then to see how they can use them effectively to create their own texts and to address audience attributes in their own writing.

To do this, I use David Wisniewski's book *The Secret Knowledge of Grown-Ups* as a model. This text consists of an introduction and then a series of "case files" that give the secret reasons for rules adults give children. The case files in this text are a variation of a genre most students will not have occasion to write; however, they are genres in the broad sense that they have regularities that respond to a specific context and audience. The procedures I use to teach this strategy practice are described in the application section also.

Peers as Audience

Another important way to help students consider audience is by using their classmates as audience, either through peer readings or through "publishing" to the class. Although I address peer evaluation in Chapter 6, I want to mention it briefly here as a way to help students think of audience. In the end-of-semester reflections for a remediation class I taught, a number of students commented that peer review was one of the best strategies they had practiced. In particular, Sid had this comment about it: "I'd like to talk about peer review, one of the most helpful strategies to me during the course of this class. It always gave me the view of the audience." Paul, a student in another class, wrote this:

> I think reading our peers' writing is one of the most important parts of being in school. Reading other students' drafts helps me because I often feel like I'm the only one that's struggling with an assignment and that mine is going to be the only paper that isn't going to be perfect. Just to know that other students have the same problems as I do is helpful. It also helps me see how my writing is unique, which keeps me motivated.

Even when students don't have an audience outside of the class— or if they have an imaginary one—if they have peer evaluation, they should consider the rest of the class as readers. Doing so helps them broaden their perspective of audience and, as students note, improves their writing by making them entertain ideas they might not consider on their own.

To expand the idea of the class as audience, some assignments can be bound in a book form and then checked out by class members to take home and read independently. The Six Traits strategy practice in Chapter 3 and the Secret Knowledge practice in this chapter are two that lend themselves to such treatment. Other writing can be shared orally, either with the whole class or in small groups. With the appropriate technology, students could also post their papers to a class Web site. Any way that teachers can help students consider their peers as at least one audience will help students develop audience awareness as a part of strategic writing.

Applications

Strategy Practice: Personality File

Declarative knowledge: Journals are places where a writer writes for himself or herself. Sometimes journals are read after a person's death to learn of the writer's life or of the time the writer lived. But the primary audience of a journal is the self. Therefore, details that matter to the person are included, as are feelings and emotions the writer might not share with others. Because of the nature of journals, different versions of the same event may end up in the journals of different people who shared an experience.

Procedural knowledge: Learn about a character in the literature by looking at evidence in the text that shows how the character feels and thinks. Take notes about the things your character says and does, what others say about her or him, and what all these clues might mean for the character's thinking and emotions. Use these to write as if you were the character you chose. Then write a letter from your character to another character in the literature about something that happened. Consider how the two characters feel about each other and how that might be reflected in the writing.

Conditional knowledge: What strategies did I use to think about my character in order to write like him or her to himself or herself? What did I do to make it seem as though it was really a journal and not for another audience? What shifts did I have to make when I wrote the letter to the other person? How might these considerations help me when I write in other situations when I have to shift audiences?

I use *Romeo and Juliet* for this assignment. Other teachers have used other pieces of literature, however. In this writing, students fictionalize audience, but this practice helps them develop both an understanding of character as well as how a single perspective (the character writing to himself or herself) influences choices in text. Irene Clark lists several benefits of having students write to fictional audiences, including "foster[ing] respect for an audience's humanity and opinions" (149). This assignment can do that well, I think.

Romeo and Juliet Personality File

We are beginning to read the play *Romeo and Juliet* in class. Completing this personality file will help you find connections with the play and increase your understanding of it as well as help you consider issues of audience in your writing. As we begin, you should choose one character you find interesting from among the main characters. Your file will be based on that character. The following guidelines should be followed.

1. The file should contain six (6) journal entries that could have been written by the character you have chosen at different points during the action of the play. The journal entries should accurately reflect the character as he or she is depicted by Shakespeare as well as show your interpretation of the emotions attached to the events occurring in your character's life. Weave a quote with the reference into each entry. Please write only one journal entry per page.

2. The file should also contain a letter the character might have written to another character in the play or to someone else of that time outside of the play. Again, the letter should accurately reflect the character's feelings, fears, motives, personality, and so on, and should consider the different audience.

3. A one-page collage of pictures portraying the character—interests, appearance, likes, dislikes, personal philosophy or beliefs, and so on—should be included in the file.

4. The whole personality file should be placed in a decorated cover that also reflects the character in some way. The character's name should be on the outside, along with your name.

Be creative! The project grade will be based on how accurately you represent the character but also on how creatively you portray your understanding and insights as well as your awareness of audience shifts.

We will pause from time to time in our reading and discussion to give you time to draft journal entries. The complete project is due at the beginning of class on _____. Have fun!

Here is one of Alisha's pages from her personality file on Juliet.

"Thy husband lives, that Tybalt would have slain;
And Tybalt's dead, that would have slain my husband" III, ii, 71–
72

Oh what a terrible, terrible day. My husband of less than a day has killed my only cousin Tybalt. How bittersweet, my cousin dies that my husband may live. I am so angry but I don't know who to be angry at. Shall I be angry with Romeo because he has killed my cousin? Shall I be angry at Tybalt for drawing Romeo into a fight even though it cost him his life? Or shall I be angry with myself for being disloyal to my new husband and speaking ill of the dead?

This has been a very eventful day. This morning I was excited to hear from Romeo. This afternoon I was married and could not wait until night to see him. And now I grieve for my cousin and wonder if I will ever see Romeo again. Here is perhaps the very worst part—Romeo has been banished from Verona. I may never see him again. He's going to Mantua and it is said that if he is ever seen in Verona again that he will be killed.

I am so very, very sad about Romeo. My parents think that I am sad for Tybalt. What they don't know won't hurt them. Besides, I probably won't see Romeo again after tonight.

It's clear that Alisha shows her understanding of Juliet's emotions as she comes back again and again to her concerns and problems—just what a writer does when she writes to herself. She also shows her sense of Juliet as a teenager with her comment that what her parents don't know won't hurt them. In her letter to Juliet's parents, Alisha reveals all and explains from Juliet's perspective her reasons for making the choices she did ("I knew that you would forbid our marriage") and her understanding of her parents' motives ("I know that you were trying to make me better by arranging my marriage"). The strategy practice allows students like Alisha to practice various stances effectively.

Strategy Practice: Postcards

Declarative knowledge: Postcards are short pieces of informative writing directed to a specific audience even if others might read it. Writers give cues that indicate what the relationship is with the audience. *Procedural knowledge:* Read literature and consider the characters and events, carefully attending to the way characters relate. At different points in the literature, have one character write a postcard to another character, commenting on an event in the literature. Consider what the addressee knows and doesn't know about the event as well the writer's relationship to him or her. Use ideas and words to suggest the relationship and characters' knowledge.

Conditional knowledge: What cues did I use to make sure the postcard could only have been written by my character to the character in the address? What did I have to think about? When might that same kind of thinking help me select ideas and language for other writing?

I usually assign the postcard writing after students have read a book of their choice. I ask them to write about their book in a series of postcards from one character to another. They should include in their postcards cues that identify the audience and the relationship to the writer. These will include naming cues as well as strategy cues.

The postcard writing also involves students in what Ryder et al. call "context cues," considering writing as part of a community or relationship. When writers write with a consideration of audience, they must carefully consider what to include and what to leave out, especially since the length of the writing is short. Such information (or lack of it) gives cues to the reader about the relationship the writer is establishing. Students could practice context cues in class by considering how they describe a party to a friend who was there, to one who wasn't, and to a parent. A lot changes: Details change, word choice changes, tone changes.

With the postcards, students practice these considerations. Does the audience they are writing to know enough to allow the writer to leave out certain details, or does the audience need to know even more? Students enjoy creating the relationship, considering the implications of the relationship, and showing it in their writing, as well as drawing the pictures for the postcards (which are generally just five-by-seven-inch index cards). Some students even design elaborate stamps that relate to the topic of the card.

I shared this idea with a junior high teacher, Anna McNeel, who used it with her students. The sample postcards shown in Figures 4.1, 4.2, and 4.3, all from one of Anna's students, reveal the way this assignment helps students consider audience and indicate that consideration through their audience cues. Mark uses pronouns to indicate relationships as well as content cues to indicate shared knowledge, both of which are good indicators of student awareness of audience. Additionally, his awareness of audience increases the voice of the writing, a bonus that many teachers will appreciate in student writing.

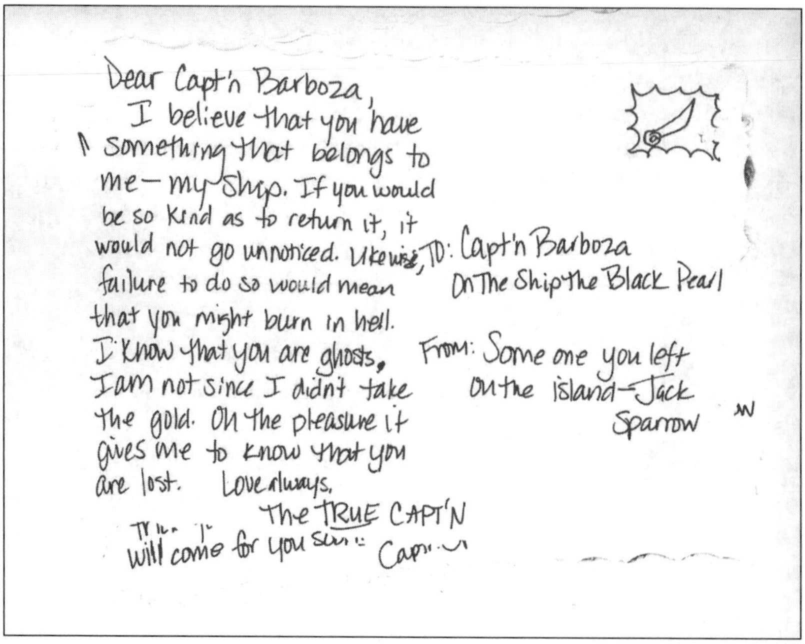

Dear Capt'n Barboza,
I believe that you have something that belongs to me—my ship. If you would be so kind as to return it, it would not go unnoticed. Likewise, failure to do so would mean that you might burn in hell.
I know that you are ghosts, I am not since I didn't take the gold. Oh the pleasure it gives me to know that you are lost. Love always,
The TRUE CAPT'N
will come for you

TO: Capt'n Barboza
On The Ship the Black Pearl

From: Some one you left
On the island—Jack
Sparrow

Figure 4.1. Mark's postcard.

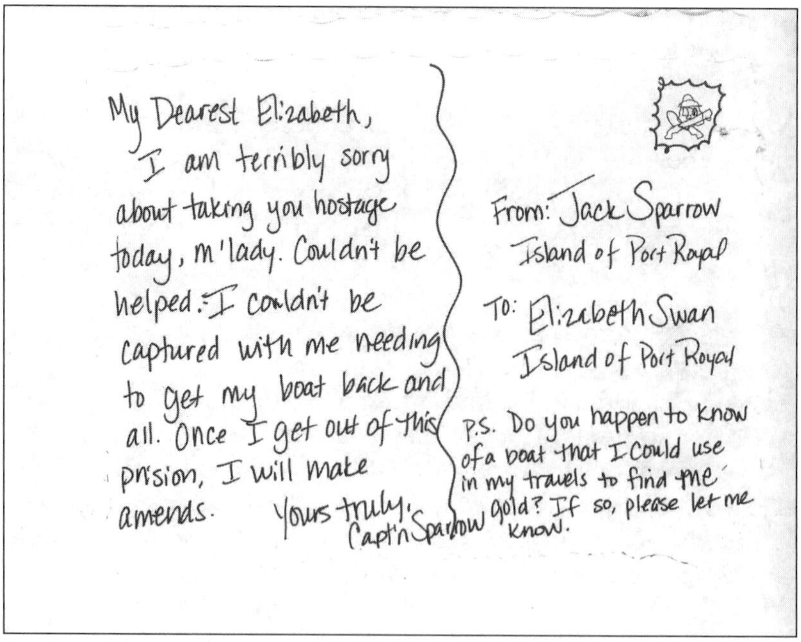

My Dearest Elizabeth,
I am terribly sorry about taking you hostage today, m'lady. Couldn't be helped. I couldn't be captured with me needing to get my boat back and all. Once I get out of this prision, I will make amends.
Yours truly,
Capt'n Sparrow

From: Jack Sparrow
Island of Port Royal

To: Elizabeth Swan
Island of Port Royal

P.S. Do you happen to know of a boat that I could use in my travels to find the gold? If so, please let me know.

Figure 4.2. Mark's postcard.

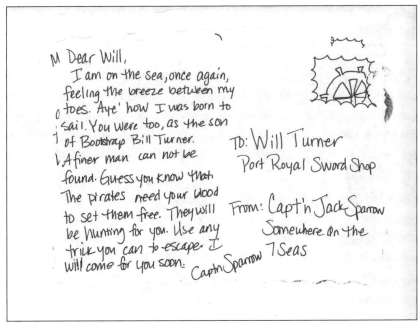

Figure 4.3. Mark's postcard.

Strategy Practice: Secret Knowledge

Declarative knowledge: When we write to persuade, we need to consider audience questions and concerns. Since much writing is persuasive to one degree or another, this consideration of audience and the questions an audience might have are important to effective writing. *Procedural knowledge:* Analyze a model text in order to understand the purpose and intended audience of a book and the cues that indicate these. Consider rules that adults give children and possible reasons for those rules. Then choose one to write about. As you draft and revise, continue to pose questions a potential reader might ask—and use those questions to help you develop your text. During revision, have peers consider what questions they might still have, and be sure to consider addressing those in your revision. *Conditional knowledge:* How did reading the case files help me consider audience and ideas for my own paper? When would this reading strategy help me in other writing? What did I do differently because of audience considerations? How did having peer readers question my draft help me revise effectively? When could I use the strategy of peer questioning in other writing?

This strategy practice is based on the book *The Secret Knowledge of Grown-Ups* by David Wisniewski. Before I introduce the book, I ask students to brainstorm a list of rules adults give children. It can be effective to limit this brainstorming to school rules or house rules; otherwise, this list can go on forever. After generating ideas, I ask students to suggest some reasons adults might give for requiring younger people to conform to such rules. Their responses are very similar to the reasons given by Wisniewski in the book, but the students don't know that yet. This activity stimulates use of prior knowledge and also provides a list of possible topics for the writing that follows.

Following the introductory discussion, I read the book to the students. The text begins by informing the reader that the reasons adults give to explain their rules are false. "The truth must be told to kids!" says the introduction. Then each "rule" is detailed, and the real reason behind the rule exposed. Wisniewski uses a genre resembling a case file for each rationale, and these files have certain characteristics that set up the "top secret" nature of the file: the location, date, and time of the discovery and a short log detailing what risks were taken to retrieve the information. Each revelation begins with the rule and the officially stated reason before detailing the "truth." The true story is told in narrative form, and the details have a sense of science but also a sense of the ridiculous. References to "authoritative" sources, lists, and charts—elements more common to scientific explanations—add a sense of authenticity to imaginative content. From the introduction, it is clear that this text is meant to be fun—and a little silly and far-fetched—but couched in terms and forms that pretend legitimacy and seriousness.

I want students to consider how these attributes are cues to the audience and also how they reflect a sense of audience, so as I read the book aloud, I ask my students to consider the audience and purpose for this kind of writing and how they know what those might be. Students first say the obvious: The intended audience is kids because the text is obviously about rules that kids don't like and the content is pretty far-fetched. But they also notice that some of the vocabulary is not for children and that some of the humor and the allusions to historical or cultural figures and events in the evidence would not be familiar to children. These cues help them understand that the author is addressing two audiences: children and adults.

After students have an understanding of the diverse audiences and the cues the author uses to address these audiences, we look again at the case files to see some of the specific characteristics of the text. I have students read the case files in small groups and answer questions on the investigation sheet that follows. When the groups have generated answers, we share them as a class and build a list of the mandatory and optional expectations for writing a case file of our own. Among the mandatory expectations are the introductory form (the log, to set the tone), a parent reason/real reason contradiction, evidence that appeals to authority, and a conclusion that reinforces following the rule—but for a different reason. Optional expectations include the types of support: stories, quotes, graphs and charts, examples, and references to history or science. With this exploration, students start to see how the author addresses audience considerations.

Secret Knowledge Investigation

1. What kinds of ideas does the author use to develop the story behind the truth? Which do you think are mandatory (must exist), and what kinds of ideas are optional (they can be there or not, but they don't make the report not a report)?

2. What organizational elements do you notice? How are ideas arranged? Are there forms? What ideas are first, second, and so on? Are these things flexible or mandatory for creating this kind of text?

3. What kinds of evidence does the writer use? Are these all words, or are some pieces of evidence visual? What is mandatory, and what is flexible? What is the tone of this kind of writing? How is it created? What words or ideas help create the tone?

In explaining an assignment that asks students to create a fictional character and then formulate a dialogue with that character as a way to discuss a topic, Irene Clark posits that such invention can help students develop "important insights associated with audience," including "help[ing] students determine which cues in their own text are likely to be effective in addressing their created audience" (149). This is one of the outcomes I have seen this strategy practice develop in my students as well. One part of Sid's Secret Knowledge case file shows this awareness. He is writing about the grown-up rule, "Clean your room." He notes that the official reason is "because your parents say so," but the truth is different: "To protect yourself from roving packs of dust bunnies!" In his first paragraph of explanation, Sid shows his awareness of his double audience—children and parents—with his choice of words and ideas that appeal to both without losing either:

If you don't clean your room, the dirty habitat provides the perfect environment for these malicious and insidious bunnies. Ever since the late 1900s they have been wreaking havoc on unsuspecting people. In the mid 1930s a huge outbreak of these bunnies occurred. Dubbed the "dust bowl," these creatures swarmed over an area that covered 3 states!

A full example by Katie can be found in the appendix.

Lesson Plan: Reversal Paper*

In my planning, I consider what my students need to know or know how to do to be successful on this assignment. Some major things they need are these:

- Knowledge of the kinds of topics that work for this kind of writing
- A perception of what the audience knows or thinks about a topic
- An understanding of the difference between writing that informs and writing that persuades
- An ability to gather information that meets the needs of this writing situation
- An ability to develop an idea that informs an audience

To help students be successful with this writing, I use the following strategies.

Teacher Plan for Inquiry Strategies

1. I use a model to introduce this assignment. I find models in a number of places. I started with one about tarantulas found in the Ramage and Bean text, but now I have student models that work. I have also found some good options in other places: airline magazines, for example. (I often tell students to consider an airline passenger as an audience. An airline passenger, thumbing through the magazine, would read if interested but would not be argumentative; instead, this reader would want to be entertained while being informed.) I sometimes also find good models in the "My Turn" feature of *Newsweek* magazine or on the feature page of the newspaper, but reversals are found in essays in many places. Whatever the topic of the model I plan to use, I first generate interest by getting students' responses to and knowledge about that

---

* Adapted from an idea in *The Allyn and Bacon Guide to Writing* by Ramage and Bean.

topic. For the model included here, written by one of my preservice teachers, Paul, I ask students what they already know about bodybuilding. We write all our ideas on the board. Then we read the model together and consider what new knowledge we gained from our reading.

Brawn and Brain

He's a weightlifter. The inevitable stereotypes follow. He's dumb; he speaks in one-syllable words and often simply grunts. He spends countless hours in pointless activity—namely weightlifting—the only issue being how big he can get. He has strange eating habits. Peanut butter, protein powder, ice cream, and bananas all mixed together in the blender with a few raw eggs added for kick. He sleeps too much. He's mean; don't even try to talk to him because he may just punch you. And—*hush*—he's probably on steroids.

Like nearly all problematic public perceptions, we can trace them directly to our Hollywood friends. Who hasn't laughed at Sylvester Stallone's Rocky and his inability to express himself? We remember him shouting, "Yo Adrian, I did it!", the climactic comment after beating Apollo Creed. We wonder how he managed to slip that three-syllable word in there. And what about Arnold Schwarzenegger, whose poor command of the English language put him in the same category? "Huge muscles equals stupid," we think to ourselves as we watch the terminator pull out another big gun. "And mean too!" Jean-Claude Van Damme hasn't helped the situation either; he's just another big man whose strict steroid regimen resulted in big money as an actor.

But not all weightlifters are seeking a Herculean build, and not all weightlifters are dumb. Weightlifters—not counting the recreational lifters who go to the gym on Tuesdays and Saturdays because the doctor said it would be beneficial—come in three main types: bodybuilders, power-lifters, and Olympic lifters. It's true that bodybuilders are looking to get large, rippling muscles. They care more about muscle *tone* and appearance than muscle *strength* and power. Ironically, bodybuilders—like our Hollywood strong men—are the least strong type of weightlifter because of their training emphasis.

Power-lifters and Olympic lifters are often much stronger than their bodybuilding counterparts, although they do not appear to be so. Power-lifting is quickly becoming the most common form of competitive lifting in the United States. Power-lifting includes competition in the bench press, the squat, and the dead-lift. These lifts don't require tone; they require pure strength. Looking pretty didn't help Dr. Frederick C. Hatfield in 1987—then 45 years old and a body weight of 255 pounds when he lifted 1014 pounds in the squat. Being strong did. Olympic lifting, as seen in Olympic competitions, may very well require the greatest strength, flexibility, and athleticism of any lifts. These lifts, the snatch and the clean-and-jerk, are the two most popular lifts in European gyms. Naim Suleymanoglu of Turkey, affectionately known as The Pocket Hercules, easily lifts 400 pounds overhead; he only weighs

130 pounds. Also, viewers may be surprised to see that the world's strongest men, usually from Russia or Bulgaria, have large guts! Again, the focus is on strength, not a pretty-boy, six-pack stomach.

Most serious competitive lifters are not looking to develop over-sized muscles. They don't care that the ladies love big biceps. They are concerned with developing raw strength.

Lifting weights overhead or on their backs? But isn't that just dumb? Can't they find something more mentally challenging to do? Weightlifters quickly realize the ignorance of such questions. High-intensity weight-training is an incredibly stimulating activity. "Smart people are drawn to the Olympic lifts," says Scott Glasgow, a Utah record holder in the Olympic lifts and a math professor at Brigham Young University. Lifters have to develop specific and particular training programs in order to achieve results and to achieve peak performance at competition time. *Let's see. I'd like to be able to clean-and-jerk 130 kilograms at the next competition. I'll probably need to attempt the weight on my second attempt so I'll have another chance if I miss it. If I make it, I'll be able to attempt a personal best. Now, what kind of training program do I need in order to be ready? On what days and what times should I do back-squats? Front-squats? Jump-squats and snatch-squats? Hang-cleans and full-cleans, hang-snatch and full-snatch . . . ? When do I rest? I have to have my sleep? When do I eat? I have to eat well. Maybe I'll go do some research. I wonder how the Bulgarians would approach this. . . .* No wonder Dr. Hatfield asks us to discipline ourselves and learn the SCIENCE of weightlifting.

There is another type of intelligence that seems innate to the serious weightlifter, and it is not the type that helps to solve a calculus problem. I can't count the number of times that I have seen otherwise intelligent individuals work in futility at programs that do nothing to further their training goals. There is a sense, an interconnectedness of body and mind, that helps a weightlifter know exactly what to do to push the body to its full potential. "How are you able to bench-press 430 pounds?" I am consistently asked. And throwing technical explanations aside, the best response I can give is: "I know exactly what training my body needs to be able to do it." Perhaps it is the smart weightlifter who comes closest to achieving Plato's ideal—a sound mind in a sound body. The order of his insight is important because in many instances the idiom is true: with "mind over matter" we can reach our full potential.

"I thought it would be just a bunch of sweaty guys screaming and grunting. I didn't think I would like it," my mom reflected after attending my first Olympic weightlifting competition. She had changed her mind; she saw something different. She saw a group of guys who enjoyed the chance to compete, the opportunity to reach for a peak performance. These guys enjoyed the competition. Yelling and screaming were at a minimum. The lifters concentrated. The crowd cheered when amazing lifts were completed. Handshakes and congratulations where offered when the competing was done. And some of the lifters even sat down together trading insights and training secrets. Dumb? Definitely not.

2. After students have some exposure to the kind of writing I'm going to ask them to do, I give them the following assignment:

Reversal or Expansion Essay

What's a subject you know more about than most people do—a place, a hobby, a group of people? Using your own experiences (and maybe a little research!), use what you know to expand your readers' view of the topic. For this assignment, imagine a general audience that holds a common view of your topic. Then, using what you know, either enlarge or reverse that common perception.

Although this assignment looks like it might be trying to change the reader's mind, your writing will actually be informative rather than persuasive since it both poses a different kind of question and considers a different kind of reader. In this case, your topic should not be controversial, as is typical with persuasive writing. Also, in persuasive writing, we imagine a questioning reader who may want to argue with your position; however, in informative prose, we can imagine a more positive reader willing to trust you and your experiences or research.

---

3. Next I have them generate possible topics. I use the list from the Ramage and Bean text, although teachers can generate their own heuristics. The categories I ask them to consider are these: people, activities, places, pets, and other. For each category, I ask students to write at least one idea, and I prompt them to get them going. For instance, with the category "people," I ask them to consider what groups they belong to: cheerleaders, basketball team, debate team, car club. They can consider religious affiliations or family configuration. (I have had students write papers on being a witch and on being a member of a large family.) For each category, I try to prompt enough to generate ideas, not to limit them.

4. When students have their lists of possible topics, I have them get into small groups to talk about their lists and see which ideas generate the most interest in the group so that they get a sense of audience right from the start. After students have done this, they freewrite about one of the topics that seems to be of interest to the rest of the group. I suggest they write about what they know that they think is unique and how they came to know it. What experiences do they have that makes their knowl-

edge unique? I ask students to think about their topics over the next few days and to ask other people what they know or think they know about that topic. Students should begin to collect ideas for both the common view and the reversal.

5. In class, we use two writing strategies to expand the students' thinking and perspectives about their topics. The first is based on synectics, which uses analogies to stretch students' thinking. "In synectics exercises, students 'play' with analogies . . . then they use analogies to attack problems or ideas" (Joyce and Weil 236). I have students number a paper from 1 to 8 and then ask them to consider their topic and answer this question for each of the following ideas: If my topic were a(n) _____, which one would it be?

1. car
2. color
3. weather pattern
4. food
5. television show or movie
6. famous person
7. country
8. animal

If a student's topic falls into one of these categories, I suggest they substitute "tool." So, for example, if a student's topic is "iguanas," for the "animal" category I suggest "tool" as an alternative.

6. The second writing strategy I use for generating ideas for the paper is a poem for two voices, as described in Chapter 2. This writing is especially useful for this assignment as it helps students consider both commonly accepted knowledge on the topic and their specific knowledge, which will be the reversal. If there are holes in the knowledge—either in what the students think they know about the audience or in what they need to enlarge or reverse the audience's knowledge—those holes often show up in the poem for two voices.

7. Before they begin drafting, I have students read another model or reread the bodybuilding model in order to discuss the kinds of evidence and ideas that are useful in this kind of writing. This is a good time to consider how the writer addresses audience considerations: How does the writer show what he or she thinks the audience already knows or

feels about the topic? How do the writer's tone and use of specialized vocabulary, pronouns, and ideas show audience consideration? At this time, we also look at the general shape of this kind of writing. It is most often a review of the common view first and then an exploration of the reversal. By looking at the models this way, students can see that the shape of the paper mirrors its purpose and content.

8. Before drafting, I also have my students consider the thesis for this kind of writing. The thesis is rather informal and is delayed until the common view is developed and explored. I provide them with several models of thesis statements that have worked for other students' papers. We discuss them, and students can use them as ideas for drafting their own thesis statements before they begin drafting their papers. What follows are a few sample thesis statements that can help students consider how to establish their reversals. In some cases, I've included a few sentences to make sense of the actual thesis statement, but these thesis statements are not as tight as traditional thesis statements and sometimes are actually more than one sentence long.

- However, appearance can be incredibly deceiving; jumping from trains is scary, dangerous, difficult, and even deadly.

- Hollywood and literature have done much to create a warped image involving mad scientists who experiment on poor, helpless animals. But as a whole, taxidermy is not quite so drastic; it is an art.

- There are no slaves now, are there? It doesn't happen. It can't. Americans are so used to the lifestyle of freedom that any other way of life seems barbarously impossible. How can a life of slavery be accepted in the world today? Who would let it happen? Maybe the answer isn't as foreign as we would imagine it to be.

- This is a common misconception of sharks that often leads to fear and mistreatment of the creature, when, in fact, sharks aren't all they seem.

Teacher Plan for Drafting Strategies

1. I usually have students draft in class, beginning with the common-view part of the paper. After they have some of this drafted, I teach a minilesson on levels of abstraction. I start by putting the following words on the board: *living creature.* I ask students to get an image in their mind, and then I ask some of them to share what they thought. Usually students name a wide range of items. Then I draw an arrow down from

living creature and write *mammal.* I repeat the procedure, eventually adding the following: cow, Holstein, Betsy; I note how more and more of us see the same things in our heads as we move down the list. (I have since found an explanation for this in Harry Nodin's book *Image Grammar*, 191. He attributes the idea to Alfred Korzybski.) We discuss how it is important for a writer to consider what moving back and forth between generalities and specifics does for the audience, and when it is a good idea to stay abstract and when it is not.

Next I have students look at a piece of writing and see how it moves from abstract to concrete and back again. In the first paragraph of the sample model essay, for example, the writer moves from an abstraction (dumb) to concrete with "he speaks in one-syllable words and often simply grunts." He talks about eating habits (more abstract) but moves into specific concrete items: "peanut butter, protein powder, ice cream and bananas all mixed together." In the next paragraph, he mentions Hollywood as an abstraction but then uses three concrete examples: Stallone, Schwarzenegger, and Van Damme.

These examples help students understand the concept; from here they can look at the paragraphs they have written and revise the content where it would improve from the inclusion of more concrete details. (Although some students need to work on the shift from concrete to abstract, for most the challenge is the reverse.) We share papers to get ideas and make suggestions to peers about similar improvements. The following paragraph from Jack's paper shows these moves from abstract (dumb) to concrete (just trying to get by) to even more concrete (easy classes) to the most concrete (floral design):

> The one athlete that people have been deluded into thinking of as big, dumb and clueless is football players. When you look at the average football player, you might think they're just trying to get by with their grades just to play football. You also might find them in easy classes, like floral design, Pre-Algebra, graphic design, and foods.

2. Next I have students work on drafting the reversal part of the paper. They need to consider how to organize this, but usually it is a response to the generally held view already developed. They can choose to start with the most obvious aspects of the reversal and move to the least known, or they can choose to organize in a way that counters each aspect of the common view as it was developed. Usually students consider what their audience knows and might want to know as they arrange the ideas in the reversal. This is another good time to have

students meet in small groups to get ideas from each other. In this way, they can anticipate the response of a wider audience through reaction of the members of the group.

3. Finally, we look at interesting ways to introduce and conclude the paper. I have students look at the models for this, but we also consider other ideas. Again, we have to consider audience. If a person sitting in an airplane pulled out the magazine and thumbed through it, pausing briefly to glance at the beginning of each article, what could make that person want to read through the essay? We discuss delaying the introduction of the topic and using pronouns for the first few sentences to create suspense and interest. I also have students consider bookending as a strategy. Bookending is beginning with an intriguing idea or part of a story and then returning to it at the end of the paper. This strategy works well for this kind of writing, and I bring in some examples for students to review.

The introductory techniques seem to be the easiest for students to grasp with this paper. Many take on a moralistic or persuasive tone at the end: *Think this instead of what you used to think!* It's almost as though some of them want to depend on the last sentence to do the work their evidence should have done. The use of evidence is a concept some get, but Sid's conclusion shows that some continue to misunderstand the tone of this paper: "So next time you hear something bad about the 'hardcore kids' tell them to stop the perpetuation of such pointless myths. After all, as the saying goes, you can't judge a book by its cover." Some students, no matter how much coaching, have trouble moving away from the types of text they are used to and depending instead on quality evidence to do its work.

However students choose to introduce and conclude their papers, though, audience consideration should be a major part of the choice. This can help students tone down the tendency to preach in the conclusion.

Teacher Plan for Product Strategies

1. After students have a draft of the paper written, we do peer evaluative readings. Following is a copy of a review sheet students use to guide their comments on others' drafts. I also teach minilessons as needed on strengthening sentence fluency (including the thesis statement, using subordination) and developing voice and word choice; these minilessons are described in Chapter 6.

Author _____   Editor_____

Reversal Essay Evaluative Reading

Editor: Read the essay all the way through first, and then answer the following questions:

1. Ideas
   - What is the general view of the topic presented in the paper?
   - Do you agree that the general view is really the accepted one?
   - In what ways does the reversal expand or counter the general view?
   - Put a * on the draft where the writer *could* move up or down on the abstraction scale.

2. Organization
   - Where is the thesis of the paper? Underline it.
   - Is that the best spot? Why does it work there—or why should it be somewhere else?
   - Rate the introduction's interest level: 5 (best) 4 3 2 1 What advice could you give for its improvement?
   - Rate the conclusion's effectiveness: 5 (best) 4 3 2 1 What advice could you give for its improvement?

3. Voice
   - Put a "V" on the draft where the author's voice shows through.
   - How do you know the author is engaged with this topic? I can't tell.
     Because . . .

4. Sentence fluency
   - Underline sentences on draft that are especially effective, and put an "S" by sentences that could use some work on fluency.

5. Which trait is the strongest in this paper? Why?

6. Which trait needs the most work in this paper? What could the writer do to improve this trait?

Author: Please score the editor on the helpfulness of his or her comments for your revision:

   10 9 8 7 6 5 4 3 2 1

What three revisions will you make based on the editor's comments (or your own feelings about what can be improved)?

2. When students turn in their papers, they reflect on their writing and the strategies they used by responding to these questions: What strategies did you use for this paper that helped you in writing it? How did they help you? What audience considerations did you apply? How might you use the strategies you practiced writing this paper with other writing you'll do in the future?

What follows is a paper written by Russell, a high school student, in response to this lesson plan presented by his teacher, Julie Larsen. Russell's selection of evidence and his organization of that evidence signal his consideration of audience concerns. His use of concrete details shows his application of the strategic options of the models and lessons.

The Computer Game—A Brain Basher or a Brain Builder?

It all started when I was young. My little friends and I were all gathered around my little Nintendo with all our fingers, legs, arms, eyes, and toes crossed, all in the collective effort to perhaps conjure up any luck for the one player who holds the paddle. We've never gotten this far in the game Super Mario Brothers 3 before, and we've spent many hours taking turns to get to this point in the game. Mario can do many things: he gonks Goompas, flings fireballs, plops through pipes, and collects coins all in his glorious quest to save Princess Peech. Mario is brave and strong; however, he stands no chance against the monster called my mom.

"Get off the Nintendo!" is a common command of many parents to their kids, and I get it occasionally from my mom or dad also. In 1999, an estimated 67% of children had a game system such as Sega or Nintendo and about 60% had a home computer (Subrahmanyam). Kids can spend countless hours pounding away at a keyboard or paddle to conquer that "bad guy" or save the world. There are plenty of constructive activities they could be participating in instead. They are neglecting their homework, and their grades are going down.

While it is probably true that many kids in the United States may play more than is healthy, is it really always just a waste of time? How come games are never perceived as a possible way to develop logic or abilities? Maybe it is because of the fact that many children become addicted to games and spend way too much time away from the real world. People often observe that many games don't seem to require much thought process or physical movement other than a flick of a thumb or a push of a finger. When some people think of video or computer games, they think of desensitized and lazy children.

However, games aren't always a waste of time because they can be involving and educational and still be fun at the same time. There are some games that are probably more beneficial than others. Now, later in my life, I occasionally play a popular game called Starcraft. My friend

Ray thinks he is pretty good at this game, but I decided to teach him a lesson. Like when I play chess, I have to figure out what strategies to utilize against this formidable foe. After playing for a short time with him, I come to realize that he is a very defensive player. I concentrate all my work effort into creating attacking forces, since I know he doesn't have a great army to attack me with because all his time and effort is going into building defensive fortifications. I gather intelligence using various methods such as satellites and probes to find any possible weak spots in his base and I execute my attack. Hooray! Ray is now defeated, but a new challenger wishes to join our next game.

Brandon is a completely different kind of player than Ray, as he utilizes a good balance of attacking and defending forces. Also, to make it even harder I now have two opponents instead of one. The game starts and I must make some very important decisions: Should I attack Ray before he has a chance to build a good defense, should I attack Brandon to lessen his smart and insidious attacks, or should I try to remain a conservative player while the other two battle it out? I have to learn how to effectively manage resources for maximum production or a specialized attack, determine the opponent's ways of thinking so that I can counteract their attacks and strike at their weak points, and micromanage as much as I can so that I am the winner. I think it is incontrovertible that strategy and competitive skills are developed when looking at what is incorporated in playing this game.

As for the perception that people who play video games are lazy, not all games are idle sit-on-the couch activities. Dance Dance Revolution is a game that I have that often involves getting tired and sweaty. Step moves that are coordinated with the songs must be stepped on a dance pad to pass levels. As people get better and better at DDR, they dance faster and faster. Brandon and his friends introduced me to this game, and it seems a lot like a sport in that there's competition, not to mention you often get a good workout. You sure get a lot more exercise than you would in Ping Pong. Like most any other sport, it's a great social activity and people can lose weight on a game like this and have fun at the same time. Not to mention I'm a dance maniac now. The coolest party animal around. The footloose crazy man. Well, at least that's what I like to think.

Now some people may ask how can video or computer games help in the *real* world? One answer to this question is simulators. There are all kinds of game simulators used in the world. These help people understand what a real life situation would be like by trying it in an imitation first. SimCity is a fun simulation game that is an excellent foundation for understanding urban planning. As mayor of my own virtual city, I enjoyed this game. It teaches money and resource management and the basics of what it takes to plan the development and care of a community, and I am excited to play it at the same time. I don't know of many kids that would want to learn that kind of stuff for fun by any other way.

There are many other kinds of simulators, too, and they can even help people prepare for future careers. Potential pilots may find a place for them in a flight simulator. The only one I've every really played is F/A–18 Korea. The game is based on the real-life physics and mechanics of a fighter jet. I take off, land, and control the plane similar to how I would in real life in various environments such as on an aircraft carrier. I learned many things from how to read a variety of radars to how to initiate emergency procedures in an airplane. I went through missions and tutorials that taught me the physics and operations in an airplane. Not only do I learn how to fly an airplane, but I also learn the strategies that are involved for fighting in one. All branches of the U.S. military use computer games or videos in some way such as to help people learn teamwork, safety, shooting, controlling submarines, flying, commanding forces, and in numerous other things. In fact, there is even a free game put out by the army called Army Operations, which teaches a variety of things like what it's like to be in the army, though I haven't played it much.

Games can also be used as a way to relive famous historical events or to visit old prominent landmarks in the world. A good example of this to me is Civilization III. It is a very educational game when it comes to understanding history. Players create maps, learn historical timelines, and research game concepts. Through this they can draw historical parallels to the real world to better understand the development of mankind and technology through history. Gaining technological advances like literacy, horseback riding, mathematics, and gunpowder help you just as they would in the real world. Players must explore different forms of government so that they can determine what type would be best for their society. Those are but few of the things I have learned from this Civilization game.

Behold the plummeting bodies into banana chairs and great beating of fist against carpet as my friends and I witness the utter defeat of Mario as he falls down that black and unexpected hole. No, maybe Super Mario Brothers 3 isn't the best example of an educational or profitable game, but there are still other good games to benefit from out there and still more to come. While it's very true that too much of any video game is usually a bad thing, video games can be good for developing skills and knowledge also. There isn't always a great availability of games that are to some extent pro-social, educational, and fun, but smart game players can make intelligent choices about what games to play and how much to play. Hopefully in the future, games will come to be great assistors in the human learning process so that it isn't as hard to pick what games to play. Some may say that computer games are worthless, but perhaps there is even a good place for a game in a classroom once in a while. The advantages of computer games may be intangible but they are real. So for now, I will put my pride aside and risk being called a nerd to defend righteous computer gaming.

———

11/6: Today a preservice teacher visited my class and presented a minilesson on types of conclusions. She had prepared a handout of possible options for conclusions. For each one, she read the description and then asked students if it would be a good choice for the essay they are currently writing (the reversal paper). The students said yes or no and discussed how each could or would not work. Their responses showed that they understood that the conclusion needs to suit the audience expectations of this paper. When she introduced the idea of ending with a forceful statement, they all said no, and Larry said the audience would just ignore everything else if we used that ending. When the preservice teacher introduced the idea of a mysterious ending and gave an example, Larry said it could work, but they'd have to "kind of work it in." Jack said that it would be better for a story. When she came to the open conclusion, Larry said this was the best one. Isac agreed. "The way you end it could still leave it up to them." "How about if I write an inflammatory conclusion?" Alec asked. (This was not an option the teacher had brought up.) He was partly showing off for the preservice teacher (at least today he didn't wear a suit, as he did the last time I had a preservice teacher in), but he was also showing the same thing as the others—that he understood the nature of the audience of this paper and that the conclusion had to be sensitive to that audience. I just hope students put the lesson into practice, since I know from past experience that many students struggle with the conclusion. The move from declarative to procedural knowledge is sometimes hard for my students. I suggested students write down their choice of conclusion, but even that might not be what ends up in the final paper.

Additional Resources

Ede, Lisa, and Andrea Lunsford. "Audience Addressed/Audience Invoked: The Role of Audience in Composition Theory and Pedagogy." *Cross-Talk in Comp Theory: A Reader.* Ed. Victor Villanueva, Jr. Urbana, IL: NCTE, 1997. 77–95.

Elbow, Peter. "Closing My Eyes as I Speak: An Argument for Ignoring Audience." *The Writing Teacher's Sourcebook.* 4th ed. Ed. Edward P. J. Corbett, Nancy Myers, and Gary Tate. New York: Oxford UP, 2000. 335–52.

Park, Douglas B. "The Meanings of 'Audience.'" *The Writing Teacher's Sourcebook.* 4th ed. Ed. Edward P. J. Corbett, Nancy Myers, and Gary Tate. New York: Oxford UP, 2000. 310–19.

5 Strategies for Drafting: Responding to Purpose

Successful writers grasp the occasion, purpose, and audience for their work.

Carl Nagin

Most of my writing in high school was traditional essay writing or research papers—and the expectations were clear and made sense to me. I usually earned A's on them. But once, in a high school class on Romantic literature, I didn't do what was expected.

I was assigned to research the life and writings of a poet of my choice and turn in a paper on my findings. The expectation was a traditional research paper, but the more I researched the poet and his life, the more uncomfortable I felt reporting my findings in that expected format. It just didn't seem to fit the poet and what he was about. It didn't seem to be a form that fit the purpose of what I was trying to say—and show—about a nontraditional poet. A new self I didn't allow out very often warred with the good-student, stay-in-the-lines self. My new self won the war.

On the due date, I handed in a poem, many pages long, imitating the style of the poet I had researched. It had the facts of his life and quotations about him and from his poetry, all the requirements of the assignment, but it was written as a poem, not as a report. I had never been so afraid in a school setting. I didn't tell anyone what I had done, but I was tense and fearful for days. More than once I considered going to the teacher and asking for the paper back, asking if I could redo it in the traditional format. But I didn't have the nerve.

Finally, the papers were handed back. There were no marks on mine anywhere until the end—and then just the letter "A" and a note on a separate sheet of paper. I still have the note. It says in part, "Debbie, I must have read your tribute (and I have to call it that) twenty times this weekend. It's beautiful. K. Goll"

I was lucky to have a teacher who understood what I was trying to accomplish—and who allowed me room to do it as I saw fit. I don't remember teachers talking to me about fitting writing to purpose. No one ever told me that a speech, written to be delivered orally, should be different in some important ways from a paper written to be read by a teacher. I can't remember teachers talking about shifting language or tone for different purposes. School writing was either report writing or, if we were lucky, something creative like poetry or a short story. On the other hand, the purpose was usually to tell the teacher how much we knew, so maybe there wasn't really a point in talking to us about strategies for addressing purpose.

My college training urged me to think of writing as primarily self-expression. My teachers came out of the expressive movement of the 1960s, and I wasn't prepared to question their perspective. But when I started teaching in my own classroom, I realized that students would need to do other kinds of writing, too—if not for me, for their science and social studies teachers, for their jobs, for their lives. I turned to the textbook our school used and found writing for a variety of purposes described as modes: descriptive, narrative, expository, and persuasive. Writing to describe, to tell a story, to inform or explain, or to persuade.

Faculty psychology, the belief that the mind can be divided into four primary faculties—understanding, imagination, passion, and will—developed in the early 1800s. George Campbell made the first connections between the faculties and types of discourse, and then in 1866, Alexander Bain published *English Composition and Rhetoric,* wherein he classified types of writing into the four forms of writing that came to be known as the modes. Albert Kitzhaber notes that "this classification was adopted almost universally in the 1890s and continued to dominate rhetorical theory well into the 1930s" (119). Certainly it dominated the textbooks I used in the late 1900s, despite the rejection of the original inspiration (faculty psychology) almost before the modes were developed. I used my textbooks and tried to teach my students to write in the modes—adapting them to the purposes of describing, telling a story, and so on—but the whole time, the students' writing and my instruction felt strained. I finally began asking myself some questions: What is the purpose of writing a description? What is the purpose of writing in any of the modes? Only persuasion seemed to have a possible answer. The others were only exercises.

I thought more about the modes and my reasons for using them. This was my thinking: I use description when I want to make someone *feel* what is happening in an anecdote I am telling: *Fog covered the ground up to my knees, swirling around me as I moved and smothering the sounds of the early morning. In a sudden shifting of white, I saw the dark, gaping hole where the door should have been in the house across the street. It was broken open, broken from the frame, but no one was around. Through the mist, I couldn't see clearly enough to tell if anyone was still in the home or not.*

Or I use description when I want someone to *understand* when the cooked frosting is ready: *Keep the icing at a slow to medium boil. That means that bubbles are forming, but not so many that your stirring can't keep them down momentarily. After you've cooked the frosting for about five minutes, stirring constantly, you should notice that it is thickening enough that your spoon will leave a trail and the color changes from an egg-and-butter yellow to a buttered-toast color. Dark specks are a bad sign.*

Or I use description when I want to *make a point* about how we do things in class: *An excellent project isn't evaluated by its glossy folder or colorful artwork, although those can certainly enhance its presentation. Instead, excellent work is distinguished by its careful thoughtfulness, its consideration of all perspectives, and its attention to detail.* In each case, I describe, but the kinds of details and the tone of the description change. My thinking told me what my intuition had suggested: Description (or narration, exposition, or persuasion) isn't a purpose in and of itself. It is used to serve other purposes. That's what I had to change in my teaching. That's what I had to help students understand.

As my thinking about purposes for writing continued, I questioned how purpose differs from genre, since genres, in the truest sense, develop out of a specific purpose within a specific context. When I considered the many forms research takes when it is published in the real world, I could see that purpose and genre don't always mean the same thing, that writers use many genres for the purpose of informing. Sometimes writers use a genre, and the reader expectations that go with it, to more effectively achieve their purpose. *The Professor and the Madman* by Simon Winchester and *The Devil in the White City* by Erik Larson are both books that inform but that read more like novels. Some books, like *Salt* by Mark Kurlansky and *The Meaning of Everything* by Simon Winchester, although primarily informational in purpose, use anecdotes to engage readers as well as to inform. *Fast Food Nation* by Eric Schlosser and *The Lexus and the Olive Tree* by Thomas Friedman are two books that use stories both to inform and to persuade. Children's books make use of many genres to present research for informative purposes: Celeste Mannis combines poetry and prose to do so in *One Leaf Rides the Wind* and *The Queen's Progress.* Leigh Ann Tyson uses an interview genre to do so in *An Interview with Harry the Tarantula,* Barbara Nichol uses an exchange of letters to do so in *Beethoven Lives Upstairs,* and Mark Kurlansky uses a variety of genres (timelines, insets, recipes, etc.) to do so in *The Cod's Tale.*

If our students understand genres, they can use them to accomplish their own purposes as writers as well. In fact, the thoughtful use of genre to accomplish different purposes shows a depth of thought teachers might hope for from all students. As Celeste Mannis uses the combination of poetry and prose in her books, she also alters the choice of poetic forms, using haiku in her book on Japanese gardens and rhymed couplets in her book on Elizabethan England. So, too, students could consider what she did: What kind of text will best accomplish my purposes? How can I use readers' expectation of a certain kind of text to better accomplish my purposes or to enhance comprehension or enjoyment?

Consideration of purpose, then, overlaps considerations of genre and audience. When I write for a specific purpose—let's say to show a teacher how much I know the subject—I have to consider audience (How will I show this teacher that I really read the chapter?) and genre (Will a poem do the job, or should I write a lab report?). Beyond audience and genre, however, or maybe within them, purpose is a separate consideration. A specific genre—a letter for instance—even with a specific audience can have a wide variety of purposes behind it. So what I want my students to do with practices like those described in this chapter is begin to see how strategies for understanding and addressing purpose can help them in their writing.

One way to help them do that is through a categorization approach I've adapted from Maxwell and Meiser (213–15), who classify levels of writing by style, audience, function, form, and evaluation. The way I present writing levels to my class abbreviates Maxwell and Meiser's definition somewhat and adds purpose and how much of the writing process is involved:

Level 1 (L1): This is writing that goes through only an abbreviated process (maybe little or no prewriting, little or no revision), that is meant for a limited audience (yourself or the teacher), or that is scored for limited traits. The purpose of L1 writing is often to explore ideas or to express feelings and ideas informally. For example, writing logs or journals are L1; in-class writings are often L1, too. These papers are scored for participation, following directions, or content.

Level 2 (L2): This is writing that usually involves either more prewriting or more revising than L1 writing. L2 writing might be shared with peers or the whole class and may be scored for more than one trait (ideas and organization, for instance). The purposes of L2 writing could include informing, interpreting, or evaluating. The occasional paper and end-of-quarter reflection are examples of L2 writing.

> Level 3 (L3): This is writing that goes through the entire writing process, that may have a wider audience (possibly published in some way), and that will be thoroughly assessed for all traits, including conventions. Although many purposes could be achieved with L3 writing, these assignments are usually more formal informative, analytical, or position papers.

As I have used the levels in my class, students have developed a clearer sense not only of purposes for writing but also of the writing process as strategy. They now understand better that process isn't something just for school or for teachers—it's really about the purposes of the writing. And using writing levels gives evaluation of writing more clarity as well.

In their textbook *Reading Rhetorically: A Reader for Writers,* Bean, Chappell, and Gillam include a table labeled "A Spectrum of Purposes" (12–13) that describes a wide variety of purposes for writing. Their table lists the following: to express and reflect, to inquire and explore, to analyze and interpret, to take a stand, to evaluate and judge, to propose a solution, to seek common ground, and to inform or explain. These purposes are much more what people really use writing for than what the modes express—and they are often what teachers are actually encouraging through student writing anyway.

Writing to Express and Reflect

Writing for these purposes is often informal (L1 or L2) and can include journals and freewriting, among other things. Students might use writing to express how they connect to the literature of the course or how they feel about the events of the day. Writing to express or to reflect might be used as a stand-alone activity or as part of the process of writing for other purposes as students express what they know or want to know prior to inquiry or as they reflect on their goals between writing projects.

After extensive research and thought on the place of reflection in a writing classroom, Kathleen Yancey concludes that "for reflection to be generative and constructive in a school setting, it must be practiced, must itself be woven not so much throughout the curriculum as *into* it" (201). Once it is woven into a course, reflection helps "students learn to know their work, to like it, to critique it, to revise it, to start anew" (201).

With these goals in mind—and with the idea that writing to express and writing to reflect can be kinds of writing that students can use throughout their lives, no matter what they do for work—it seems important that teachers incorporate writing for these purposes in strategic ways throughout a course. And since all aspects of L1 writing are not assessed, it's not a big burden for teachers to assign more writing for these purposes in their classes.

Writing to Inquire and Explore

Writing to inquire or explore can include note taking, questioning, brainstorming, webbing, or charting—as well as freewriting. Much of this writing could be considered writing to learn, as described in Chapter 2, since its purpose is to help students think and learn, not to show what they already know or to show how effectively they can polish writing. Despite what it isn't used to show, writing to inquire or to explore is very important in a strategic writing class since it helps students learn that writing for some purposes, especially personal ones, is valid and important even if it isn't the kind that gets polished and weighted heavily in final grades. Again, most of this writing would be L1.

Writing to Analyze and Interpret

Like many English and language arts teachers, I ask students to analyze and interpret the course literature. Students may write about character, symbolism, or theme, or sometimes I ask them to interpret the ideas of the literature in terms of their own worldview and perspective. My only problem with this writing is that it sometimes seems artificial in genre since I rarely read essays that analyze literature outside of my role as a teacher or English major. As teachers, I think we persist with these assignments because we hope such writing will develop students' thinking and reading abilities as well as their writing, as it connects various activities in our courses. And those aren't bad reasons, since we believe that the thinking that students develop will transfer into analysis and interpretation outside of class, too. We often begin that transfer with assignments that analyze advertisements, for example, or interpret political speeches.

In the application section of this chapter, I describe a strategy practice (Literary Brochure) that allows students to analyze and interpret within the larger purpose of taking a stand.

Writing to Take a Stand

Bean et al. describe writing to take a stand as writing that "states a firm position, provides clear reasons and evidence, connects with readers' values and beliefs" (13) and whose success depends on reasons that convince the reader. Although this sounds like persuasive writing, it really isn't, as taking a stand isn't necessarily about a controversial topic or written to an antagonistic audience. This is the kind of writing that is often prompted by large-scale assessments in which students respond to questions such as "Do you favor year-round school?" (What student would ever say yes?) or "Should your school have vending machines to support extracurricular activities?" (Students will say yes either because they want the vending-machine food or because they want the after-school activities). Most of the time, these large-scale-test questions ask students to write an opinion without enough significant evidence to develop a convincing position; what is evaluated as L3 is often written as L1. Inquiry strategies with class assignments that ask students to take a stand (letters to the editor or opinion papers, for example), though, can help students develop the ability to marshal evidence when writing for this purpose.

In one high school remediation class I taught, the students had written several occasional papers (Martin) about entertainment that led to a discussion and an essay about the value of entertainment to American culture. After addressing a news item about teens imitating a video game and making the point that entertainment influences behavior, Sid, in this excerpt of his essay, uses personal experience as a way to support his stand on the issue:

> One such occasion worth mentioning is when I strolled into a movie called *The Texas Chainsaw Massacre*. Lovely title, isn't it? As I was watching the ending credits do their thing, I caught sight of something a little disturbing. Next to me was a couple. The father was holding an infant no older than 6 months, while another child no older than 6 years was sitting next to him. Yet again the question arises. Is entertainment to blame or are the parents to blame? It seems both have a little guilt in the situation. There are good parents, and there are bad. There are meaningless, destructive ways to entertain ourselves, but productive ways as well. Media does have an impact on the youth of today, but I strongly believe that parents play a bigger role.

Sid's practice in this assignment helped him learn how to take a stand and support a position with meaningful personal experience.

In a class I took once, a teacher presented the idea of using stamp designs to connect students to literature. I was intrigued by the idea and did further research. In the course of my research, I learned that stamp designers not only draw the stamp design (as a piece of art) but also make a written case for why the stamp design is worthy of being developed (since the cost is so high for each design that makes it through the decision process). This intrigued me. Since I was unsatisfied with my students' background knowledge of the setting for *To Kill a Mockingbird,* I wanted to provide them with an assignment that would help them gain that knowledge at the same time that they practiced writing that took a stand and asserted a point. In the application section of this chapter, I describe the strategy practice, Stamps, that does this.

Writing to Evaluate and Judge

Writing to evaluate and judge can include a number of writing assignments, usually L2 or L3: case files, annotated bibliographies, editorials, and reviews, to name a few. The genre can vary, but the purpose is similar. These types of writing require students to gather evidence and then make judgments based on that evidence. When students in my classes write comparison/contrast papers, a common assignment, I insist that they use the prompt, what in classical rhetoric was a "method of probing one's subject to discover possible ways of developing that subject" (Corbett and Connors 19), for the purpose of evaluating. Too many students think they write comparison and contrast as an exercise, because the teacher said to, as a kind of listing exercise: the two things are alike in this way and different in this way.

But in the world outside of school, we compare to evaluate: which jeans to buy, which restaurant to go to, which movie to see. Having students compare two characters to determine something about them encourages evaluative thinking beyond just saying how they're alike and how they're different. One year, my juniors and seniors chose their topics for writing for this purpose by considering a major purchase they planned to make in the next year and comparing and contrasting different options. Their inquiry and interest were certainly authentic—and their conclusions were useful. Another type of writing to evaluate that students understand and enjoy is a review of a book or movie.

Writing to Propose a Solution or Seek Common Ground

Writing to propose a solution is more like what teachers traditionally consider persuasion because it suggests opposing views and proposes some kind of change in thinking or behavior. Possible assignments (L2 or L3) to write for this purpose may include proposals or editorials, letters to the editor, or traditional arguments. This purpose is similar to writing to take a stand, but the expected outcome is different. Writers might choose this purpose not only to express opinion but also to inspire action. Since the topics and genres might be the same, though, much of the difference lies in the position the writer takes. Justine, writing on the same topic as Sid about entertainment's value, takes this stance —not just stating a position but proposing a solution to a problem:

> There are two ways to get rid of the violent entertainment in our lives. First, we could shame those who make the violent television shows, video games, and movies, and teach them a better way to do their jobs, or we could simply solve the problem ourselves by turning the page and changing the channel. Entertainment surrounds us on a daily basis. Instead of wasting time going after the source, it should be incumbent upon us to take matters into our own hands and change it one day at a time. By doing that, maybe entertainers will think more about what they put out there for their viewers.

Sometimes teachers ask students to write research papers but to use the research to accomplish the purpose of proposing a solution or seeking common ground, thus moving the paper out of the realm of simple reporting. Writing to propose a solution or to seek common ground requires students to consider multiple perspectives and audience concerns in order to be effective, so it is a better way to develop good thinking than reporting. Large-scale writing assessments sometimes pose these kinds of questions, too, but the readers don't usually evaluate on the validity of the proposed solution or even on the effectiveness of the perspectives assumed or the evidence provided for the argument (Hillocks, *Testing* 136). Despite that, students can still learn to write effectively for these purposes through strategy practices on topics that matter to them, in class where readers do care about the quality of the ideas.

Writing to Inform or Explain

Most people would consider writing to inform or explain as the most common purpose for school writing of those listed by Bean et al. Although some school writing may truly serve this purpose, I might rename most of what counts for this purpose in schools as writing to show what you know. Realistically, many teachers assign what they call informative writing with the real intent of measuring students' knowledge. Teachers aren't really informed by this writing, and students generally understand the difference, which means they rarely really write to inform.

Writing to show what you know is unique to school, and what makes it effective may not be what is effective for writing in other places or for other audiences and purposes. When students write essay answers in content classrooms, for example, teachers are mostly interested in students' knowledge of the material that's been studied or read—as well as students' clear presentation of that knowledge. Writing for the sole purpose of assessment, although it's often called writing to inform or explain, is a different purpose altogether—and I address it separately in another section.

Writing to show what you know could be any level of writing: L1, L2, or L3. Often, however, it's L3 because teachers also measure the writing's quality. These assignments are often book reports, summaries, research reports, or answers to questions posed by the teacher or the book. Another less common way to show what you know through writing is to use dialogues (Pirie). Although this may not work in testing situations, dialogues allow students to present ideas interestingly, even allowing multiple perspectives to be shown. The format of a dialogue allows students to learn and practice strategies for effectively incorporating information in a more engaging format, which should lead to better learning. I describe two versions of this in the application section with the strategy practice Dialogues.

Research-Based Writing

A particular type of show-what-you-know school writing is the research paper. I understand the rationale behind the research paper. It's meant to help students

- gain knowledge about a topic,
- learn to use the library and research strategies,
- learn to evaluate sources (hopefully!),
- learn the conventions of academic writing, including bibliographies and citations, and
- learn how to incorporate others' words and thoughts with their own ideas in writing—goals that matter in school but matter less once our students leave school.

Despite these valid goals, Richard Larson calls the research paper "a non-form of writing" ("Research" 216) and claims that teaching it is not only "not defensible" but also "misleads students about the activities of both research and writing" ("Research" 217). He makes the point that research is much broader than simply looking up topics in the library or on the Internet and that almost all writing is based on research in one form or another, both points with which I have emphasized my agreement in previous chapters. By assigning research papers, Larson asserts, we may suggest to students that this is the only paper so informed. He concludes with these recommendations, which I endorse: Students should

> understand that in order to function as educated, informed men and women they have to engage in research, from the beginning of and throughout their work as writers. . . . [T]hey should be encouraged to view research as broadly and conduct it as imaginatively as they can. . . . [T]hey should be held accountable for their opinions and should be required to say, from evidence, why they believe what they assert. . . . [T]hey should be led to recognize that data from "research" will affect their entire lives, and that they should know how to evaluate such data. . . . And I think they should know their responsibilities for telling their listeners and readers where their data came from. ("Research" 220)

Notice what he does not say they should do: Although students can conduct research and share what they learn, they do not have to do so in traditional research papers.

Years ago, before I had read Larson or thought much about the nature of research papers, I assigned them. I tried a number of ways to make the assignment more palatable for both me and my students. They were able to choose the topic (within limits). The papers were completed in conjunction with the social studies class and counted for both courses. Still, one spring break, as my husband and I headed back from a weekend at the coast, I cried as I packed the mostly ungraded research papers back into the car for the trip home. I had carried them with me to the beach thinking that I would feel more inclined to grade them there. Instead, the one or two I had managed to read had so discouraged me that I had left the rest untouched for the weekend. Now, unable to avoid the reality of going home, I had to face what I couldn't put off any longer: six class sets of research papers, many of them poorly written explorations of topics about which students cared little, completed mostly because I had required them. Why did I ask them to write these papers? What did I hope students would gain? Why did I think what they would gain would be worth what I went through to read and grade them? Was this the only way to accomplish some of the learning goals I hoped this project would accomplish? Why did I require them to be so darn long?

I have experimented since then and found myself and my students much happier with shorter, more creative, research-based writing. I now require inquiry of some type with every paper, so that no one paper is singled out as a "research paper." By making inquiry part of all writing and by creating more variety in my assignments, I allow students to practice strategies that prepare them to write effectively for other college and public school teachers who might want traditional library research papers. These alternative research-based assignments create a much more pleasant experience for both the students and me at the same time that they achieve the goals I originally had for research papers.

Several writers and teachers have written about a form of research paper called the multigenre paper (Allen; Romano, *Blending*). I can see value in the concept and will leave those writers to write about what they know better. From my own experience and observation, having students write in genres they do not fully understand seems to reduce the concept of genre to form. And having students write in many genres limits what I have time to teach about genres—especially that part of genre is a response to a social context that goes beyond form. Instead, I find that if I limit such papers to a few genres, as in a strategy practice described in this chapter, students have a better chance of success, and I have a better feeling about what they learn about writing, about genres, and about their topic.

A key to effectively and creatively writing research lies in the teacher's ability to help students understand that the creative form doesn't negate the need for solid research and good thinking—and that those should be evident in the finished product, whatever its form. I like to emphasize this point by having students look at nonfiction picture books. Students can identify what information moves beyond general knowledge in these books, thus also identifying how writers incorporate research into alternative forms such as letters, diary entries, poems, and so on. Some possible books for students' exploration include the following:

Byrd, Robert. *Leonardo: Beautiful Dreamer.* New York: Dutton Children's Books, 2003.

Cheney, Lynne. *America: A Patriotic Primer.* New York: Scholastic, 2002.

Cole, Joanna, and Bruce Degen. *The Magic School Bus Inside the Earth.* New York: Scholastic, 1987.

Cronin, Doreen. *Diary of a Worm.* New York: Joanna Cotler Books, 2003.

Frith, Margaret. *Frida Kahlo: The Artist Who Painted Herself.* New York: Grosset and Dunlap, 2003.

Fritz, Jean. *Leonardo's Horse.* New York: Putnam's, 2001.

Herzog, Brad. *K Is for Kick: A Soccer Alphabet.* Chelsea, MI: Sleeping Bear Press, 2003.

Hicks, Peter. *You Wouldn't Want to Live in a Wild West Town!* New York: Scholastic, 2002.

Kurlansky, Mark. *The Cod's Tale.* New York: Putnam's, 2001.

Mannis, Celeste Davidson. *The Queen's Progress.* New York: Viking, 2003.

Martin, Jacqueline Briggs. *Snowflake Bentley.* Boston: Houghton Mifflin, 1998.

Rubin, Susan Goldman. *The Yellow House.* New York: Harry N. Abrams, 2001.

Sis, Peter. *Starry Messenger.* New York: Farrar Straus Giroux, 2000.

Stanley, Diane. *Leonardo Da Vinci.* New York: Morrow, 1996.

Wright-Frierson, Virginia. *An Island Scrapbook: Dawn to Dusk on a Barrier Island.* New York: Aladdin Paperbacks, 2002.

Yolen, Jane. *Roanoke: An Unsolved Mystery from History.* New York: Simon and Schuster, 2003.

In addition to seeing these books as ways to present information interestingly, students could discover how the authors (and illustrators) of picture books conduct research, and the extent of that research, by reading the notes in the back of the books or by writing letters to those authors and illustrators and asking them. Deborah Hopkinson, for example, has a note in the back of her book *Birdie's Lighthouse* indicating that the main character of the book is really a composite of five different women, all lighthouse heroines whose lives she researched. Jean Fritz, author of *Leonardo's Horse,* notes that reading an announcement sparked her interest in the subject. Her research took her to two countries. Using one of the books from the list, I have students practice using alternative forms to inform or to show what they've learned through research. One of those alternative forms, One Leaf, I describe in the application section. Teachers can find more ideas for preparing to teach students about effective research-based writing in *The Best in Children's Nonfiction: Reading, Writing, and Teaching Orbis Pictus Award Books* (Zarnowski, Kerper, and Jensen).

Writing for Tests

Assessment is a specific purpose for writing that teachers now need to prepare students to address; while we don't want to teach only to the test, to ignore students' needs to write for this purpose would be negligent. Since a majority of students today can expect to participate in large-scale writing tests, and since, whether it is stated directly or not, these tests often value a format like the five-paragraph essay (Dean, *Current-Traditional* 116–17; Gere, Christenbury, and Sassi 153; Hillocks, *Testing* 193), teachers should address its use in specific situations.

The challenges connected to teaching the five-paragraph essay are probably best addressed through a consideration of purpose rather than a general censure of the form or a total capitulation to it. Although the five-paragraph form suggests that writing can be reduced to a kind of fill-in-the-blank simplicity, if students need to know it to accomplish certain purposes, we should teach it strategically—as a response to those purposes. If we focus on the principles of the form as we address purpose and foreground ideas when practicing the form, we should be able to avoid the worst effects of teaching this kind of writing for tests.

To help my students understand the principles, I teach them that the five-paragraph essay developed as a school genre over a hundred years ago, a genre meant to help overburdened teachers read lots of papers quickly. That's why important ideas need to be in key positions in the five-paragraph essay: so readers can find them easily. The basis of the form is a tight thesis statement at the end of the introductory paragraph, an explicit topic sentence at the beginning of each body paragraph, and a summary conclusion paragraph. With this brief background, it's easy for students to see how busy readers can be guided by the skeleton frame. Certainly the audience for essay tests is often most interested in a coherent piece of writing that can be read quickly to see if the writer has anything to say on the assigned topic. In referring to state writing tests, George Hillocks notes that

> the need for strong reliability and for high speed have the effect of drawing attention to the most obvious features. . . . They must be looking at the amount of writing and skimming for certain features that appear in the opening and are followed up in the paper. (*Testing* 120–21)

Considering purpose and audience in any testing situation then, students might choose to use the five-paragraph format; it can work as a default organizational strategy if the writer knows the reader will be looking for specific pieces of information more than development of ideas or if the writer doesn't have time to develop a more appropriate organization. However, as teachers we also need to impress on students the limitations of the genre to address other purposes. After students have a chance to practice some of the aspects of the five-paragraph form, they should both talk and write about the conditions under which the form would be useful, when it would not, and why. In this manner, they can begin to develop their own rationale for its appropriateness at the same time as they develop an understanding of how writing for different purposes shapes how we write.

If we need to teach the five-paragraph form to prepare our students for tests, though, we can teach the principles of it without the rigidity of the form. The principles are key ideas in prominent places and grouping of ideas, which I've helped my students understand visually. After a unit on heroes, I ask students to define a hero, but to do it visually rather than in writing, a poster rather than a paper. The students choose three or four attributes they believe a hero must have. For each attribute, students select a variety of types of supporting evidence from newspapers and magazines: pictures, headlines, and articles that exemplify and elaborate each characteristic. These they group on a poster, much as similar ideas are grouped in paragraphs. I add an additional element of priority by asking students to decide on the order of importance of the attributes and then represent this order three-dimensionally by placing the most important attribute raised from the poster the most, with the least important attribute flat on the poster.

Through this visual manipulation of ideas and evidence, students learn some of the principles of the five-paragraph essay without actually writing one (Dean, "Visual"). Additionally, the Literary Brochure strategy practice described in this chapter functions somewhat like a five-paragraph essay with the title as thesis and the three panels as body paragraphs. Student response is certainly more positive than for writing a traditional essay, but students practice the same set of skills as they would in writing a five-paragraph essay.

Finally, when my students practice writing the five-paragraph essay, I try to soften the form's rigidity somewhat by playing with it a little. I encourage students to move the thesis statement around sometimes to see what that does to the overall piece. I teach about implicit topic sentences or topic sentences that come at the end of the paragraph instead of the beginning, although some students are more ready for this than others. I've also encouraged students to incorporate elements of alternative style or Grammar B (Weathers) or to mix genres in with the five-paragraph form, thus creating surprise and interest, while still practicing the principles of the form (Dean, "Muddying"). Playing with the elements of the five-paragraph form can still teach the principles without students' becoming too rigidly focused on the structure.

Another way teachers can try to make sure the teaching of the five-paragraph essay minimizes its inherent problems is to emphasize inquiry in the writing process and ideas more than organization. Encouraging more inquiry prior to writing can help students focus on ideas before form instead of the other way around, which is what often happens with five-paragraph essays. George Hillocks notes that a common problem with five-paragraph essays is that they tend to encourage empty development—opinions with little substance to support them, reasons repeated in various iterations as evidence. He encourages the teaching of inquiry and questioning strategies to help students first conduct substantive thinking about their topics: "[A]sk students to examine a set of data of some kind in order to identify a problem, develop hypotheses, consider and test alternative explanations, marshal evidence, explain why the evidence supports one or more possible conclusions" (*Testing* 201).

One of my attempts to do this included presenting definitions of close encounters, then having students read reported experiences with aliens, classify them as first, second, or third, depending on the aspects of the experience, and support their classifications by referring to the definitions. (I no longer have my source, but http://www.unexplained-mysteries.com now lists five categories of close encounters. A Web site that has a similar practice on classifying galaxies can be found at http://www.smv.org/hastings/galaxy.htm.) The assignment required my students to examine both the story and the category definitions and use evidence to support a conclusion, generalizing from an experience that wasn't distinctly one category or another. This process is similar to the kind of inquiry Hillocks suggests that can develop thinking prior to writing, and this kind of inquiry can alleviate some of the vacuous thinking the five-paragraph essay seems to allow. By foregrounding inquiry and prioritizing ideas over structure, teachers can minimize the challenges of teaching the five-paragraph essay when they need to teach it for test-taking purposes.

Applications

Strategy Practice: Literary Brochure

Declarative knowledge: Brochures can inform, persuade, or take a stand. We can analyze a piece of literature and frame that analysis within one of these larger purposes.
Procedural knowledge: Before reading, consider the purpose of the analysis and what the brochure will do. Read a piece of literature, keeping in mind the questions that will ultimately be addressed in

the analysis or interpretation. From time to time, freewrite on aspects of the literature that make text-to-text, text-to-self, and text-to-world connections. Keep notes of ideas that might be pertinent to the ultimate purpose the writing will serve.

Conditional knowledge: What strategies during reading helped me prepare for writing? How did I consider purpose during my writing process? How might those same strategies help me in future writing of analysis or interpretation?

One brochure assignment I give goes along with our reading of *Brave New World,* when I ask students to consider if we are becoming the society envisioned in the novel or not. Their response is to be written in a brochure. The title on the front panel should provide an indication of the purpose of the evidence they present inside (a kind of thesis). Then each inside panel addresses how one of the aspects of society—identity, community, stability—is portrayed in the book and in current society, referring to both the text and current events. The back panel contains the student's name and class period and a place for me to respond to the brochure, while the remaining panel is a kind of conclusion piece that can be visual (an illustration or collage) or verbal (a paragraph or letter to the editor or whatever else the writer feels is appropriate).

My students enjoy writing these brochures and produce more text than they usually do for an essay. And the writing is interesting. With this title for her brochure, "A Brave New World: We Are Similar to *A Brave New World* in Community, Identity, and Stability," Naomi frames her interpretation/analysis in a brochure that takes a stand. What follows is one of the panels from her brochure, an example that shows her synthesis of ideas from the novel and modern culture and that presents evidence in support of her stance:

> Society today, along with *Brave New World*'s society, raves over identity. Both societies group themselves by what they wear, how they look, and where they work. *Teen Magazine* says, "True beauty is everything." In *Cover Girl* we find tips on how to dress or how to do our hair in order to make our bodies look more appealing. In *People Magazine* we see how one's place of employment is considered a good way to gain identity since society today also identifies people by social classes. Just as social classes mold our identity, castes mold a *Brave New World*'s identity. We find castes set apart by spoiled Alphas and Betas, Gammas, Deltas and uniform Epsilons. Throughout the novel we also see jobs, clothing, and

living locations shaping identity. Some may agree with *Teen Maga-zine* when it says, "Ultimately, identity is everything."

Strategy Practice: Stamps

> *Declarative knowledge:* Stamp designs are decided on by the Citizens' Stamp Advisory Committee (CSAC), which receives thousands of proposals each year but recommends only about 25 to become stamps. Proposals must be submitted in writing, and because of the intense competition, the proposal should provide solid reasons for the proposed stamp design to be accepted.
> *Procedural knowledge:* Research a time period. Then select topics and research more deeply to develop solid reasons for proposing a new stamp design. Draw the proposed design and write the rationale. Conduct evaluative readings and revise.
> *Conditional knowledge:* How did I choose reasons that I felt would be convincing to the committee? How did my research help me in my writing? What other strategies did I use in my writing? How might I use these strategies in writing based on research in other circumstances?

The assignment is a group project to create stamps commemorating a time period, particularly in these categories: people, events, daily life, and spirit of a particular time period. Students conduct general research first, generating possible topics to fit the period and categories. Once they've settled on ideas for each, they conduct specific research. Because stamps are expensive to develop, students need enough evidence to write a paragraph-length rationale for each stamp's design, defending each choice as important enough and legitimate enough to warrant selection and production. This pattern of broad research first to select a topic followed by deep research to develop evidence is an effective strategy for many writing situations. After inquiry, students design the stamps on nine-by-twelve-inch paper and attach them to the rationale paragraphs. What follows is Mariellen's paragraph about a stamp in the category of daily life of the 1930s, in preparation for reading *To Kill a Mockingbird:*

> One of the most important black figures in American history was Martin Luther King, Jr. He spent his life fighting for equal rights for African Americans nation wide. In 1935, King experienced his first dose of racial segregation. At the age of six, King had two best friends that were white. To them, color didn't seem important when choosing friends. The next fall, the three boys were

ready to start school. Because King was black, he and his friends were separated into different schools. Also, the two boys' mother no longer permitted King to play with them because he was a "negro." This event ignited King to question civil rights and equality. This stamp shows how blacks and white were separated into different schools during King's childhood. Segregation in schools was common in the South during the 1930s.

From her research, it's clear that Mariellen was ready to consider some of the issues in the novel that she might not have understood prior to this assignment and to take a stand on what she learned.

Alisha's stamp for the category of the Spirit of the 30s was titled "A Common Hope."

After the 1929 stock market crash, unemployment soared while wages plummeted. But during these turbulent times when people had no money, the price of the things necessary to daily life did not come down with the income of the population. Thousands of people went hungry all over America. Many charity groups opened soup kitchens and gave out dry bread and thin soup in an attempt to curb hunger. Haggard men and women waited in line for hours to receive the meager portions given to each, each hoping that the bread would sustain them until the next day. But with each passing year, hope grew that America would again regain its former greatness. It was this hope held by each person that carried America through the troubles of the thirties to times of great prosperity.

Her stamp design (see Figure 5.1) depicts the long lines waiting for food; her knowledge of the setting of the novel helped her (and the class) understand some plot events better during our subsequent reading of it.

Strategy Practice: Dialogues

Declarative knowledge: Dialogues are written reports of people talking. Just as speech can reveal what people think and believe and feel, so can written dialogues.
Procedural knowledge: Inquire to gain substantive knowledge about a topic. Consider whose voices would best represent different ideas. Portray the ideas as if they were the words of characters you've chosen.
Conditional knowledge: How did using dialogue help me both understand and portray my knowledge? What strategies did I use in writing the dialogue that were useful to me? How might those same strategies be useful to me in other writing, especially since much writing to inform or to show what I know can't be written in this way?

Figure 5.1. Alisha's stamp design.

I ask my preservice teachers to try writing dialogues on a difficult topic: writing theory. In a dialogue among teachers in a faculty setting, they are to accurately represent four approaches to writing instruction (Soven) that develop from Berlin's ideologies and Fulkerson's philosophies. The interplay of the characters allows students to present abstract ideas in a concrete way that clarifies their thinking and helps them articulate what they have learned about writing theory and practice. What follows is part of Katie's response to this assignment:

> This is a dialogue among four teachers at Westside High School. The district has just sent a memo requiring an additional writing assignment from the sophomore students. This assignment is open ended and left up to teacher discretion. Here Cleavis (correctness) a veteran teacher, Patricia (personal growth), Rhett (rhetorical), and Sarah (sociocultural) all younger teachers, discuss the memo and ideas for how they will structure the writing assignment.

> *Rhett:* So, did you all receive the latest district memo?

> *Cleavis:* (grimacing) Another assignment for the students to despise.

> *Patricia:* (throwing a tie-dyed scarf around her neck) Oh Cleavis, stop being so pessimistic. I'm thrilled. Finally the chance to be inventive. The students will finally be able to use their innate creativity and discover themselves through personal writing! This has the potential to be a transcendental experience for the kids.

> *Sarah:* (fumbling with a "Save Tibet" bumper sticker) I agree. Lately the writing assignments have been so unrealistic. Our students will learn so much more by writing about something they know, something practical. They have to be equipped with writing skills that will be applicable in the real world. I'm thinking some sort of resume would be a good idea. It makes the kids look at their inner qualities but also focuses on organization and real life skills.

> *Rhett:* Don't you think some sort of persuasive letter would be better? This would engage the kids in analytical thinking, as well as choosing a subject they enjoy and practicing practical skills. This would be the best assignment in my opinion. It's a well-rounded assignment, where an audience has to be clearly identified. As teachers our main concern should be teaching our students to communicate effectively. If you want to teach effective communication, this is the way to do it. Don't you think so Cleavis?

Cleavis: Communication is the least of my problems. The kids in my class can barely spell, much less communicate persuasively. It doesn't really matter what they're writing about as long as in the end they produce a grammatically polished product. We all know the district wants correct grammar, punctuation, and spelling. This is exactly what I intend to deliver.

Patricia: No wonder your students are so unresponsive. You extract all the fun and creativity out of the art of writing. Say it with me Cleavis, Process over product, process over product.

Sarah: I agree, Cleavis. Stop being so old fashioned. This is a chance to engage the students in something practical, like a social issue, and then let them conference with each other about it instead of ripping apart their sentence structure with a red pen. You've got to give students freedom instead of restricting them. Get with modern times and indulge in some student-centered learning.

Patricia: Amen!

Although this example is on a subject students in secondary schools will not address, it shows the possibilities for secondary students to write about other conceptual topics. For an end-of-the-year project with ninth graders, I have students write dialogues to show what they've learned about characters and literature. I have them choose three characters from three different pieces of literature we have read during the year and one historical figure they have studied in social studies (since the classes are teamed). Students are to put these four people together in some kind of problematic situation and write a dialogue for them. In groups, students choose the characters and write the dialogues, showing how the four handle the problem. The characters can be moved from their original time period for the sake of drama; my primary requirement is that characters must act in ways consistent with literature or history.

All the dialogues, about ten to fifteen minutes long, are acted out, but many students videotape theirs ahead of time. The resulting work is effective as a culminating review and clearly reveals the students' knowledge of characters. By putting Scout with Lincoln, Odysseus, and Romeo, all trying to find their way out of the Bermuda Triangle, for instance, students explore implications of character and plot. Some of the most interesting dialogues put Atticus and Hitler together, confronting some of the basic conflicts two such ideologically opposed men would face. The dialogue format allows students to show what they know in a more interesting—and sometimes more insightful—way than traditional show-what-you-know writing does.

Strategy Practice: One Leaf

Declarative knowledge: Different genres provide different lenses on a topic, so information that fits best in a paragraph might not be the best for a poem, and vice versa. Because of that difference, writers may need to learn more than they will use in the final written product.

Procedural knowledge: Read two kinds of texts to determine which kind of information goes in which text. Research broadly first and deeply second. Practice forms of poetry to determine which best fits the topic. Write up the information in one of the two types of text, using the counting book as a frame.

Conditional knowledge: What did I learn about adapting information to fit textual expectations? In what other writing could I use that knowledge, and how would I use it? What did I learn about researching? In what other writing could I use that knowledge, and how would I use it?

One Leaf Rides the Wind, by Celeste Mannis, is an informative picture book that combines short prose paragraphs with haiku poetry to provide information (and a feeling) about Japanese gardens. The book is written in a counting-book format, so the topic of each page is partly determined by the associated number. The book is a good model of how writers can write to inform (as a purpose) in an interesting way. Using this book as a model, students can research a topic and produce counting books of their own (Dean and Grierson). Most students find the assignment interesting, and teachers find students engaged with research and writing in interesting ways.

Because of the counting-book format, a frame already exists for beginning research. Students decide on a topic and then research possible ideas for each number, one through ten. Many students pick a country or state, but some have picked holidays, animals, hobbies, or professions—anything they want to learn more about. After they have decided on the topics for the numbers, they conduct deeper research on each topic (in books or through interviews; this doesn't have to be traditional) in order to develop the paragraph and poem for the page. Finally, they draw or generate illustrations to fit the writing.

2

Two countries in one
Surrounded by fortress walls
Both are very small

Two countries inside of their own, each with culture and different
customs. San Marino, for instance, is one of the smallest countries in the
world. Almost everyone is related. It is known for it's fortress walls, cakes
and wine, festivals and postage stamps. In all it is only 24 square miles in
size. The second country is Vatican, which is found in the Apennine
Mountains, North Eastern Italy. Their palace has over 1,000 rooms inside.
Vatican is about the size of an average city park, 109 acres.

Figure 5.2. Sample page from Brittney and Kaitlyn's One Leaf strategy practice about Italy.

For a seventh-grade class book on Italy, Brittney and Kaitlyn produced the page shown in Figure 5.2. It's interesting to note the specific facts and details that reflect their research. Although the paragraph shows that some work is still needed on polishing the writing, the girls show they can conduct research and write about that research in an in-

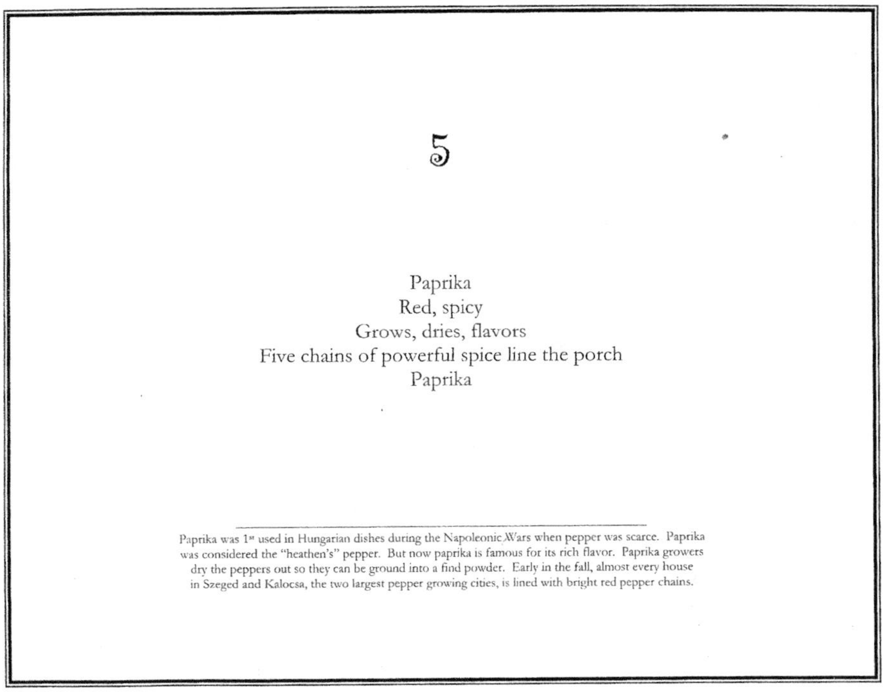

5

Paprika
Red, spicy
Grows, dries, flavors
Five chains of powerful spice line the porch
Paprika

Paprika was 1st used in Hungarian dishes during the Napoleonic Wars when pepper was scarce. Paprika was considered the "heathen's" pepper. But now paprika is famous for its rich flavor. Paprika growers dry the peppers out so they can be ground into a find powder. Early in the fall, almost every house in Szeged and Kalocsa, the two largest pepper growing cities, is lined with bright red pepper chains.

Figure 5.3. Sample page from Jeanette's One Leaf strategy practice about Hungary.

teresting manner. Certainly the voice of the writing suggests they were engaged in the writing.

An older student, Jeanette, produced a book by herself about Hungary, a country she had visited and wanted to know more about. She choose a different poetic form, one she felt more suited to her topic. A page from her book appears in Figure 5.3. Once again, the writing shows engagement and reflects research beyond general knowledge. And it's interesting and informative to read!

Lesson Plan: Brochure

In my planning, I consider what my students need to know or know how to do to be successful on this assignment. Some major things they need to have or know are these:

- An understanding of the nature and design of brochures
- A way to learn what an audience might want to know about a topic
- Methods for gathering and recording information about a topic

- Ways different information can best be expressed (lists, paragraphs, etc.)
- Ideas for how to make information visually appealing and accessible

To help students be successful with this writing, I use the following strategies.

Teacher Plan for Inquiry Strategies

1. I begin by asking students to use their existing knowledge of brochures. Our discussion addresses the anticipated audience: interested people who might or might not know much about the topic. Possible purposes include to inform, to persuade, to advertise, or to take a stand.

2. When we have addressed the purposes of brochures, I have students investigate several brochures in small groups. I provide them with an investigation sheet (below) so that they can identify salient features more effectively. After they have reviewed several brochures, together we make a descriptive list of characteristics and discuss how these accomplish the purposes of a brochure.

Investigation Sheet

List of names of brochures your group reviewed:

-
-
-
-

- What is/are the purpose(s) of brochures? What is the tone?
- What is the intended audience like? That is, what characteristics do they have?
- What kind of content is found in brochures?
- How does this kind of content fit the purpose of a brochure?
- How does this kind of content fit the audience of a brochure?
- How is the text organized in brochures?
- How do these aspects of organization fit the purpose of a brochure?
- How do these aspects of organization fit the audience?
- What aspects of formatting do you notice? How do these connect to the purpose and audience characteristics?

---

3. If students are deciding on a new topic, this would be the place for them to do it. When I teach brochures, I have students write one on the same topic they selected for their reversal paper (described in Chapter 4). This is my way of helping them see how different purposes might require different content as well as different forms. I give them the assignment in the form of a brochure: These are sample panels.

Writing Brochures

An Assignment for Strategic Writing

Mrs. Dean

What does a brochure do?
As we discovered in class, a person selects a brochure because the cover indicates visually and with words what the brochure contains. Thus, the audience is already somewhat interested. They want more information. That is what you will give them in the inside of the brochure.

Your topic needs to be developed around four or five main questions or aspects of your topic that an audience might want to know more about. For each of those aspects or questions, you should provide a clear, concise, informative answer. You don't have room for a lengthy response, simply one that is accurate, makes sense, and answers the questions.

Your content can be arranged in paragraphs, lists, graphs or charts, or a number of other choices of text or graphics. The arrangement should lead the reader to find what he or she wants to know quickly and easily.

The overall appearance of the brochure should be neat and appealing. The use of white space and graphics should appeal to and guide the reader efficiently through the content.

---

continued on next page

When is everything due?	How will I be graded?	Word Choice (8) ___

When is everything due? You will ask other people to help you determine the main aspects or questions to answer about your topic. Then you will conduct research about those. In class on ____ we will begin drafting. On ____ you will need to have two sketches of layout designs to get feedback on. Your first draft of the brochure is due ____, and the final is due ____.

How will I be graded?
Ideas (30) ___
• Content is researched, interesting, and informative.
• Ideas are presented in effective formats—whatever works best. (At least two must be in paragraph format; the others can be in lists, graphs, charts, diagrams, etc.)
Organization (25) ___
• Ideas are arranged effectively to guide the reader efficiently through the information in the brochure.
• Paragraphs are coherent (chaining), and lists use parallel structure.

Word Choice (8) ___
• Precise words help the reader understand more about the topic.
• One vocabulary word is used effectively.
Voice (7) ___
• Tone is informative and objective.
Conventions (10) ___
• Brochure is mostly free from errors in spelling and punctuation.
• Bibliography is correct.
Presentation (20) ___
• Overall presentation is neat and appealing, meets requirements.
• Design follows principles discovered from inquiry.
TOTAL (100) ___

4. Once students have a topic, they have inquiry homework: interviewing three people who might be interested in the topic. They bring their names and the five most important questions each of those people has about their topic to class, where we find patterns and commonalities that help us determine the areas to address in the brochure.

Inquiry Sheet

Name: _____

Topic: _____

What do you think are main ideas or questions about your topic?
1.
2.

3.
4.
5.
Before the next class, talk to three other people and get their responses
to the same question: What are the main ideas or questions you have
about _____? (You can add more than the five that are
listed here if you need to.)
Person 1: _____
1.
2.
3.
4.
5.
Person 2: _____
1.
2.
3.
4.
5.
Person 3: _____
1.
2.
3.
4.
5.
Synthesis: What are the key ideas or questions related to my topic?

5. Next, we conduct inquiry. Students begin by filling out a form somewhat like the KWL teachers often use as a prereading strategy (see Table
5.1). In the first column, students list the ideas or questions they have
decided to address in the brochure. In the second column, they write
what they already know about each idea or question. At this point we
go to the library, and as students conduct research, they record what
they are learning and their sources for each of the areas or questions
identified on the guide. Students, of course, are encouraged to conduct
inquiry outside of class by talking to knowledgeable people and going
to places that might have information to add.

Table 5.1. Brochure Research Guide

Main ideas or questions (one in each box)	What I already know about this idea or question	What I need to find out—notes and sources

Teacher Plan for Drafting Strategies

1. Before students begin drafting, we revisit brochures to discuss content types we can choose from. In each brochure, students see content types such as lists, charts, graphs, maps, paragraphs, and illustrations with captions. We review these to determine not only what options are available but why a writer might choose one over another: What purpose and information might best be served by one text type rather than another?

2. Next I have students list each idea or question they will address in the brochure and which content type they will use for each one and why. This is often a good time to allow students to work in small groups to bounce ideas off one another to determine if they've made effective choices. I encourage them to consider appropriate visual elements at this time, too. Now students are ready to being drafting the pieces of the brochure.

Teacher Plan for Product Strategies

1. Once students have text pieces but before they put them together in the brochure, they sketch two different options for the design of the brochure. I encourage them to begin to consider how to use font and white space to help guide the reader's eyes. We review the sample brochures to decide on effective strategies: Which are most effective visually, and why? How does design contribute to the brochures' effectiveness in achieving their purposes? How do the fonts and graphics contribute to the flow of the brochure, so that readers are led through and can easily find what they want to know? Students share the sketches in small groups to get feedback, finally selecting one of the designs based on that feedback.

2. When students have drafts of text, we have minilessons on parallel structure, looking at our drafts of lists to ensure parallelism. I also encourage students to look for conjunctions in their paragraphs and captions to identify other places where they should check for parallel structure.

3. With drafts written, we can also use chaining to check for coherence (Hansen). Chaining requires students to highlight or draw circles around key words in the paragraph. In the concise nature of brochures, these key words should make a chain of ideas that uses synonyms and phrases to create a logical progression of ideas. To practice, we work through example paragraphs. Here is one from *Seabiscuit* by Laura Hillenbrand, already marked to show chaining:

> Seabiscuit may have been trapped in the barn, but his idleness didn't hurt his **celebrity.** He was the **hottest name** in the nation. **Fans thronged** into the Uptown Theater in Pasadena to see *The Life of Seabiscuit,* a compilation of the horse's newsreel footage. The film relegated a much anticipated Jimmy Stewart movie to second billing. The stylish "Seabiscuit" ladies' hat, with a fishnet veil, was **all the rage** in department stores on Manhattan's Fifth Avenue. The hat was the first of **myriad lines of signature products:** toys, commemorative wastebaskets, two varieties of oranges. **All kinds of businesses** from hotels to laundries to humor magazines were using the horse's likeness in their ads. The horse even had his **own parlor game,** the first of at least nine. (305)

For this example, I ask students to look at the first sentence and guess what the paragraph will be about. They guess that it will be about Seabiscuit's celebrity, so that begins the chain. Then we look for words that show celebrity or are evidence of celebrity. Those are the ones highlighted above. If a sentence doesn't have a highlighted word or phrase, we check it to see if it fits with the paragraph, either in ideas or order. In the paragraph above, the sentence beginning "The film relegated . . ." does not have a direct chaining link to the other sentences. We discuss its purpose and decide that it is further evidence of the previous sentence, at a deeper level, so it works in the paragraph. Next I ask students to do the same thing with their own paragraphs to determine if they are as unified and tight as they can be. Sometimes this check is more effective if a peer does the chain or at least checks the writer's chain.

4. When drafts are ready, we conduct evaluative reading. Because of the nature of brochures, this is a little more complex, and I have to plan more time for it in class. This is the form I use to help students evaluate one another's brochures.

Brochure Evaluative Reading

Author _____ Reviewer _____

1. Spread the brochure out and look at it overall from a visual perspective. What works in the layout design? What doesn't seem to work—or what do you have a question about in terms of layout?

2. Overall, consider the following elements:

   - Are the main topics or questions arranged in the most logical order—in the order a reader might want to know the information? If not, make suggestions for moving them.

   - Is there a place where the main idea isn't clear or accessible?

   - Is the brochure too crowded, or is there too much empty space?

   - Are there illustrations? If so, do they fit the content? What suggestions can you make for improving selection or placement of visuals?

   - How would you describe the overall tone of the brochure?

   - Is a vocabulary word used effectively? Are there any errors in conventions you can help with?

3. Now look at each topic or question one at a time. For each one, answer the following questions:

Topic:_____

- Is the format (paragraph, list, graph, map, etc.) the best for this type of information? Why or why not?

- Is the content informative? List two specific details you didn't know before reading this passage.

- Are the ideas in this passage arranged in the best order? If you see another place where an idea might work better, draw an arrow from the idea to that place.

- If the passage is a paragraph, circle the main idea in the topic sentence, and then circle all the words or phrases that restate or rename the idea (synonyms) in the rest of the paragraph (chaining, as we did in class). Could the paragraph be tighter?

- If the passage is a list, check for parallel structure: Underline the words of each item in the list that should align. Give suggestions if parallelism could be improved.

Use another sheet of paper to answer these questions for each section.

5. When students turn their brochures in for grading, they complete a reflection. The questions I use to prompt this reflection are these:

   a. The topic for the brochure was the same as for your reversal paper. What did you have to do differently with that topic to write about it for a brochure? Why did you need to do what you did? How might your adaptations be useful to you in other writing situations?

   b. For this assignment, I provided you with a number of hand-outs that asked questions or prompted your thinking in ways that I hoped could be helpful in completing the brochure effectively. In what ways were those handouts helpful strategies to you? In what ways were they not? How might you use what was helpful as a strategy for yourself in other writing when I'm not there to provide the handouts?

   c. What strategies besides those you've already mentioned were helpful to you in writing the brochure? How might they be useful to you in other writing situations?

The students' responses to the reflection questions show the value of these strategies. In responding about what strategies were helpful in this paper, Justine noted, "Research, research, research. That was a big help to get facts on my topic. Also planning it out and asking lots of questions were useful. The idea of asking people questions about the topic made it easy to know what to write about." Isac wrote that he appreci-ates the note-taking strategy: "I would use the column notes if I was writing a paper because if you use this method you can stay on your topic and not go off into something not even related." Larry noted that making more than one design plan before drafting is useful: "I've never done that with any assignment. It took longer, but I felt more confident with my final product. I was able to see that my initial ideas weren't as good as I had thought."

In response to the reflection question about the handouts, Justine wrote the following:

> Even though it seemed like a lot of handouts, they turned out to be very helpful. We did things that none of us would go out and do/ask on our own. They were easy to refer back to. In the fu-ture, I would probably ask people questions about my topic and find examples of what I was doing.

Figure 5.4 shows Justine's brochure on teenagers. Through her inquiry, she learned that people who might read a brochure on teens were interested in driving, jobs, and increased risk of suicide. As a re-sult, she had a panel on each and two panels on driving: one on why teens are more likely to have accidents and one on how parents might help teens drive more responsibly. She arranged her brochure in re-sponse to key questions. Despite a problem with parallel structure (prob-ably because of an effort to make use of a vocabulary word), Justine's brochure was informative and served the purposes of a brochure on this topic.

11/04: How can I help my students think about the purposes for their writing and how those purposes influence that writing, especially when almost everything they do for school has at least one purpose of earn-ing them a grade? I thought by having them use the same topic for the brochure as they had for the reversal paper, they would start to under-stand what I was teaching about strategies for considering purpose. Some of them did. But some of them just complained—they'd already done some inquiry on the topic for the reversal paper and they didn't want to do more for this. And why did they have to write on the same topic? They were tired of it. They are just so used to seeing assignments as ends, not as means. When they finish one, they want to move on and forget it, even though they can revise it if they want to. I have to remind myself again and again that teaching writing is hard work and learn-

What makes teenagers more at risk to commit or attempt suicide?

Suicides among young people nationwide have increased dramatically in recent years so that today thousands of teenagers commit suicide each year. They experience feelings of stress, confusion, self-doubt, pressure to succeed, and other fears while growing up. For some teenagers, divorce, the formation of a new family with step-parents and step-sibling, or a move to a new community can be very unsettling. In some cases, suicide appears to be a "solution." Parents should be aware of the following danger signs:

- changes in eating and sleeping
- not being loquacious with family
- violent actions and rebellious behavior
- drug and alcohol use
- marked personality change
- frequent complaints about physical symptoms, often related to emotions.

Sources

http://www.psych.org/public_info/teenag~1.cfm

http://www.qvpl.ca/youth/teens/teenlinks.htm

Teenagers

A guide to the life they live

Justine
Period 1
November 25, 2003

Figure 5.4a. Justine's brochure (panels 5, 6, 1).

What are some teenage jobs beyond a lemonade stand or babysitting?

A cleaning service. Maybe teens hate doing chores at home, but getting paid for doing them is completely different.

A yard maintenance service. There is always something that needs to be done in a yard. Mowing lawns and weed control, raking leaves in the fall, and shoveling snow and planting for the spring in the winter.

A car-detailing business. With so many people having such busy lifestyles, few people have the time to really take care of their cars. Teens could offer a service of washing, waxing, vacuuming, etc.

A catering service. In these busy times, teens could help neighbors and family out through the holidays.

Are teenagers the worst drivers of any age group?

Teenagers are involved in more car accidents than any other age group and are more likely to be the responsible party in an auto accident. In an analysis of vehicle accidents that involved teen drivers, the following factors were found to be true:

1. Teenagers tend to avoid wearing seat belts and yet they also tend to engage in more risky driving habits such as speeding.

2. Teenage drivers often tend to drive at night when driving conditions are more challenging.

3. Although teenagers are less likely than adults to drive after consuming alcohol, when they do, they are more likely to be in an accident due to inexperience.

How can we help teenagers drive more responsibly?

The first step is to make sure that you set a good example. Then talk to your teen and explain why they tend to be involved in more accidents.

It is also important not to let them drive alone for the first three to six months after they get their driver's license. Make sure that there's always an experienced driver with them. Also for the first six months, consider restricting night driving to a minimum.

Getting a driver's license is exciting. It's natural that teenagers want to share their freedom with friends. Unfortunately, too many passengers in the car may contribute to driver distraction. Consider restricting the number of passengers that you will allow your teen to have in the car.

Figure 5.4b. Justine's brochure (panels 2, 3, 4).

ing to write well is a process as slow as a glacier moving. Sometimes we don't see its effect until a long time has passed. So I'll keep on. Meanwhile, if there are ways to help students consider other purposes, what are they, and how can I implement them in my classes? What assignments do I already give that might work or that could be adapted to help students learn strategies that apply to purposes for writing and how those strategies can be useful in writing outside of this class or even outside of school?

Additional Resources

Gere, Anne Ruggles, Leila Christenbury, and Kelly Sassi. *Writing on Demand: Best Practices and Strategies for Success.* Portsmouth, NH: Heinemann, 2005.

Hillocks, George, Jr. *The Testing Trap: How State Writing Assessments Control Learning.* New York: Teachers College Press, 2002.

Jago, Carol. *Beyond Standards: Excellence in the High School English Classroom.* Portsmouth, NH: Boynton/Cook, 2001.

Pirie, Bruce. *Reshaping High School English.* Urbana, IL: NCTE, 1997.

6 Strategies for Product: Rethinking Revision

Revision takes you from self to society, from the writer's concerns to the readers' concerns.

Wendy Bishop

I *had a writing conference scheduled with my professor. He was supposed to have comments for my paper. Since I'd been a successful writer for classes in the past, I didn't have any reason to think he would have major problems to discuss.*

When I entered his office, he seemed distracted. It took him a few minutes to rifle through the stacks of papers and books on his desk to find mine. (I couldn't help but think, "Didn't he know we were meeting? Didn't he think more of my paper than to lose it in a stack of papers as though it were meaningless?") He skimmed over the paper for about thirty seconds, refreshing his memory, I suppose. Then, he ripped off the first eleven pages of the fifteen-page paper, tore them in half and dropped them in the trash.

"That was garbage," he said, nodding toward the trash can. "About page 12 you begin to get interesting. Start there and do it over again."

With that, he handed me the skeletal remains of my paper and turned back to his desk. He was finished with the conference, so I got up and left. Dazed.

I think now that, perhaps, there was more conversation when I first walked into that professor's office, but if so, I honestly can't remember it. The main point of the conference for me was his utter dismissal of my paper. I revised because I had to. And it was the most extensive revision—re-seeing—I had done to that point. It was good practice for later, for writing the dissertation (he was the chair of my committee) and for editors returning manuscripts, but it was hard at the time. And I had some experience as a writer.

That experience has made me consider how I help my students revise. Certainly I didn't ever—wouldn't ever—physically rip one of their papers apart. But are my comments—any teacher's comments— as unhelpful as his were to me? Richard Beach seems to think so: "In short, because students do not know how to assess their writing, much of our seemingly helpful feedback may not necessarily help them to critically assess their writing" (128). Although we know that revising (in some form) takes place all through the writing process, this chapter focuses on strategies that students can use after some words are down on paper to help them learn to assess writing and find ways to improve it.

Students and Revising

What do we know about revising and student writers? First, most students resist revision. Margot Soven, citing Weaver's report of a study by the National Assessment of Educational Progress, notes that when given a specific time to rewrite, about 90 percent of the students "did nothing" (44). My own experiences with state and district tests of writing confirm this. The test (at least in my state) allowed time for pre-writing, drafting, and revision—at least theoretically—by providing two hours for the writing. I supervised a group of twenty-five students, only one of whom did anything besides drafting. The rest of the group finished in under twenty-five minutes. This behavior is partly a factor of attitude and partly a factor of ability.

Brock Dethier lists attitudes students have about revising that suggest reasons they might resist it, including feelings that revision is nitpicky, unnecessary, a waste of time, not creative, or a sign of failure (2–3). Elaine, one of my university students and a more experienced writer, indicated that her feelings exemplify some of what Dethier notes. After a peer review session, she wrote the following in her reflective response:

> Well, to be honest, I don't like when people make suggestions for improvement or change. Of course I want to improve my writing, but I also don't like to be told that I really don't know what I'm doing. This may stem from knowing it needs to be fixed, but not knowing how to fix it. This creates a lot of anxiety for me. A good writer either shouldn't make major "mistakes" or should be able to see them themselves and know how to fix them.

Certainly if more-experienced writers have some of these attitudes, teachers should consider that less-experienced writers might feel similarly. All of this suggests that teachers might make some efforts to improve attitudes about revision along with providing strategies. Although Donald Murray is commenting on editing and not revision, perhaps we can help students gain his attitude: "It is not an admission of failure when you have to edit. . . . Editing is not punishment, but opportunity" (173). Revision should be an opportunity, too.

We know that the ability to revise, to step back from a paper and see it with a new perspective, is somewhat developmental and therefore also linked to ability. Students may not be able to revise because revision is hard. It requires a writer to consider many aspects of the writing at once: audience, genre, purpose, ideas, organization, and tone—at the very least. Writers are expected to figure out what isn't working with a draft and know how to fix it and then have the ability to do so. These are complex tasks. Sometimes, even with years of experience, I know a piece of writing isn't working, but I can't figure out why. Sometimes I don't even know a piece of writing isn't working until someone else reads it and tells me. Then I have to figure out what's wrong when I couldn't see it myself. These are challenging issues—and I have experience and thick skin and a number of available strategies. Soven points out that "beginning writers often don't know what to think about when they are revising" (46) and suggests that "there is no point asking students to revise for features of writing they have not yet learned" (47). I agree. Revision expectations must be developed along with writing strategies, allowing students to develop as revisers while they develop as writers.

Looking at the revision differences between novice and experienced writers (summarized from research by Schriver and Fitzgerald) might help us understand what strategies would best help student writers. Novice writers

- begin revision at the beginning sentence and stay mostly at the sentence level,
- may try to revise for everything at once,
- fail to look at the overall goal of a piece of writing,
- lose track of audience needs in the revision process,
- don't revise much,
- focus on correcting "errors" in revising,
- make isolated revisions that don't connect to other revisions,
- have fewer strategies,
- respond better to explicit suggestions by teachers, and
- revise only what teachers suggest.

Experienced writers

- consider the whole text before revising,
- revise multiple times, each time for specific needs,
- consider the goal of a text before revising,
- think of audience before and during revision,
- might revise more during composing than novices,
- detect more problems,

- possess more strategies for revision, and
- respond better to less explicit suggestions from the teacher.

Considering the attributes and behaviors of novice writers compared with experienced writers can help both teachers and writers. I tell my students that sometimes I behave as though I have not had the writing experience I have. Sometimes, even with experience, I forget strategies I have for revision, I can't seem to see the whole piece, or I want to avoid revision altogether. What I benefit from, however, is the experience of past revisions, of having used multiple strategies so I have options available. And I have enough experience with revision to know that it *does* improve my writing. Giving our students opportunities to practice revision strategies so that they also see its benefits may be one of the best ways to help them become more effective at revision.

Time can be a revision strategy we can provide our students. My students' best revision occurs when I am thoughtful enough to plan ahead for multiple days of revision so that students don't have to consider so many aspects of text at once. Time works for me as a writer as well. Sometimes I just need time away from the piece of writing to see it the way a reader will. If I want my students to consider time as a possible strategy, I can encourage this through my planning for their writing.

One problem many of my students have with revision is that they often don't have a very good draft to begin with. Revision is difficult to accomplish with inadequate or undeveloped text, so developing a draft can actually be a precursor strategy for revising. I use questions to help my students develop drafts, but I recently found Wendy Bishop's concept of "fat drafting" to be useful for my students ("Revising Out"). In the application section of this chapter, I describe her ideas and mine for developing drafts before we begin refining or revising them. Barry Lane, in *After the End,* gives more ideas for developing drafts: exploding a moment, digging for details, and "thoughtshots."

Although my students will get suggestions for revision from peers, ultimately revision decisions belong to the writer. I teach my students to use the grading rubric as a way to reconsider revision. They are given the rubric sometime during the writing process. The timing is one of my strategies as a teacher: not so early as to inhibit thinking and creativity, but not so late as to prevent students from benefiting from knowing the evaluative criteria. Timing changes with each assignment, but the grading rubric is always in students' hands before the last revision. I see the grading rubric as a kind of contract with students. I'm aware of the many associated issues—the philosophical foundation of the rubric, the vagueness or specificity of the language, the number of criteria, and so on—but I agree with Ed White that scoring guides can help students both in evaluating each other's writing and in assessing their own for revision: "Students do not revise their work because, in their heart of hearts, they don't really think there is anything wrong with it. . . . This is at heart an assessment problem" (212).

Because an effectively written grading rubric (and that's a whole other topic) can help students develop as writers, I find it rewarding (even though it's also a little frustrating) when students can't turn in their grade sheets with their papers because the grade sheet's at home by the computer where they used it to revise the writing. I have a journal entry celebrating a day Jon forgot his grade sheet at home. He'd finally learned to use it to guide revision, and he could tell me specifically what he'd revised because of it. The incident reminds me how a well-written grading rubric can be strategic:

- I can use it to guide instruction.
- Students can use it to help them revise.
- It can teach students awareness of audience considerations.
- Students learn that revising for audience concerns is strategic.

Another important part of teaching revision as strategy is helping students see that revision has layers. It seems pointless to talk about revising for sentence-level concerns when students still need to generate sentences as they revise for ideas or organization—although I've done this with my students before I thought it through. By separating revision into levels and spreading it out over more than one day, my students improve their abilities both to revise and to produce effective final products. The next section explains the two levels.

Revising Globally

Less-experienced writers often think of revision as "correcting" a paper, worrying about conventions and formatting. Experienced writers usually consider more global issues first, issues related to development of ideas, to organization, to voice, audience, genre, and purpose. As teachers, we often try to teach this to our students by advising them not to worry about spelling during drafting, for instance. I've done the same thing, although many less-experienced writers can't really separate the two. Some of my students are so disturbed by the green and red lines on the screen that they are literally halted by them. They can't continue until the lines are gone—and then they have lost the thought and often the momentum of their writing. If I can, I have students disable the spelling and grammar checker, but that isn't always possible. It's up to teachers to try to help students consider global issues first. Our focus on these issues, through the comments we make and the strategies we have students practice, can help students learn this important aspect of revision.

Alice Horning notes that "expert writers understand the differences in genres and have the skill to move flexibly from one genre to another" (45). For students to gain that flexibility, they should have chances to write the same information in more than one genre, much as I suggested earlier with the reversal and brochure practice sequence. Such switching can help students see how genre shapes ideas and organization, tone and language. The same idea can be applied to audience switching and purpose switching.

Horning suggests a specific exercise that secondary students would find interesting and that could be adapted for a variety of genres. Her suggestion is to read Lewis Carroll's "Jabberwocky" and then have students rewrite it as a news story or research report (45). I have used a similar idea. We read Robert Frost's poem "Out, Out" along with the news story he had read that prompted the poem. My students then find news stories that catch their interest and bring them to class, where we work on rewriting them as poems. Considering aspects of genre, once students are familiar with the idea, can help them revise their own papers more effectively because it helps them consider generic expectations as part of revision.

Many teachers have used a strategy of outlining after a draft is written to help students see the general flow and shape of a paper. Dethier suggests a version of that strategy to help writers revise for ideas and organization. Essentially, students make an informal outline of their draft by numbering the paragraphs; on a different sheet of paper, they write a brief summary of the paragraph next to each number. Students then group the numbers together by idea using boxes or colors or another technique (12). These procedures can help students see if their paragraphs are unified (If they are difficult to summarize, could the problem be that they address more than one point?) and if the ideas are in an order that makes sense (if the paragraphs don't block together, some ideas might need to be moved). A strategy practice I use to help students revise for paragraph unity and organization, Questions, is described in the application section.

In order for my students to revise for organization, I have them cut a draft apart by paragraphs and then have a peer tape the paragraphs together in the way that makes the most sense. If the writer disagrees with a choice of the peer reviewer, I suggest that he or she might need transitions to help the reader see the flow from the previous idea into the next one. This reinforces for my students the writer's responsibility to cue the reader as to how to read the paper.

Revising Locally

Local revision strategies generally address revising for sentence fluency and word choice, and this revision is not about correctness but about effectiveness. In the editing section I address issues of correctness with sentence boundaries and grammar. Here, I look at other issues.

In an older book I found at my school, *The Lively Art of Writing* by Lucile Vaughan Payne, I was intrigued by the discussion of sentence rhythm. Payne provides two short paragraphs that I share with my students and ask them which sounds like writing and which sounds like speech. One of them is a parent's voice telling a child to be home by a certain time, so the answer seems obvious, but that's not the point. Even if I read the written one about acting first, they all say it's writing, not speech. I ask them how they know, but they have a hard time expressing how. I then have students help me count sentence lengths and compare the two passages that way. The paragraph that sounds like writing has four sentences with these word lengths: 16, 12, 17, 18. The paragraph that sounds like speech has six sentences with these word lengths: 9, 14, 3, 3, 21, 3. The wider variety is quite evident. Then Payne does something interesting: She revises the written paragraph so that its sentence rhythm is more like the speech paragraph. Here is that paragraph:

> Few things are so essential to an actor as a sense of timing. Without that, nothing else about him matters very much. He may have a handsome face. He may have a splendid voice. But unless he has an innate sense of timing, the finest director in the world cannot make an actor of him. He can never be more than a puppet. (107)

After we discuss this short example, students can see how sentence length variety can add interest to writing. Students count the word lengths of their sentences. I tell them that the inner ear can't really "hear" a difference in writing unless the difference is four or more words (I don't know where I heard that, but it works), so students need to consider variety from that perspective. If they have lots of sentences close to the same length, they should find ways to revise them. I give them these guidelines: Short sentences will give an idea some punch. Save those for the ideas you want to drive home. Long sentences are good for background and depth. Although there is no specific formula for balancing short, medium, and long sentences, if students are aware of the idea and if we bring it to their attention when we are reading something that uses the idea effectively, they will become more sensitive to it and revise more effectively for sentence fluency.

Much of the revision work with word choice and sentence fluency in my class is built around the regular daily work we do in class with vocabulary and sentences. Those practices are described here.

Building Basic Tools: Word Work

It has been reported that today's average students (ages 6–14) have about 15,000 fewer words in their written vocabulary than students from 1945 (Fletcher 142). Without words, how can students write effectively? And yet most vocabulary work simply has students memorize lists of words and show their word knowledge by choosing the appropriate synonym from a multiple-choice list on a test. Even explicit instruction in vocabulary isn't always effective in helping students make large gains (Nagy and Herman 257). Such practices might—at best, I believe—provide students with an increased receptive vocabulary, the kind of knowledge that helps them understand their reading and what they hear. That kind of vocabulary instruction rarely provides students with increased expressive vocabulary, however, and that's what they need as writers.

Significant research exists that helps teachers understand how to improve students' vocabulary. The problem is how time-consuming such instruction can be and how much effort it takes on the part of the teacher. Much of the time, vocabulary activities are what teachers have students do at the beginning of class so teachers can take care of the myriad other tasks necessary at the start of class. In some ways, teachers hope (and I understand this) that the individual work will build vocabularies while it engages the students for a few minutes. It needs a little more.

Vocabulary instruction, at its best, should be derived from the needs of the students and the class; prepackaged plans, although they save time, are not of as much value as teacher-developed programs. I've used prepared plans and found that good ones can do what motivated students could do on their own if they were studying the dictionary or any number of handbooks. What such programs can't do is help students get a sense of the words and how to use them. That requires a lot of talking and writing. It requires a teacher who wants to talk about words and what they mean and how they mean and how they feel coming out of our mouths and into our heads, about how they can mean more than they seem to mean in the dictionary. It requires some passion. What I describe here is an overview of what I do in my class (Dean "Learning").

I choose my words either from the reading we are doing or to suit the kind of writing we will be doing (adjectives, for example, for poetry or creative writing). I begin by introducing students to the idea of Latin influences in the language. Through a few minilessons, students can see how knowing a little about Latinate origins can help them understand words, even though there are limitations, which we also explore. For each list of words we study, then, I begin by giving students a short list of Latin bases and prefixes and their definitions that students will find in the words of the current lesson and that I think will help them understand the words and word families. I use Ayers's *English Words from Latin and Greek Elements* as my source. Before we even look at our words, we brainstorm words that contain each base or prefix and discuss their connections.

I introduce the words to my students in a list of sentences with the words italicized, so that the students don't see the words in isolation. While I read the sentences aloud, students make guesses as to the meanings of the words, relying on context clues and the discussion of the Latin, if that applies. When we've finished, the students look up the words in dictionaries and write a definition—*in their own words*—that works for the word in the meaning of the sentence. This is an idea I read in *Words Work* by Thomas Carnicelli; I've found it very successful, as students have to think more than copy—and they can't just write down the first definition.

After they've finished, we review the words and what students think they mean. This is just the start of our talking about words. Over several days students work with the words, writing sentences and paragraphs as well as captions to comics. We use drawing and pictures from magazines to make visual connections to the words.

And every day, no matter what else we do, we talk about the words. Students share their sentences, their sketches, and their pictures. Talking is the most effective aspect of vocabulary instruction—and the most neglected. During the talking, teachers can learn whether students really are internalizing the words or not. A recent discussion had us all laughing as we tried to help a few students in the classroom understand how "redundant" was not the same as "repetitious" by providing examples and non-examples: If you mow the lawn one direction and then the other is that redundant? If you clean your room and then do it again because your dad says it wasn't good enough, is that redundant? Students started generating humorous examples just for fun. Because we talk about the words in these ways, students become more word conscious. They start to hear and see the words we discuss everywhere, but I am also concerned that they can use the words. It's always a reward when some of the students start to bring the words up in class to describe a character or situation.

Because I want all my students to use the words, they are required to use one or two vocabulary words appropriately in each L3 writing. I don't ask them to use more because then the effort leads to their misuse of the words as they try to force words where they might not fit. After a while, most get better at including their vocabulary words in early drafts. But if they don't, one step in their revision for word choice—in addition to considering if they've used the best word in each spot—is to consider when a vocabulary word might be effective, too.

Building Basic Tools: Sentence Work

I often stop in my reading to reread a sentence that pleases my inner ear with its fluency, that tickles my mind with how its structure enhances its ideas. I recognize now that this is something I have done since I was a child, who, when sent outside to "get some exercise," would carry books into the woods behind our house and read instead of run. I can remember leaning back against the trunk of a tree and looking up through leaves, running a sentence through my mind for the music of it. Despite this pleasure I have received my whole life from sentences artfully constructed, I had not really considered sentences as strategies that good writers had access to and inexperienced writers did not.

I stumbled on Corbett and Connors's *Classical Rhetoric for the Modern Student* and discovered that sentence imitation has been a writing strategy for centuries. Why hadn't I ever heard of it? Probably because working on writing process often means not working at the sentence level, and that was the way I was taught. I can understand that, especially if the instruction focuses only on correctness. But Corbett and Connors's book made me think of teaching sentences as stylistic options, as strategies students could learn and store to use when they seem applicable. I have read a large number of books on style and sentence combining, trying to find an approach that would work for me and my classes. I eventually came up with my own approach that blends ideas from others.

I want my students to learn to enjoy language and the multiple ways it can play in sentences, to develop sensitivity to sentences and patterns in language and their effects on readers, and to consider these patterns and play as options for themselves as writers. I recently stumbled on another teacher/writer, T. R. Johnson, who expresses my goals for this instruction more articulately than I have been able to do:

> An immersion in style is a microcosm for what an education in rhetoric tries to achieve, for it can open the student to the possibility that becoming a better writer means, at least in part, learning how to use writing to become a healthier, stronger participant in the world. (61)

This is what I want to achieve—and, to a certain extent, it is what I think some students gain from my efforts.

I have described my first attempts with sentences as strategies in an article published in *English Journal* ("Grammar"). Since then, I have tried more work with sentence combining and imitation. From reading and practice I have developed three overriding principles that seem to work best for me when I use them strategically instead of simply as activities.

1. First, I have to be engaged. I have to be interested in sentences and what they do and how they work. I have to continue my love affair with them at a conscious level. No matter how many books or resources I have, I have to be the instigator and the example for my students. I have to be fascinated by language—and I have to share this fascination with them. This should be mutual pleasure. So, when I read, I keep sticky notes handy to mark sentences that I could use for one reason or another, and I use those sentences in class when they are appropriate. I have all kinds of books marked up this way—and many of them are the books I read with my students, so I have more than enough for all occasions, and I can connect our reading to our sentence work. Then we discuss sentences in class. We talk about what they do, about what works, about what we like (and what we don't), and why. I tell them the names of structures we work on—polysyndeton, apposition, parallelism, anaphora—but I never test them on the names. I want my students to see me savoring sentences, showing them the power of language. The way to undermine this sentence work is to consider it as what students do while the teacher takes roll (or whatever other beginning-of-class business needs taking care of) before either moving on to other work or simply "correcting" the sentences.

2. Second, this work with sentences shouldn't be about right and wrong but about what effects different structures and patterns have on meaning and on audience. It should encourage students to think this way about sentences: *Yes, there are some things we do with sentences that cloud*

communication, that don't do what we hope they will do. There are some is-sues of correctness, but these are not for this play time unless they come up in the play. This is a time to try to imitate what effective writers do and see if we can succeed—and to then decide what the effects of our efforts are and when they would be appropriate. Sentence time should be a place to try—and then to discuss those tries and see what could be improved. Risk tak-ing should be encouraged by providing a grade-free zone for trying. Students get participation points for playing with sentences in my class, but eventually they don't really even worry about that. Even with my most remedial class, I have students who eventually share sentences that they aren't sure are working, just to see if they can get ideas about im-proving them. That's when I know the practice is working.

3. Third, what we do with sentences has to connect to what students are currently writing. This is essential for ensuring that the work with sentences is strategic and not just an activity. I used to use any kind of writing to practice imitation but found that certain styles of writing didn't work well when imitated in other kinds of writing. So, for in-stance, sentences imitated from Kennedy's Inaugural Address—al-though very effective sentence structures—didn't work well as models for the sentences my students were writing for much of their own work; those Kennedy structures were often too formal. Now I try to use effec-tive sentences from models of the same genre my students are reading and writing so that structures match in genre, tone, and topic. The imi-tations are practice for writing and should be used as such. Just as my students who are basketball players don't practice shooting hoops with-out anticipating a game, my writers don't practice sentence strategies without anticipating a place to apply them.

I have found a number of books and articles useful in informing my teaching of sentences. Although I don't use any of them exclusively, they have all helped me shape how I work with language and sentences with my students. I include the list here in the hope that they might be help-ful to other teachers as well.

Corbett, Edward P. J., and Robert J. Connors. *Classical Rhetoric for the Modern Student*. 4th ed. New York: Oxford UP, 1999.

Ehrenworth, Mary, and Vicki Vinton. *The Power of Grammar: Unconventional Approaches to the Conventions of Language*. Portsmouth, NH: Heinemann, 2005.

Hale, Constance. *Sin and Syntax: How to Craft Wickedly Effective Prose*. New York: Broadway Books, 1999.

Haussamen, Brock, with Amy Benjamin, Martha Kolln, and Rebecca S. Wheeler. *Grammar Alive! A Guide for Teachers.* Urbana, IL: NCTE, 2003.

Johnson, T. R. *A Rhetoric of Pleasure: Prose Style and Today's Composition Classroom.* Portsmouth, NH: Boynton/Cook, 2003.

Killgallon, Don. *Sentence Composing for High School.* Portsmouth, NH: Heinemann, 1998.

Kolln, Martha. *Rhetorical Grammar: Rhetorical Choices, Grammatical Effects.* Boston: Allyn and Bacon, 1998.

Noden, Harry. *Image Grammar.* Portsmouth, NH: Boynton/Cook, 1999.

Paraskevas, Cornelia. "The Craft of Writing: Breaking Conventions." *English Journal* 93.4 (2004): 41–46.

Schuster, Edgar H. *Breaking the Rules: Liberating Writers through Innovative Grammar Instruction.* Portsmouth, NH: Heinemann, 2003.

———. "Sentence Comparison: An Activity for Teaching Style." *English Journal* 94.5 (2005): 94–98.

Strong, William. *Coaching Writing: The Power of Guided Practice.* Portsmouth, NH: Heinemann, 2001.

Weaver, Constance. *Teaching Grammar in Context.* Portsmouth, NH: Boynton/Cook, 1996.

Editing, Not Revising

Revision differs from editing. It seems so obvious that I am surprised when even my preservice teachers, the semester before they student teach, tell me they haven't heard the distinction before. Revision is about re-seeing the paper, changing its shape or its meaning at either deep or more surface levels. Editing has to do with cleanup. It's about making the paper conform to expectations of correctness. It's important for students to know the difference. And especially with L3 writing, writers need to work on editing, on fixing up the surface errors that might distract or interrupt a reader.

In working with sentence boundaries, a particular problem some of my students have, I have had them read their writing sentence by sentence from the end to the beginning. They find the period (or other end punctuation) before the last one and read what's in between. They repeat this for the whole paper. My experience has been that fragments and run-ons often occur because students don't really understand sentence boundaries, so reading a paper in the normal order allows the ideas to mingle, thus complicating the students' ability to "hear" those boundaries. Reading what they've counted as sentences backward forces the ideas apart and helps students hear boundaries more effectively.

My students can recite the definition of a sentence, so I find it particularly interesting how many texts and self-help books use the definition of a sentence (which is problematic itself) to help less-experienced writers correct sentences. Knowing that a sentence has a subject and predicate and expresses a complete thought doesn't help most of my students. Instead, I've collected sentence-boundary tests that can help my students find sentences. Two of them follow:

1. Tack the group of words under question to the end of this starter: "They refused to believe the idea that . . ." If it makes sense, the words are probably a sentence. If not, they are probably not (Noguchi 55–56).

2. Make the words under consideration into a yes/no question by adding a tag question to the end or by inverting the word order (Noguchi 53–54). "I was tired" becomes either "Was I tired?" or "I was tired, wasn't I?" Students who are learning English as a second language may find this test more challenging until they've learned how to form such questions in English.

In teaching sentence boundaries, sometimes it also helps students to read their paper aloud while a partner follows along on another copy. When the writer/reader's voice sounds like the end of a sentence or pauses significantly (not just a comma pause), the partner makes a slash mark on the paper at that point. Then the two trade copies, and the writer reads the marked paper aloud again, pausing at the slashes as if they were ends of sentences. If the writer/reader and listener agree that the text makes sense, the writer can put in appropriate end punctuation; if not, the process can continue until the writing makes sense. Again, reading aloud can help students edit for sentence boundaries.

At the secondary level, I teach punctuation and grammar in minilessons as needed by students and the assignment. When students' writing shows patterns of problems, I prepare lessons to address and practice the problematic issue. For these lessons, I move from declarative knowledge (explaining what the concern is and how to fix it) to procedural knowledge, which might involve students' practicing on prepared sentences first but which must eventually have students practice with their own writing and their own sentences. This type of language instruction is challenging because it means I can't rely only on a textbook. I can use a number of resources, but I have to determine what my students' difficulties are, how they can best learn to identify and address them, and what I can do to help. Rarely can I just use ten sentences from a grammar book as practice. I borrow and modify, so it means a little more time for me but usually more effective instruction for my students.

Sometimes different kinds of writing assignments require different kinds of language structures from student writers, so I prepare lessons or imitations to correspond to the unit as well. For instance, students practice appositives when they write book or movie reviews (appositives are plentiful in that genre), and this practice allows me to review the use of commas around ideas that interrupt at the same time. The point I try to make in my lessons about punctuation is this: Punctuation is not all about rules. Certainly, rules apply—but the important thing about punctuation is that it is the writer's way of helping the reader read the way the writer intended. It's a control issue and an understanding issue, not necessarily only a rule issue. Rules are standardized ways for the writer to direct reading, and they should be understood as that. Students appreciate this approach more—and it brings a dynamic to my teaching that makes it more interesting: If we put a comma here, how does that change the way a reader would read? Is that how we want this part read? Writers make choices and think about readers. Punctuation helps them do that. That's strategy.

Evaluative Reading

I used to call this peer review, but a colleague, Kimberly Johnson, in speaking to graduate instructors, noted that most students don't see *review* as suggesting improvements. They see *review* as reading and making a response, perhaps "I liked it" or something equally unuseful in revising. She suggests the term "evaluative reading" since it implies reading for the purpose of evaluating: deciding what works and what doesn't. I think the choice of words matters.

We want students to see the value of others' opinions about their writing. Such a perspective sharpens audience awareness and puts substance behind our belief that writing is a social activity rather than an isolated one. Still, it can be a scary prospect. When I first started sharing my writing with colleagues, I would break out in cold sores from the stress of it. I learned not to get quite so nervous—and I learned the value of others reading my writing before it was ready to be submitted. Even so, it was hard and remains so still.

Training

Even when it's not scary, students need to feel that the person doing the evaluative reading will provide something of value to the writer, will give some ideas that will be useful in revising the writing. This is one of the most challenging concerns to overcome with student writers: how to train them well enough that their comments instigate meaningful revision and a more effective piece of writing. I'm sure I'm not the only teacher who's had students come to the desk when it's time for "peer review" and ask if I could read the paper. Students don't believe their peers really can give them the advice and help they need. Or, if some have found that a few students can give helpful feedback, those few are swamped with requests to "trade papers with me" so that the most helpful evaluative readers are overwhelmed.

Students need to be trained as evaluative readers—but I don't have any magic solutions except a belief that it matters and that persistence pays off. Modeling how evaluative reading should work is a good idea. If I have students I can work with, I have them pretend to be a group with me and work through a draft of my own writing in front of the class. Then the class can analyze the experience for examples of how evaluative reading should work. If I don't have those students, I put a draft I wrote on an overhead and model what questions I have and ask students for comments to improve my writing and answer my questions. By doing this, I can comment on the responses and show how they can be helpful or modified to become more so.

Gloria Neubert and Sally J. McNelis describe evaluative reading training using a handout that lists possible peer comments and then provides room for students to evaluate the comments for their effectiveness (55). Although it takes time to complete and then to discuss these comments (I do small groups first and then the whole class), the time spent is worth it in helping students develop a sense of the type of comments that help fellow writers and the type that don't.

Sample Response Group Comments

Read each of the following comments and evaluate the effectiveness of each.

Response/comment	This is effective because . . .	This is not effective because . . .
You need to give the readers more information to convince them. Why is it better in North Carolina than Maryland?		

First sentence is too
short. A few words are
misplaced.

I liked your story, but you
began practically every
sentence with "but" or
"so."

Try to shorten your first
sentence; it is a good topic
but too long.

Exactly why did your teacher
pick on you?

What happened when you made smart
remarks back? After you accepted
defeat? More specific detail
is needed to get the whole
story.

Good word choice, detail, and
facts. Sentence structure is
not too good in some places.

Your topic sentence needs work.
I don't take French and anyone
who does not wouldn't understand.

Good description of your feelings
when you lost your cat.

From Gloria A. Neubert and Sally J. McNelis, "Peer Response: Teaching Specific
Revision Suggestions," *English Journal* 79.5 (1990): 55. Copyright 1990 by the National Council of Teachers of English. Reprinted with permission.

In general, my approach to evaluative reading has been to be
persistent, not to give up just because the process doesn't work as well
as I'd like the first or second or fifth time. It does get better, even if it's
not perfect. Each time I use peer evaluative readings, I try to ensure that
students are respectful, and then I implement other strategies to improve
the quality of commenting that goes on. I have learned that my students
do best if they have prompts to respond to during their evaluative readings. The worst experiences I've had or witnessed have been the open-
ended read-a-neighbor's-paper-and-tell-him-what-you-think kind of
peer readings. Once I observed a student teacher give those directions
and face open rebellion. "Why do I have to make two copies of the same
paper?" a boy asked. When the student teacher said they wouldn't be

the same, that the peer reader would give suggestions for revision, there were hoots and snorts from all over the room. These students had previous experiences with peer reviews and had found that nothing beneficial happened. They started yelling about wasting paper and killing trees and wasting time. The student teacher hadn't planned for effective evaluative reading: She hadn't trained her students and hadn't prepared prompts that could guide less-experienced writers as they helped each other through revision.

Prompts

Prompts for evaluative reading are important. First, I try to make them both structured and open. That is, prompts need to direct students to the features of text most important to the successful production of whatever genre students are writing. In this way, students are also trained to read for certain attributes that they can consider when they are reading their own papers again. But the questions also need to be open-ended instead of yes/no questions that ask for whether something exists or not. For example, "Is there a topic sentence at the beginning of the paragraph?" asks a reader to identify the existence of a structure but not to evaluate the effectiveness of that structure. Instead, asking students to evaluate a topic sentence for its ability to focus the ideas of a paragraph or to rate an introduction for its ability to interest and engage the reader (excellent, very good, good, could use some improvement, not at all) encourages students to become somewhat evaluative. Getting students to focus on traits other than conventions in evaluative responses—and getting them to be specific—can be a good learning experience.

One prompt I have used, shown in Table 6.1, asks peers to read and rate the paper on its ability to hold the reader's interest paragraph by paragraph. Although some students treat it as superficially as they do other prompts, others use the marks they receive to reconsider certain paragraphs for revision. I have found that if I ask students to explain their evaluations, they are less likely to provide cursory evaluations.

I have also learned to make the evaluative reading prompts interactive, that is, to have the writer respond to the comments made on the draft. Sometimes I have the writer give the peer evaluator a score on the effectiveness of his or her comments, but I always have the writer note three specific revisions he or she will make for the next draft based on the peer's comments. After training peer evaluators, it's important that writers pay attention to their comments and consider them when revising. Such behaviors help both writers and peer evaluators value the process—and that's a big step in the right direction.

Even with better prompts and with training, it is still possible for students to provide feedback that is not helpful. I've had students mark everything on a peer's paper "excellent" just so they don't have to write so many comments. I usually resolve that by giving some value (points or a grade) to evaluative reading. I skim the drafts and reader's comment sheet when the paper is turned in, and with a quick glance I can get a good idea of the effectiveness of a reader's response. But I don't always wait until the paper's been revised before considering the peer responses. I initial the evaluative reading response sheets we do in class before they go back to the writer. That way I can stop most of the rush-through jobs before they get back in the hands of the writers. This also gives me a chance to remind students that the more helpful they are to others, the more likely they are to get beneficial responses to their own papers—and the more likely they are to learn to be effective readers of their own writing.

Another way I help improve student responses and the way writers value them is by my response to them when I evaluate a paper. I skim the evaluative reading sheet before I read the paper; then I try to note when the writer has followed the reader's advice to create a more effective paper or when he or she should have. This acknowledgment of the reader's comments shows that I value the advice other students give and reinforces the idea that students can provide helpful suggestions. And these practices don't take that much time to do. Preparation

Table 6.1. Prompt for Evaluating Reader's Interest

Paragraph	1	2	3	4	5	6	7	8	9
I can't wait to read more									
I'm very interested									
I'm still interested									
My mind's starting to wander									
I'm distracted									
I'm bored									

and thoughtfulness—and persistence—are keys to success with peer evaluative reading.

Applications

Strategy Practice: Fat Drafting

> *Declarative knowledge:* Revision is even more challenging when drafts don't have much substance to them. With more generous drafts, writers are often able to select what's important more effectively and then work with that for their revisions and rewriting.
>
> *Procedural knowledge:* Use at least one "fat draft" technique to bulk up a draft you have already written. Reconsider your paper and its purposes, and revise it using the ideas generated by the fat draft.
>
> *Conditional knowledge:* What aspects of the fat drafting did I use in my final paper? Why? What did fat drafting do for my thinking on the paper and during revision? When would it be a useful strategy in future writing? How will I know to apply it?

Wendy Bishop, a noted writer and teacher of writing, insists that, since "novice writers tend to write little" ("Revising" 17) and since "to have options in revising, you have to get text. An abundance of it" (16), students should first be given strategies that help them build up a text before they begin revising it, which she calls fat drafting. "Fat drafting encourages writers to add significant detail, to explicate ideas, and to explain what they thought might not be needed by a reader (but so often *is* needed)" (17). She provides forty-four strategies to help students develop fat drafts. Among them are the following:

- Mark the "center-of-gravity sentence" from each paragraph, the sentence that seems "core, crucial, provocative, evocative, and so on" (19). Somewhere else, list these sentences, and then use each one as a prompt, delving more deeply into those core ideas.

- Expand "mindfully" (20): Between each paragraph, write a new paragraph—or if the writing is only a paragraph long, add a sentence between each sentence. See what is buried in the draft.

- Put subtitles into your text, and then before and after each one, add interesting transitional sentences: summarize, forecast, expand, connect, contextualize. "Think of yourself talking to a friendly, interested listener" (20). Later, you can take out the subtitles if they are not needed.

- "Insert a list into your text and then explore the items in the list. Instead of using the list to compress an idea, use it to open up ideas" (21).

- Select two places in your draft where expansion seems to be invited. Write in those places, even if it seems off-topic, and see where the writing leads (21).

- Circle five important or thought-provoking words in your text. "Freewrite on each one. Do the same with five sentences" and then five quotations. See if any of what you wrote might be important to your paper (22).

- "Collect five media images—ads, family photos, sound bites, and so on—that illuminate your text in some way. Freewrite in response to each of these (and in relationship to your text). Insert written (perhaps even visual) material from this exercise into your text" (22).

- Revisit models of the genre during revision, and look at introductory strategies in four different ones: "Revise your opening paragraph to echo the four experts you've found. What does each new paragraph 'predict' you will need to change in your entire text? If some of these predicted changes offer you expansion ideas, incorporate them into your most recent draft" (23).

- Reconsider your draft as if it were a hypertext (24). With markers, indicate where you would create a link—and then write the text of those imagined links. Consider how you might insert this material into your text, maybe as sidebars or notes.

A strategy I use to help students expand text before revision is to list actions writers might take during drafting and ask students to choose one or more of them and apply them to their own draft:

- Explain a detail.
- Clarify a point.
- Generate an example.
- Extend an idea.
- Add a story or anecdote.
- Insert a contrary point—and argue with it.
- Change your voice.
- Find a new connection.
- Reorder parts.
- Condense ideas.

Although fat drafting is beneficial, especially for inexperienced writers, those writers sometimes resist what they see as *more* writing. But once they try it, they can usually see its benefits. Megan, who was already a good writer, wrote this in her reflection on a paper where I required students to practice fat-drafting options:

> The fat drafting was an interesting and beneficial experience as well. While I was doing the fat drafting exercises I was feeling a little annoyed because I thought my paper was already the way I wanted it, but when I read back through my rough draft I started to see all of the places some of my fat drafting ideas would fit really well. After doing the fat drafting, I felt like my rough draft was missing a lot of details, and I found those details in my fat drafting.

Strategy Practice: Questions

Declarative knowledge: Paragraphs are sentences that group themselves around a main idea.

Procedural knowledge: Read paragraphs to determine what the main idea is by pretending that the paragraph is the answer in a Jeopardy! square and that you have to give the question it answers.

Conditional knowledge: What does this questioning help me do as a writer? How can I use this strategy when I am drafting or revising my own writing?

My students often have trouble paragraphing, so I use this strategy to help them both during the reading of model texts and again during revision (as found in the lesson plan at the end of this chapter). For example, when students are reading models from *Jazz: My Music, My People* by Morgan Monceaux, I have them use the Questions strategy by putting sticky notes next to each paragraph and then writing the question that the paragraph answers on the note next to the paragraph.

For the paragraph that follows, Brady wrote this question: "How did she start into jazz?" By considering a single question for a paragraph, students see that one paragraph of their own papers can tell a story or provide background details.

> Like Billie Holiday, Ella Fitzgerald got her start at a young age. Orphaned at the age of fifteen, she was making the rounds of amateur talent contests in Harlem when she was discovered two years later. A saxophonist in Chick Webb's big band heard her and made her promise to audition with Webb. But Webb wasn't excited about having a singer in his band. When he heard Ella, though, he changed his mind. (Monceaux 39)

This strategy can help students generate ideas for writing (questions that could be answered) when used during inquiry or drafting. During revision, students write in the margin of the draft, beside each paragraph, what question is answered by the paragraph. If more than one question is being answered—or if the peer can't figure out a question—the writer may have a signal that revision for organization is needed.

Lesson Plan: Writing about a Person

Students are used to writing biographies. They write them from the time they are in elementary school—and they all sound alike. Just like encyclopedia entries. Boring. I was trying to teach my students that good writing holds some element of surprise for the reader and tried this short writing as a way to reinforce the concept.

In my planning, I consider what my students need to know or know how to do to be successful on this assignment. Some major things they need are these:

- An understanding of how the model differs from more traditional forms—and how it's similar
- Knowledge of the kinds of information they should look for during inquiry
- An ability to group ideas into effective paragraphs
- Ideas for how to incorporate quoted material in their writing

To help students be successful with this writing, I use the following strategies.

Teacher Plan for Inquiry Strategies

1. I start by discussing celebrities and the idea of celebrity. We talk about what makes a person famous and why we are interested in famous people's lives. We brainstorm some of the famous people most interesting to us right now and then students choose one to freewrite about: Who is it? Why are you interested? What do you know about the person? What questions do you have about the person?

2. I bring in models of traditional biographies. Before we look at them, I ask students what they expect. They accurately name characteristics: date and place of birth, parents' names, lists of events in that person's life. We look at the model and see how close they were and what they might have left out.

3. Next I have students read models of less traditional biographies. My favorites are from *Jazz: My Music, My People* by Morgan Monceaux. I have students practice the Questions strategy described earlier in this chapter in order to understand the ideas the models discuss.

4. After reading a few models (and these are short), students generate a list of ways these models are similar to traditional biographies and ways they are different. Students note the following different characteristics:

    a. Influences on the person's life and big changes

    b. How they became famous—made into a story

    c. Details of professional life, nothing personal unless it connects to the professional

    d. No dates—stories instead of lists of facts

    e. Comparisons and contrasts

    f. The introduction: a personal connection, why the writer is interested in this person

5. Next I give the assignment. I want students to know that the aspects of the nontraditional biographies we have listed will be the expectations for this writing. I add one aspect not in the models: incorporating a quote. Since much writing students do for school requires this, I want to teach it strategically. I agree with Tom Romano that

> quoting others gives writers the opportunity to include multiple voices in their writing and to build upon words of others to illustrate a concept, strengthen a point, introduce a counterclaim. A pertinent quotation can add variety and energy to the texture of writing. Sometimes the words of another cannot be improved upon. Admitting the voices of others into our writing doesn't have to steal our voices, silence us in deference to another, and make for a numbing kind of academic writing that no one I respect wants to read. (*Crafting* 93)

I want my students to practice this, so I include the requirement in this writing. Here is the assignment:

Writing about a Person

Biographers write about people who matter or who are interesting to others. (Some famous people even have *official* biographers!) We are going to practice strategies for writing about information, using a biography as our content. You can choose the person you want to

---

write about, with these restrictions: the person has to be real, although he or she may not be alive now; the person should be famous enough that you can find information on him or her; and you need to have some reason for being interested in this person.

Like the sample short biographies we read, you will not write a report on this person. Instead, this will be an interesting essay/biography that tells about the main achievement of your selected person and the influences that led toward that achievement. You will use many of the strategies you've noted from your group readings and in your notes: stories instead of a list of facts or dates, a focus on the person's professional life (personal details only when they relate to the professional), contrasts and comparisons, surprises that interest the reader. You will need to have one direct quote either from the person or about the person that matters to the story you are telling.

6. Students choose a person, usually from their freewriting, and conduct inquiry, practicing note-taking strategies as they do. I remind students to consider the kinds of information they will need for this writing so they don't go back to old practices and take notes on information that won't be useful here: Skip the common. Look for surprises.

Teacher Plan for Drafting Strategies

1. After inquiry and before drafting, I remind students of the Questions strategy. We go back to the models they have with sticky notes. They should consider the questions as possible ways to arrange and group their ideas for their own paragraphs.

2. In preparation for drafting, I also teach a minilesson on using quotations in text. I remind students to look for effective quotations during inquiry. I have examples of good quotes woven into text that we review and discuss. We talk about ways to make the quote part of our voice and not lose our voice to the quoted material. This isn't simple; it's subtle and challenging. If necessary, students may need to consider cutting the quote to the core of what makes it useful in the writing. They can sandwich the quote with their own words before and after. But they need to make sure that the words before and after are meaningful and not fluff—or they still lose their voice. Ashley tries these ideas in her paper about Amy Brown, an artist who paints fairies:

> When she was older, she worked as a custom picture framer at a local gallery. While she was working, her good friend and boss, Shawn, handed her a frame and said, "Here. Paint something to fit in this frame. . . . Maybe a little fairy or something." She was up all night.

Ashley's use of ellipsis cut her quote appropriately to what she needed to say and allowed her to emphasize the almost accidental way this artist got her start.

3. Because our models begin with a personal connection, a story that explains why the writer is interested in the subject of the paper, I encourage students to start their drafting there. We know the story has to be short, but it also needs to be specific, not "I liked listening to Billy Joel as a child" but a specific memory that connects: "When I was staying at my grandma's house one summer, she let me pick out any music I wanted. I liked her Elvis Presley music, even though I didn't know who he was. When she'd play it, she'd stop her work and we'd dance while it played. I've liked Elvis ever since." Tanner's paper (given at the end of this lesson plan) is a good example of this use of specific stories.

Teacher Plan for Product Strategies

1. After students have drafts, they meet in small groups and read their papers aloud to one another. The papers are short enough that this doesn't take long. The listeners keep track of questions that come to mind during the reading. These questions should not be about facts but about ideas the information raises. When the writer is finished reading, the listeners share the questions they still have so the writer can consider more inquiry to answer the questions or clarification if the answer was there but unclear.

2. In pairs, the students complete evaluative readings of each other's papers. These are the directions and prompts I give them:

Writing about a Person Evaluative Reading

Editor _____   Author _____

Editor: Read the whole paper through first. Then answer these questions and complete these tasks as you read it the second time.

    1. Do the Questions strategy: In the left margin beside each paragraph, write the main question this paragraph answers. If it answers more than one main question, write the other ques-

---

tions it answers so the writer can make decisions about paragraphing during revision.

2. What information surprises did you find? And don't make this up! Think of how a teacher might read it to find surprises. If you don't find any, say that, but read carefully for interesting information surprises and list the ideas briefly here:

3. What information in the paper looks as though it came from inquiry and what seems as though most people would know it? Put an I above information that seems beyond common knowledge and a C above information that is probably common knowledge. (Writer: Remember that this writing should have information surprises that reflect research! Too many C's and not enough I's are a clue for you to do what?)

4. What questions do you still have about the person? List them here. (Writer: Consider answering these!)

5. What could the writer do to make the introduction more interesting? the conclusion?

6. Did the writer use a vocabulary word? If yes, is it effective? If no, put a * where he or she could use one.

Writer: What three revisions to ideas or organization will you make as a result of these comments?

1.

2.

3.

3. After the students have revised their drafts, they work on local-level revision strategies. I make sure to have a minilesson on punctuating direct quotes so that students will be able to punctuate their papers correctly. We graph sentence lengths to help students create a lively tone through sentence length variety. I also use reading aloud as a strategy to find sentence boundaries.

4. When students turn in their papers, they complete reflection questions: What strategies did you use on this writing assignment that you found helpful?

- Strategies for process
- Strategies for product

Why were they helpful to you? In what future situations might you use those same strategies again?

Here is the paper Tanner wrote in response to this assignment. Despite the requirement that the person had to be real, Tanner insisted on writing about Mickey Mouse. I okayed his topic, partly because I really wanted him to write (and he was actually interested in writing about Mickey Mouse) and partly because I thought he could complete the rest of the assignment with that topic, given the information available. And he could. Although he didn't incorporate a quote, Tanner effectively used several of the other strategies he had garnered from his reading of models.

> My family was constantly on the move in the early 1990s due to the fact that my father was a doctor in the US Air Force. It was a special occasion whenever we got to go out of the house. Yet I didn't consider it a very special occasion when we got to go to Disneyland in California and I was confronted by a five-foot giant mouse who tried to touch me with his big white gloves. Not even my two-year-old thumb-sucking powers would protect me from the mouse.
>
> Mickey was first known as Oswald, the Lucky Rabbit, a creation of Mr. Walt Disney. But Oswald the Lucky Rabbit didn't turn out to be too auspicious; he crashed Walt Disney's dreams. Then on the way to a business meeting, Walt Disney sketched a few quick circles and created a new character. He called him "Mickey Mouse." Over the years the mouse's body design was changed. His eyes have been altered, his tail length, his ear size, his smile, his shirtless body. But the Mickey we know today highly resembles the original Mickey.
>
> His first appearance was in a black and white, short film called "Steamboat Willie." Critics were unsure what to think about a whistling, dancing mouse. Then in his second appearance ("The Opry House") Mickey showed off his stylish white gloves, amazing voice talent, and soon-to-be co-character Minnie Mouse.
>
> Maybe I'll never get to meet that same mouse I came across 16 years ago. But if I ever do I'd ask him why he only wears pants and nothing else. Then I'd congratulate him on getting so far in the career of a cartoon star. After all, Mickey Mouse is the only cartoon character with a star on the Hollywood Walk of Fame.

———

10/26: Several students came without drafts today. They were mostly the ones I couldn't get going in class last week, even though they promised me they would have drafts today, would write them at home. I get discouraged sometimes because I think I've given them time and strategies to accomplish what should be done, but they still don't always do it. The ones who were ready went into their evaluative reading groups very well. I was pleased with the way they worked and how they helped each other. They *are* getting better at it; today I wasn't able to help them or prompt them at all. I had the ones without drafts on the other side of the room, writing. I was reminding them of the strategies for drafting that they could use to get going. Sometimes I wonder if they forget the strategies when they go home, but they seemed to remember them as soon as I'd bring them up. So, if they don't forget them, what is the problem? I guess I need to remember how hard writing is, especially for some of these students. They've had years of failure. Their reading scores are below the basic level, so I don't think they spend that much time with written text. In that way, I guess I should be excited that they get as much done as they do, that they risk what they do when they write in this class. Still, revision strategies for writing aren't useful without writing to begin with. Maybe I need to consider revision strategies for my teaching. What should I, could I, do differently that would help these students move forward in their writing? Revision. It's a wonderful concept, and not just for writing.

Additional Resources

Bishop, Wendy, ed. *Acts of Revision: A Guide for Writers.* Portsmouth, NH: Boynton/Cook, 2004.

Ehrenworth, Mary, and Vicki Vinton. *The Power of Grammar: Unconventional Approaches to the Conventions of Language.* Portsmouth, NH: Heinemann, 2005.

Heard, Georgia. *The Revision Toolbox: Teaching Techniques That Work.* Portsmouth, NH: Heinemann, 2002.

Lane, Barry. *After the End: Teaching and Learning Creative Revision.* Portsmouth, NH: Heinemann, 1993.

Murray, Donald M. *The Craft of Revision.* 3rd ed. Fort Worth, TX: Harcourt Brace, 1998.

Romano, Tom. *Crafting Authentic Voice.* Portsmouth, NH: Heinemann, 2004.

Schuster, Edgar H. *Breaking the Rules: Liberating Writers through Innovative Grammar Instruction.* Portsmouth, NH: Heinemann, 2003.

Appendix: Student Papers

The following student papers are available for teachers to use as models with their students when they teach some of the strategies explained in this book. As student papers, they are not perfect, but they still serve as good models for many of the features and strategy practices mentioned.

Says-Does: Hilary

My Name

I am sandwiched by sisters named for extraordinary people. My older sister bears the name of one of the most angelic characters in all of literature. My parents, hoping that she would intrinsically inherit those same qualities, even jazzed up the spelling as well. Melynie. Unique to be sure. My younger sister was named for the faithful wife of Father Abraham; Sarah—the mother of nations. After writing what seemed an average of one paper per year on my name with no special background, my mother tried to console me by telling how she'd always loved the meaning of my name—"cheerful one." It was little consolation to my 15-year-old ego that my name was found in the boys' section of our 1970s copy of *Name Your Baby*.

Hilary.

A difficult sound at times for a young shy girl with allergies. It never rolled off my tongue smoothly, and when I spoke, everyone always thought I said Lori. "What? Lori?" they'd ask. Painfully, I'd shake my head no and repeat it. On about the fourth time, they'd get it.

As I've gotten older, my name has become more beautiful to me. It is somewhat unique and seems to have taken on a solid, more meaningful tone. More like the wind singing gently around the tops of Mt. Everest and then suddenly whipping over the ragged clefts and barreling down a narrow canyon. Sir Edmund Hilary was the first man (yes, man) to conquer the giant. After I learned that, it gave me some delightful images. When I hear my name, it seems to flow with a gentle motion with a strong foundation. Just as I, Hilary, although quieter than I'd like to be, have the strength to climb my own Everests.

I-Search a Word: Emily

Picture a funeral. Now, picture your family's Thanksgiving dinner. Which picture is solemn? I found out that they *both* are, depending on which century you live in! I couldn't believe that the original Latin word *sollemnis* actually meant customary, festive. After seeing that, I had to find out how it had come to having its current meaning: religious, serious.

My quest for this treasure of trivia had several stages, much like the mythical hero's journey. Only, I am not very heroic and the horrible dragon happened to have a big square head, many cord-like tails and a crazy little mouse that followed him everywhere. My only weapon was a handy assignment sheet with helpful instructions about how the dragon could be tickled into producing the needed information. Still, the task was not simple and I had several fights with Dell the Dragon's sidekick, Printerthanus. Luckily, the gods stepped in and gave me further assistance—probably because I was about to go crazy in public—in the form of my trusty helper, Andy. He taught me Dragon Smooth-Talk, a narrowly known sub-dialect, which when used properly, will tame any dragon out there. Perhaps this whole ordeal wouldn't have been so hard had I not forgotten the book of magic spells (the readings packet) that contained even more detailed information about my quest. Anyway, dragon beaten, I obtained the ultimate prize: an encounter with hidden knowledge.

This path to knowledge had many tributarial trails. The first of these that I followed led to the Oxford English Dictionary. It gave several definitions of solemn as an adjective. It means "having religious character," "of days or seasons," "performed with formality," "uniform," "customary" and the list goes on. These seem unusually dark and dreary as do some of solemn's synonyms: serious, grim and somber. As I mentioned earlier, these denotative and connotative meanings haven't always been prevalent.

The lineage of solemn traces itself through current English, to Middle English, to Old French and all the way back to Latin, where *sollemnis* meant merely customary, established and festive. Surprisingly, the jump from celebratory to sacred and religious isn't as far-fetched as it seems. As the Western world was Christianized, all the heathen feasts were made into Christian holy days (holidays). Thus, the word unnecessarily but understandably took on the personality of the Christian religion. By the time the word actually reached English in the 14th Century, it already carried with it a log of today's sentiment.

I found it interesting, however, that even when the King James Version of the Holy Bible was published in 1611, an element of the Latin meaning was still present. For example, in Psalms 92, the Psalmist is singing because the "Lord hast made [him] glad through they [the Lord's] work . . ." The Psalmist is obviously joyful and describes playing the harp "with a solemn sound" for the occasion. So, even as late as 1611, the translators still recognized the first meaning of the word.

A more modern interpretation of solemn seems to have carried the religious significance one step further. In his article "Biff! Bam! Boom!" R. Z. Sheppard delineates solemn as perhaps over-serious or too religious. While describing Michael Chabon's *The Amazing Adventures of Kavalier Dr. Clay*, he makes sure we know it's "serious but never solemn." In other words, "don't worry, it won't bore you to death." It is apparent, then, that solemn is diverging from its synonym, or at least becoming the superlative form of it. It is almost as though, subconsciously, modern authors are rebelling against having one segment of the society—religious in this case—have such an impact on the language.

Solemn takes another such punch in Robert Frost's poem "Blueberries." In this work, solemn becomes a byword. Frost couples solemn with an antonym that sharply undercuts its meaning: "And the air of the youngsters! Not one of them turned, And they looked so solemn—absurdly concerned." Pairing these two words takes the idea of being solemn and satirizes it. To be solemn (religious, ceremonious, somber) is absurd. This seems in line with the general social attitude toward religion. Words that are merely *associated* with religious worship are mocked as well as the act itself. I find it sad that to be serious and righteous and uniform in character—solemn—must equal being boring, pompous and restrictive, as well.

Despite my third-year-English-major status, I was still surprised at the metamorphosis of solemn. What impacted me the most as I thought about the implication of a changing language, was the idea that language is truly a product of the society that uses it. It is like a baby being raised by millions of different parents. This search forced me to see language as a living organism and to therefore approach writing as a changing art form, working with a dynamic medium.

Secret Knowledge: Katie

Location: Parent's Room
Date and Time: October 10, 8:47 p.m.
Log: Snuck into parent's room and hid in the chest drawer disguised as a pencil. Later, got out safe and sound.
Grown-up rule #372: Do homework before you go to bed.
Official Reason: Don't stay up all night doing your homework, you'll lose sleep.
The Truth: Homework gets tired after around nine p.m. and then it won't let you write anymore research on the paper.

What do you usually think when your parents tell you to do your homework before bedtime? Well, our parents say they don't want us to stay up all night doing it. They want us to get our sleep. The real reason is that homework gets very tired at night. Probably at about nine o'clock p.m. You're writing an important answer, and then at nine, the pencil won't write anymore. You keep writing, but the paper has given up for the night.

One day, I was disguised as a pencil and got into my parent's room. I found this piece of paper and it told me its life story. He hated how people would just write on him all night. It just drove him crazy. He said that some of his friends were thrown away because of the damage that was done.

Story from the Past
Back in the late 1700s, Thomas Edison and others would stay up late and finish their research. Edison found that after nine the paper and pencil would just die because they were tired. So Edison figured to do his work before nine to get all his research and also get a good night's sleep.

HGTV! Homework guides throw vengeance!
Many kids have stayed up all night doing research and doing their homework. Procrastinating isn't the way to go. A group of high school students got together to finish their study guides for their science class. It got really late, and the study guides were so tired that they ripped themselves up and threw themselves away!

I was up late last night finishing my English paper. Something came to me that I should have done it earlier. Oh well, it's too late now. The time passes by and I'm coming to the climax of my story and my pencil breaks. *Maybe I should go get another one,* I thought. So I did, and started to write again, but the pencil broke again. Grabbing a pen this time, I wrote down what I was going to write, but there was a big ink stain on my paper. The homework just smeared ink all over itself. I'm thinking that I should've done my work earlier.

Ten people in Provo High School were interviewed on if they are able to finish their homework late at night. Eight of them said they have had a hard time finishing it all up. The other two said they've been having no problems. When Bill Johnson was asked how he felt when his homework wouldn't let him finish writing the end of his report, he said this, "Man! I had put so much thought into my report. I worked like a total maniac doing it and was so sure I could get an 'A' on my assignment."

So as it has been said, homework has feelings too.

My House Has Stars: Kelley

My house is nestled among rolling grasslands. My house is small and warm. In the nearby village, men work all day long fishing for our meals. My house is distant from icy fjords that threaten to melt during the long summer days. The sun rarely sets on my house during the summer. Endless days. The day blazes on through the night like a too-bright nightlight that keeps me away even when I'm ready for sleep.

In the winter, we feast on fishy laks, reker, and torsk, all preserved from the summer fishing harvest. My brothers and sisters and I gather around Mother and Father for music and storytelling. Father tells us scary stories of trolls and mystical stories of Vikings and their ships. I gaze out the window at the still, crystal night. I imagine the Vikings on their long wooden ships. I wonder if at night they had calm times like the ones I have with my family. I see thousands of twinkling lights that seem to stop time. I wonder if these are the same stars that the Vikings looked on, long, long ago.

My house has stars.

Reversal: Saramarie

Not the Brightest: Jumping from Moving Trains

Tuck and Roll. That's what everyone says you should do if you happen to be on a moving train and need to get off. At least that's what Hollywood tells us. Images come to mind of adventurous heroes and heroines jumping from trains, escaping from the bad guys. Western and adventure movies employ the tuck and roll maneuver—the cowboy or renegade tumbles down a sagebrush-covered hill after a calculated jump from the train. He stands up, brushes himself off, apparently unhurt. From *The Great Train Robbery* made in 1903 to *Hidalgo* released last year, movies employ the spectacle of death-defying leaps from trains. Even Indiana Jones jumps from train to train without problem. More spectacular, Hidalgo jumps from a moving train while riding a horse. These action figures make it look so easy—no one is ever harmed and the velocity of the fast moving train merely provides the jumper with the needed momentum.

However, appearances can be incredibly deceiving; jumping from trains is scary, dangerous, difficult, and even deadly. I know this because I have jumped from a moving train in the middle of the English countryside. My friend Lindsey and I were traveling to a small town in Surrey, England to live with an English family for five days as part of our study abroad experience. It was an hour journey from London on a rickety old train. We arrived at our stop in Milford, England, but no matter how hard we tried, we could not get the small doors open. Lindsey and I felt like dumb American girls. By the time we got the door open, the train had started moving. It was almost past the platform, and we were stuck on the train. Lindsey, thinking she could just step out of the train, jumped off. I watched as she flew through the air, skidded on the ground, and came to a halt. Apparently the train was moving faster than she thought.

My mind raced with question after question: Is Lindsey hurt, do I have any contact information for our family, when would another train be headed back, what if I was not able to make connections, could I really jump, would I get hurt or break something, would my jeans rip? I decided in that instant that I would have to jump. So, wearing my backpack, dragging my duffle bag behind me, I jumped. Instead of doing the standard tuck and roll, I supermanned it, flying through the air, smacking down on hard ground. My body pumped with adrenaline, my palms bloodied, my knees skinned, but I had made it. My jeans even survived without a single rip—this was a good thing because I had only brought one other pair of pants for the five days. Lindsey and I grabbed each other, happy to be alive, but also realizing our stupidity.

Jumping from a moving train was not as heroic as it is portrayed in the movies, at least not for me. I really could have gotten hurt. If I would have attempted the tuck and roll maneuver, I likely would have broken something, maybe even my neck. People die or get seriously injured by jumping from moving trains. For example, it was reported that an Australian woman, Candice Maree Webb, died from injuries sustained by jumping from a moving train. Webb "forced open a carriage door of a Pakenham-bound train as it left Dandenong railway station. She fell and hit the ballast next to the tracks more than two metres below and suffered extensive head injuries" (Heasley). The train had just started moving in the accident that killed Candice, just like when I jumped from the train in England. Loyola University summer safety guidelines state, "Never 'hopoff' a train while it is moving. Trains move about 75 mph. Jumping from a moving train will result in death or serious injury" (O'Day). I would advise against the tuck and roll method, because in real life, it could be quite harmful. I would actually advise against jumping off moving trains, in any case.

In addition, most of the movie scenes of train jumpers are performed using camera tricks or stunt doubles. In *The Great Train Robbery*, it is actually a dummy that is thrown from the train (Mitchell). Additionally, in *Hidalgo,* "A slow moving truck towed the train car at approximately two miles per hour, and a stunt rider actually rode the horse off the train. The camera angle made the jump look higher than it really was, and pick up riders as well as trainers on foot surrounded the train car" (American Humane Society). The stunt doubles are professionals, often filming the scene many times in order to get the jumping from moving train scenes just right. Further, I did not have time to think out and carefully execute or choreograph my jump like they do in the movies. I could not reshoot it, nor would I have the desire to pull a stunt like that again.

Like most things in the movies, jumping off trains is mostly effect and little reality. Jumping off trains is dangerous; your favorite movie star likely does not do it him or herself. Don't be a dummy like the ones used in movies, or dumb like me or Candice Webb. Even if you are strongly tempted, don't jump from moving trains. Your life may be in danger.

American Humane Society. 8 Nov 2004 http://www.ahahilm.info/movies/moviereviews.phtml?fid=7563.

Heasley, Andrew and Andrea Petrie. "Woman Dies After Jumping Off Train," *The Age*. 12 Feb 2004. 8 Nov 2004 http://www.theage.com.au/articles/2004/02/11/1076388442030.html?from=storyrhs&oneclick=true>.

Mitchell, Rick. "First Cut: The Great Train Robbery," *The Editors Guild Magazine* Vol 24 Sept/Oct 2003. 8 Nov 2004 http://www.editorsguild.com/newsletter/SepOct03/sepoct03first_cut.html

O'Day, Kathy. *BreakPoint!* Vol 3, June 2000. 9 Nov 2004 http://www.luhs.org/depts/injprev/Breakpnt/bp-v3-6.htm

Reversal: Hilary

Of Mice and Molds

It's really not as bad as you think. At least that is the reason I gave my mom in easing the shock of my new job. "Oh honey," she said, and then I heard the word that would become standard in many similar conversations to come, "really?" The word was uttered with a mixture of surprise, admiration and mild disgust. Future conversations would typically emphasize one of the three emotions. I grinned to myself. "Are you sure that there isn't something else you can do, or do you not mind?" Her plea was actually more of a formality denoting a mother's concern for my happiness than an urge to change my mind. But in reality, I had relatively little choice.

Here I was, newly back from a two-year sabbatical to Hong Kong arriving in the States just twelve days before school. Most campus jobs had been secured months before and it had only taken a few hours into the job hunt to recognize the fact. On a desperate whim, I filled out an application for hostess at the life science museum, which I'd stepped foot in only once before. The disappointment must have shown when it became clear that my schedule wouldn't fit, because the secretary looked carefully at my face, paused a moment, and then almost apologetically suggested, "They might be hiring in the taxidermy department. I don't think they have any girls, but if you don't mind blood and guts . . ." In an instant I had assured her that both were like second nature to me and that I'd always wanted to work with . . . dead animals. Before I knew it, I was in the office of Skip the taxidermist, surrounded by heads of all sizes with glassy eyes while he chatted about the panda bear project he was hoping to head up in a year or so. A few birds lay on the table next to the small white freezer. I wondered briefly what was in the freezer. Muddled piles of fur expending an odd smell sat in the sink. Was I going to be the one working with those furs? What exactly did my job entail? Would I regret this? It wasn't until the next day that it hit me; I was apprentice to a taxidermist.

The only previous exposure I had had to taxidermy was a short story in my seventh grade English class featuring the owner of a bed and breakfast who liked to stuff her pets after they were old, including her guests. Hollywood and literature has done much to create a warped image involving mad scientists who experiment on poor helpless animals. But as a whole, taxidermy is not quite so drastic; it is an art.

Taxidermy comes from the Greek words, *taxis* (movement), and *derma* (skin) (http://www.taxidermy.net/information/history1.html). At its simplest, the art involves mounting animal skins for permanent display as realistically as possible. Sometimes it is the entire animal preserved, but often only the skin stretched over man made molds and sometimes there is nothing at all natural about the mount as is the case with fish. Any life science museum visitor has seen hundreds of mounts in their visits, however brief they may be. From birds to elephants, each specimen has had to be prepared individually.

Skip started us off easy. My first assignment was to prepare the birds for display. Because I was the only girl, I was given the hummingbirds, the smallest ones. Wires for their legs were so slender and fine that getting them in the legs was worse than any needle I'd ever threaded. Admiration for the delicate beauty of the birds turned to loathing for their smallness. Sliding the wire down the leg, through the fat (an extremely relative term) part of the foot and then wrapping the wire around a branch took 10 minutes a foot. Extraordinary care to not break any of the small bones or destroy any brittle tissue took patience and control. When the birds were groomed to perfection and mounted properly, we took them to the dry freezer for their final mold. It was then that appreciation for nature's beauty returned as I placed each lifelike mount on the freezer shelf. They lay in an array of splendid colors as if they'd chosen to pose in harmony with the universe and at any moment might flutter away, each one an individual.

Very few of the animals we worked with were hunted. As we worked, Skip told us the story of each bird. My hummingbirds had been found dead under a tree after a thunderstorm. Romar's falcon had been found at the side of the road and died a few hours later. Mark's lark had flown into a window in Terry's (the secretary) neighborhood. The deer in the freezer (I was right about the deep freeze) had been road kill and the black bear had died at the zoo. Part of me was relieved that these animals had not only died of "natural causes," but were being preserved for the education, betterment and awareness of the public.

The exception was the mice. Every Wednesday we worked with Dr. Duke Rogers. He would go down to South America twice a year and trap mice for his DNA research. When we arrived at work, we would go to the freezer, pull out a few sandwich bags of the frozen little carcasses, and let them thaw in our pockets while we prepared the rest of our equipment: scissors, twee-zers, needles and thread, tags and string, wires and cotton. Duke could com-pletely skin, tag, and mount a mouse in twenty minutes. He'd been doing it for years. I had worked my way down to forty minutes and once even only thirty. That was only when conditions were perfect. If the mouse had been in the freezer for too long, he was drier and more difficult to skin. Sometimes, because they were dry, they would lose an appendage (or two or three). Once I had a mouse lose all four legs and his tail before I was through. I'd sheep-ishly sewn them back on before mounting them with cotton. Of course it was always at that moment that Duke would come to check on us. He'd solemnly look over my lumpy mouse, and after pointing out a few of the bazillion things that could be improved upon, declared me improving.

I'd always wanted to be a nurse, so blood and guts really didn't bother me; it was like undressing the mice out of their little coats. But often it tugged at my heart strings to see the darling mice frozen in a huddled clump. One that had the cutest little nose and pretty ears had been frozen in a praying position. It seemed like he could be alive, just curled and sleeping in my hand and might at any minute start moving. I would try to do my work quickly so that he could look like that again as soon as possible.

After a little while the work became mindless and the lab seemed cozy. Happily snipping away to the soft radio music, we'd chat about school, foot-ball and our dates while the first winter flurries danced outside the narrow window. It became satisfying to see the row of sleek mounted mice boasting our initials on their tags, each one nicer and more properly mounted than the last. We started having races to see who could do the fastest work the best. Gradually we did improve, but our ignorance still flaunted itself more than we'd have liked.

Once towards the beginning of my time there, we were setting up a display of ducks. Some of the tail feathers on the mallards were curling up. I semi-scornfully wondered how old these mounts were, and asked Skip if we had any glue to stick them down. Shockingly, his response was laughter, and he promptly shared the joke with another professor. I now will know forever that mallard tails curl naturally.

Under Skip's tutelage our eyes slowly started to sharpen to the details of mounts. We took pride not only in our own work, but in distinguishing the better mounts of the museum. To those who saw only a deer head on the wall, we saw a deer whose nose was not quite shaped correctly or whose eyes were too small so the eyelids had been oversized to compensate. Skip was even better. He could tell if a bobcat had been mounted using a lion's mold or if the torso was far too long. He knew exactly what materials the taxidermist had misused and could repeat almost step by step what he had done wrong. Pres-ervation, I learned, is not enough. Preservation in excellence, beauty and care will suffice.

The wealth of skill in a taxidermist is incredible not only for their ani-mal knowledge, but their keen eye of beauty, symmetry and detail. Because it is an unusual job, most people ask what it entails, and afterwards, what I like about it. After countless reflections on the many questions, I think I have an answer. The creation of beauty is one of the most satisfying things one can do.

It may not be the traditional beauty that one thinks of in landscape paintings, but a part of nature that all can enjoy as well. Taxidermy is not only a skill, but an art.

Works Cited

http://www.taxidermy.net/information/history1.html

Reversal: Amanda

A young woman belts out a hair-raising scream as an oversized gorilla with a fetish for blonde women stomps down the street. The woman gracefully places the back of her hand on her forehead, gently closes her eyelids and sighs as she faints into the arms of the best looking guy in the entire city. The muscle-bulging hunk lightly taps her cheek while whispering her name in her ear. Her eyes flutter open and she gazes into the face of her hero.

My experience was not quite so romantic. Sitting next to my date in the cushioned velvet red seats at the theater, I struggle to watch the action scenes unfolding on the big screen. No. King Kong does not storm down the street of Manhattan. Instead, a man fighting to save his friend while hiking Mount Everest stabs a needle filled with a life-saving liquid into the friend's chest. By this time I have seen all I can bear. I cross and uncross my legs, repeatedly tuck my hair behind my ears, wipe my hands on my pant legs—all in an effort to take my mind away from the gruesome image. I place my head on my date's shoulder hoping his cologne will distract me from performing the inevitable and that which I fear most. My stomach turns in pain, the actor's voices echo inside my head; the lights begin to spin . . .

I open my eyes to the white mountains on the movie screen blocked by the silhouette of my date's head. Dozens of concerned faces stare at mine. My date is still fearfully shaking my shoulders and shouting my name. I gaze into his eyes, trying to remember who he is. When I finally realize what has happened, I hang my head in shame. I have done it again. Tears roll down my cheek. My body shakes, but not as much as my date's, who has most likely decided that he cannot handle a girl cursed with asthenophobia—fear of fainting.

Many have never passed out before or even seen it actually happen for that matter. In this case, they rely on stories from friends or Hollywood representations to better understand how or what happens when somebody faints. From swooning into another's arms to slamming face-first into the pavement, fainting is often portrayed as endearing or humorous.

Kids find it entertaining. Through the grapevine they learn the procedure for making themselves pass out. Breathe in. Wrap your fingers around your neck. Squeeze. Tilt your head upside down. Touch your toes. Do the hokey-pokey. Apparently it works (except for the hokey-pokey part). One of my sixth grade classmates decided to give it a try while standing on the sidewalk during recess. He showed up in class 20 minutes after the bell had rung with a bandage covering the two-inch gash on his forehead. We thought it was great. Mrs. Peters didn't.

My classmate was lucky he only received a minor cut. Some can recall the horrifying details of their unconscious state. One boy recalls the time his friend made himself pass out. Upon losing consciousness, the friend pounded on the floor and then charged toward the other boy. In an effort to wake him, the boy punched his friend. The friend awoke in fear and claimed that while in faint, he saw a young girl asking for help. He never tried to pass out again (Archive X).

I, too, can recall the feeling of sheer horror while in an unconscious state. Images spin around in my mind. It seems as though I am drowning in darkness. Invisible arms and hands pull me in every direction, and I unsuccessfully fight to free myself from their grip. I scream, I sweat, I try to call for help. When finally regaining consciousness, I cry—not only from embarrassment, but from the shock of what my mind has just endured. I become angered that I, a 20-year old independent college student, cannot control my own consciousness.

To many college students, passing out is simply the stage between partying and awaking the next morning to a hangover. Losing consciousness is all part of the weekend ritual. Party, drink, puke, pass out, repeat next weekend. The passing-out part is just one aspect that is easily ignored and quickly forgotten by both drinker and onlooker.

Passing out after drinking, however, could indicate danger. A fellow drinker may find a friend unconscious, thinking he/she has passed out. In actuality, the friend is dying from alcohol poisoning. The National Institute of Alcohol Abuse and Alcoholism found that averages of 1,393 deaths per year are a result of alcohol poisoning. Drinkers force so much alcohol into their bodies that they pass out . . . and never wake up.

Yet many find passing out comical and even useful. For example, Tennessee goats (also known as scare or nervous goats) faint dead away when startled. In the past, shepherds have used them to protect their sheep. By putting a scare goat outside the sheep herd, a wolf will focus on the unconscious goat, giving the sheep time to flee. The CNBC newscast in Boston filmed a short clip of a farmer chasing his goats until they fall on their backs and stick their feet in the air like dead bugs. It is funny and even newsworthy. The farmers claim that it is not harmful to the goats.

Yet medical research has found that excessive fainting leads to a higher risk of death. Of the 987 human patients studied at the Mayo Clinic, 18.4 percent were found to have several potential causes of fainting. On average, these patients died earlier than those with a single potential cause of fainting. The tests, however, were conducted based on fainting related to medical conditions instead of fear.

This research and the fainting horror stories are often overlooked or never mentioned. Fainting produces laughs and a good story, or it is portrayed as romantic and endearing. Women dream of the day when they will gracefully swoon into the arms of a Brad Pitt look-alike. I, on the other hand, have passed out 15 times since I was ten years old. I have "swooned" enough to know that fainting is not as romantic, fun or comical as many think. Fainting is a horrifying experience that I cannot control and that causes me and other asthenophobics to avoid any situation that may invoke another frightening, life-threatening and embarrassing faint. When King Kong comes storming down the street, I will be the woman fainting—not into the arms of a hunk, but into the grip of an experience I fear above anything else.

Archive X. "Fainting Friend" http://www.wirenot.net/X/Stories/obe/ OBE%2000-F/faintingfriend.shtml 28 Oct 2004.

Mayo Clinic. "Patients Who Have Multiple Potential Causes For Fainting Have a Higher Risk of Death" 28 Apr 2003 <http:// www.sciencedaily.com/releases/2003/04/030428082341.htm>

Works Cited

Allen, Camille A. *The Multigenre Research Paper: Voice, Passion, and Discovery in Grades 4–6.* Portsmouth, NH: Heinemann, 2001.

Anderson, Gaylyn Karle. "'I-Search a Word': Reclaiming the Library's Reference Section." *English Journal* 79.1 (1990): 53–57.

Antinarella, Joe, and Ken Salbu. *Tried and True: Lessons, Strategies, and Activities for Teaching Secondary English.* Portsmouth, NH: Heinemann, 2003.

Apol, Laura, and Jodi Harris. "Joyful Noises: Creating Poems for Voices and Ears." *Language Arts* 76 (1999): 314–22.

Ayers, Donald M. *English Words from Latin and Greek Elements.* 2nd ed. Tucson: U of Arizona P, 1986.

Bain, Alexander. *English Composition and Rhetoric: A Manual.* New York: D. Appleton, 1866.

Baines, Lawrence, Colleen Baines, Gregory Kent Stanley, and Anthony Kunkel. "Losing the Product in the Process." *English Journal* 88.5 (1999): 67–72.

Baker, Russell. "Slice of Life." *English: Orange Level.* Evanston, IL: McDougal, Littell, 1989. 218–20.

Bawarshi, Anis. *Genre and the Invention of the Writer.* Logan: Utah State UP, 2003.

Beach, Richard. "Showing Students How to Assess: Demonstrating Techniques for Response in the Writing Conference." *Writing and Response: Theory, Practice and Research.* Ed. Chris Anson. Urbana, IL: NCTE, 1989. 127–48.

Bean, John C., Virginia A. Chappell, and Alice M. Gillam. *Reading Rhetorically: A Reader for Writers.* 2nd ed. New York: Pearson/Longman, 2005.

Belanoff, Pat. "What Is a Grade?" *The Subject Is Writing.* 2nd ed. Ed. Wendy Bishop. Portsmouth, NH: Boynton/Cook, 1999. 147–55.

Berlin, James. "Rhetoric and Ideology in the Writing Class." *The Writing Teacher's Sourcebook.* 4th ed. Ed. Edward P. J. Corbett, Nancy Myers, and Gary Tate. New York: Oxford UP, 2000. 9–25.

Bishop, Wendy, ed. Introduction. *Acts of Revision: A Guide for Writers.* Portsmouth, NH: Boynton/Cook, 2004. v–x.

———. "Revising Out and Revising In." *Acts of Revision: A Guide for Writers.* Portsmouth, NH: Boynton/Cook, 2004. 13–27.

Burke, Jim. *Writing Reminders: Tools, Tips, and Techniques.* Portsmouth, NH: Heinemann, 2003.

Carlson, Nancy. *How to Lose All Your Friends.* New York: Puffin, 1994.

Carnicelli, Thomas. *Words Work: Activities for Developing Vocabulary, Style, and Critical Thinking.* Portsmouth, NH: Boynton/Cook, 2001.

Charney, Davida H., and Richard A. Carlson. "Learning to Write in a Genre: What Student Writers Take from Model Texts." *Research in the Teaching of English* 29 (1995): 88–125.

Cisneros, Sandra. *The House on Mango Street.* New York: Vintage, 1984.

Clark, Irene L. *Concepts in Composition: Theory and Practice in the Teaching of Writing.* Mahwah, NJ: Lawrence Erlbaum, 2003.

Collins, James. L. *Strategies for Struggling Writers.* New York: Guilford, 1998.

Cope, Bill, and Mary Kalantzis, eds. *The Powers of Literacy: A Genre Approach to Teaching Writing.* Pittsburgh: U of Pittsburgh P, 1993.

Corbett, Edward P. J., and Robert J. Connors. *Classical Rhetoric for the Modern Student.* 4th ed. New York: Oxford UP, 1999.

Darrow, Clarence. "Why I Am an Agnostic." *Of Bunsen Burners, Bones, and Belles Lettres: Classic Essays across the Curriculum.* Ed. James D. Lester. Lincolnwood, IL: NTC, 1996. 3–10.

Dean, Deborah. *Current-Traditional Rhetoric: Its Past and What Content Analysis of Texts and Tests Shows About Its Present.* Diss. Seattle Pacific University, 1999. Ann Arbor: UMI, 1999. 9951865.

———. "Framing Texts: New Strategies for Student Writers." *Voices from the Middle* 11.2 (2003): 32–35.

———. "Going Public: Letters to the World." *Voices from the Middle* 8.1 (2000): 42–47.

———. "Grammar without Grammar: Just Playing Around, Writing." *English Journal* 91.2 (2001): 86–89.

———. "Learning Vocabulary, Accessing the World." *Ohio Journal of English Language Arts* 45.1 (2005): 16–20.

———. "Muddying Boundaries: Mixing Genres with Five Paragraphs." *English Journal* 90.1 (2000): 53–56.

———. "Partnering Reading and Writing: Connecting with Models." *Kentucky English Bulletin* 53.2/3 (2004): 5–10. *Classroom Notes Plus.* Urbana, IL: NCTE 22.3 (2005): 7–10.

———. "Visual Essays." *IDEAS Plus: A Collection of Practical Teaching Ideas,* Book 16. Urbana, IL: NCTE, 1998.

Dean, Deborah, and Sirpa Grierson. "Re-envisioning Reading and Writing through Combined-Text Picture Books." *Journal of Adolescent and Adult Literacy* 48 (2005): 456–68.

DeJoy, Nancy C. "I Was a Process-Model Baby." *Post-Process Theory: Beyond the Writing-Process Paradigm.* Ed. Thomas Kent. Carbondale: Southern Illinois UP, 1999. 163–78.

Dethier, Brock. "Revising Attitudes." *Acts of Revision: A Guide for Writers.* Ed. Wendy Bishop. Portsmouth, NH: Boynton/Cook, 2004. 1–12.

Devitt, Amy. *Writing Genres.* Carbondale: Southern Illinois UP, 2004.

Dewey, John. *How We Think.* 2nd ed. Boston: D. C. Heath, 1993.

Dillard, Annie. *An American Childhood.* New York: Harper & Row, 1987.

Dobrin, Sidney I. "Paralogic Hermeneutic Theories, Power, and the Possibility for Liberating Pedagogies." *Post-Process Theory: Beyond the Writing-Process Paradigm.* Ed. Thomas Kent. Carbondale: Southern Illinois UP, 1999. 132–48.

Drake, Ernest, and Dugald A. Steer. *Dragonology: The Complete Book of Dragons.* Cambridge, MA: Candlewick, 2003.

Duke, Charles R. "Strategies for Stimulating Informal Writing to Learn." *Assessing Writing across the Curriculum.* Ed. Charles R. Duke and Rebecca Sanchez. Durham, NC: Carolina Academic Press, 2001. 1–14.

Ede, Lisa, and Andrea Lunsford. "Audience Addressed/Audience Invoked: The Role of Audience in Composition Theory and Pedagogy." *Cross-Talk in Comp Theory: A Reader.* Ed. Victor Villanueva, Jr. Urbana, IL: NCTE, 1997. 77–95.

Elbow, Peter. "Closing My Eyes As I Speak: An Argument for Ignoring Audience." *The Writing Teacher's Sourcebook.* 4th ed. Ed. Edward P. J. Corbett, Nancy Myers, and Gary Tate. New York: Oxford UP, 2000. 335–52.

———. "Writing First!" *Educational Leadership* 62.2 (2004): 8–13.

———. *Writing without Teachers.* New York: Oxford UP, 1973.

Emig, Janet. *The Composing Process of Twelfth Graders.* Urbana, IL: NCTE, 1971.

Finding Forrester. Dir. Gus Van Sant. Columbia Pictures, 2000.

Fitzgerald, Jill. *Towards Knowledge in Writing: Illustrations from Revision Studies.* New York: Springer-Verlag, 1992.

Fleischman, Paul. *Joyful Noise: Poems for Two Voices.* New York: Scholastic, 1988.

Fletcher, Ralph. "A Love of Words." *Language Development: A Reader for Teachers.* Ed. Brenda Miller Power and Ruth Shagoury Hubbard. Englewood Cliffs, NJ: Prentice-Hall, 1996. 139–45.

Flower, Linda S., and John R. Hayes. "A Cognitive Process Theory of Writing." *College Composition and Communication* 32 (1981): 365–87.

Freedman, Aviva, and Peter Medway, eds. *Learning and Teaching Genre.* Portsmouth, NH: Boynton/Cook, 1994.

Friedman, Thomas L. *The Lexus and the Olive Tree: Understanding Globalization.* New York: Anchor, 2000.

Fritz, Jean. *Leonardo's Horse.* New York: Putnam's, 2001.

Fulkerson, Richard. "Four Philosophies of Composition." *The Writing Teacher's Sourcebook.* 4th ed. Ed. Edward P. J. Corbett, Nancy Myers, and Gary Tate. New York: Oxford UP, 2000. 3–8.

Gabler, Neal. *Life the Movie: How Entertainment Conquered Reality.* New York: Knopf, 1998.

Gardner, Howard. *The Unschooled Mind: How Children Think and How Schools Should Teach.* New York: Basic, 1991.

Gere, Anne Ruggles, Leila Christenbury, and Kelly Sassi. *Writing on Demand: Best Practices and Strategies for Success.* Portsmouth, NH: Heinemann, 2005.

Graves, Donald. "An Examination of the Writing Processes of Seven-Year-Old Children." *Research in the Teaching of English* 9 (1975): 227–41.

Greene, Stuart. "Exploring the Relationship between Authorship and Reading." *Hearing Ourselves Think: Cognitive Research in the College Writing Classroom.* Ed. Ann M. Penrose and Barbara M. Sitko. New York: Oxford UP, 1993. 33–51.

Hakaim, Charles J., Jr. "A Most Rare Vision: Improvisations on 'A Midsummer Night's Dream.'" *English Journal* 82.7 (1993): 67–70.

Hansen, Kristine. English 315 style packet. Brigham Young University, Provo, UT. 1997.

Hillenbrand, Laura. *Seabiscuit: An American Legend.* New York: Ballantine, 2001.

Hillocks, George, Jr. *Research on Written Composition: New Directions for Teaching.* Urbana, IL: National Conference on Research in English, 1986.

———. *Teaching Writing as Reflective Practice.* New York: Teacher's College P, 1995.

———. *The Testing Trap: How State Writing Assessments Control Learning.* New York: Teachers College P, 2002.

———. *Ways of Thinking, Ways of Teaching.* New York: Teachers College P, 1999.

Hobbs, Catherine. "Learning from the Past: Verbal and Visual Literacy in Early Modern Rhetoric and Writing Pedagogy." *Language and Image in the Reading-Writing Classroom.* Ed. Kristie S. Fleckenstein, Linda T. Calendrillo, and Demetrice A. Worley. Mahwah, NJ: Lawrence Erlbaum, 2002. 27–44.

Hopkinson, Deborah. *Birdie's Lighthouse.* New York: Atheneum, 1997.

Horning, Alice S. "Revising Research Writing: A Theory and Some Exercises." *Acts of Revision: A Guide for Writers.* Ed. Wendy Bishop. Portsmouth, NH: Boynton/Cook, 2004. 38–50.

Johnson, T. R. *A Rhetoric of Pleasure: Prose Style and Today's Composition Classroom.* Portsmouth, NH: Boynton/Cook, 2003.

Joyce, Bruce, and Marsha Weil, eds. *Models of Teaching.* 5th ed. Boston: Allyn & Bacon, 1996.

Kitzhaber, Albert. *Rhetoric in American Colleges, 1850–1900.* Dallas: Southern Methodist UP, 1990.

Kurlansky, Mark. *The Cod's Tale.* New York: Putnam's, 2001.

———. *Salt.* New York: Penguin, 2002.

Lane, Barry. *After the End: Teaching and Learning Creative Revision.* Portsmouth, NH: Heinemann, 1993.

Langer, Judith A., and Arthur N. Applebee. *How Writing Shapes Thinking: A Study of Teaching and Learning.* Urbana, IL: NCTE, 1987.

Larson, Erik. *The Devil in the White City: Murder, Magic, and Madness at the Fair That Changed America.* New York: Vintage, 2004.

Larson, Richard L. "Revision as Self-Assessment." *Self-Assessment and Development in Writing.* Ed. Jane Bowman Smith and Kathleen Blake Yancey. Cresskill, NJ: Hampton, 2000. 97–103.

———. "The 'Research Paper' in the Writing Course: A Non-Form of Writing." *College English* 44 (1982): 811–816. Rpt. in *The Writing Teacher's Sourcebook.* 4th ed. Ed. Edward P. J. Corbett, Nancy Myers, and Gary Tate. New York: Oxford UP, 2000. 216–21.

Lee, Harper. *To Kill a Mockingbird.* New York: Warner, 1960.

Macrorie, Ken. "The Reawakening of Curiosity: Research Papers as Hunting Stories." *Practical Ideas for Teaching Writing as a Process.* Ed. Carol Booth Olson. Sacramento: California State Department of Education, 1987. 127–38.

Mannis, Celeste. *One Leaf Rides the Wind.* New York: Viking, 2002.

———. *The Queen's Progress.* New York: Viking, 2003.

Martin, Bill. "A Writing Assignment / A Way of Life." *English Journal* 92.6 (2003): 52–56.

McComiskey, Bruce. "The Importance of Being Accurate." *Ideas Plus: A Collection of Practical Teaching Ideas, Book Nine.* Urbana, IL: NCTE, 1991. 63–64.

McDonald, Megan. *My House Has Stars.* New York: Orchard, 1996.

Maxwell, Rhoda J., and Mary Jordan Meiser. *Teaching English in Middle and Secondary Schools.* 4th ed. Upper Saddle River, NJ: Pearson/Merrill/Prentice Hall, 2005.

Meeks, Lynn Langer. "Making English Classes Happier Places to Learn." *English Journal* 88.4 (1999): 73–80.

Miller, Carolyn. "Genre as Social Action." *Quarterly Journal of Speech* 70 (1984): 151–167.

Monceaux, Morgan. *Jazz: My Music, My People.* New York: Knopf, 1994.

Murray, Donald M. *The Craft of Revision.* 3rd ed. Fort Worth: Harcourt Brace, 1998.

Nagin, Carl, and National Writing Project. *Because Writing Matters: Improving Student Writing in Our Schools.* San Francisco: Jossey-Bass, 2003.

Nagy, William E., and Patricia A. Herman. "Incidental vs. Instructional Approaches to Increasing Reading Vocabulary." *Issues and Trends in Literacy Education.* Ed. Richard D. Robinson, Michael C. McKenna, and Judy M. Wedman. Boston: Allyn & Bacon, 1996. 255–66.

Neubert, Gloria A., and Sally J. McNelis. "Peer Response: Teaching Specific Revision Suggestions." *English Journal* 79.5 (1990): 52–56.

Nichol, Barbara. *Beethoven Lives Upstairs.* New York: Orchard, 1993.

Nodin, Harry. *Image Grammar.* Portsmouth, NH: Boynton/Cook, 1999.

Noguchi, Rei R. *Grammar and the Teaching of Writing: Limits and Possibilities.* Urbana, IL: NCTE, 1991.

Nokes, Jeffery D., and Janice A. Dole. "Helping Adolescent Readers through Explicit Strategy Instruction." *Adolescent Literacy Research and Practice.* Ed. Tamara L. Jetton and Janice A. Dole. New York: Guilford, 2004. 162–82.

Ong, Walter J. "The Writer's Audience Is Always a Fiction." *Cross-Talk in Comp Theory: A Reader.* Ed. Victor Villanueva, Jr. Urbana, IL: NCTE, 1997. 55–76.

Park, Douglas B. "The Meanings of 'Audience.'" *The Writing Teacher's Sourcebook.* 4th ed. Ed. Edward P. J. Corbett, Nancy Myers, and Gary Tate. New York: Oxford UP, 2000. 310–19.

Payne, Lucile Vaughan. *The Lively Art of Writing.* Chicago: Follett, 1965.

Petraglia, Joseph. "Is There Life after Process? The Role of Social Scientism in a Changing Discipline." *Post-Process Theory: Beyond the Writing-Process Paradigm.* Ed. Thomas Kent. Carbondale: Southern Illinois UP, 1999. 49–64.

———. "Writing as an Unnatural Act." *Reconceiving Writing, Rethinking Writing Instruction.* Mahwah, NJ: Lawrence Erlbaum, 1995. 79–100.

Pirie, Bruce. *Reshaping High School English.* Urbana, IL: NCTE, 1997.

Piven, Joshua, and David Borgenicht. *The Worst-Case Scenario Survival Handbook, Student Edition.* New York: Scholastic, 2001.

Porter-O'Donnell, Carol. "Beyond the Yellow Highlighter: Teaching Annotation Skills to Improve Reading Comprehension." *English Journal* 93.5 (2004): 82–89.

Pugh, Sharon L., Jean Wolph Hicks, and Marcia Davis. *Metaphorical Ways of Knowing: The Imaginative Nature of Thought and Expression.* Urbana, IL: NCTE, 1997.

Ramage, John D., and John C. Bean. *The Allyn and Bacon Guide to Writing: Brief Edition.* Boston: Allyn & Bacon, 1997.

Reither, James. "Writing and Knowing: Toward Redefining the Writing Process." *The Writing Teacher's Sourcebook.* 4th ed. Ed. Edward P. J.

Corbett, Nancy Myers, and Gary Tate. New York: Oxford UP, 2000. 286–93.

Rentschler, Kay. "Accessorizing the Scoops of Summer." *New York Times* 30 June 2004. 30 June 2004 <http://query.nytimes.com/gst/abstract.html?res=F40617F93E5C0C738FDDAF0894DC404482>.

Romano, Tom. *Blending Genre, Altering Style.* Portsmouth, NH: Heinemann, 2000.

———. *Crafting Authentic Voice.* Portsmouth, NH: Heinemann, 2004.

Ryder, Phyllis Mentzell, Elizabeth Vander Lei, and Duane H. Roen. "Audience Considerations for Evaluating Writing." *Evaluating Writing: The Role of Teachers' Knowledge about Text, Learning, and Culture.* Ed. Charles R. Cooper and Lee Odell. Urbana, IL: NCTE, 1999. 53–71.

Schlosser, Eric. *Fast Food Nation: The Dark Side of the All-American Meal.* New York: Perennial, 2002.

Schriver, Karen. "Revising for Readers: Audience Awareness in the Writing Classroom." *Hearing Ourselves Think: Cognitive Research in the College Writing Classroom.* Ed. Ann M. Penrose and Barbara M. Sitko. New York: Oxford UP, 1993. 147–69.

Sebranek, Patrick, Dave Kemper, and Verne Meyer. *Writers Inc: A Student Handbook for Writing and Learning.* Wilmington, MA: Great Source Education Group, 2001.

Siu-Runyan, Yvonne. "Writing Nonfiction: Helping Students Teach Others What They Know." *Making Facts Come Alive: Choosing Quality Nonfiction Literature K–8.* Ed. Rosemary A. Bamford and Janice V. Kristo. Norwood, MA: Christopher Gordon, 1998. 169–78.

Smagorinsky, Peter. "How Reading Model Essays Affects Writers." *Reading/Writing Connections: Learning from Research.* Ed. Judith W. Irwin and Mary Anne Doyle. Newark, DE: IRA, 1992. 160–76.

Smith, Gary. "The Ball (An American Story)." *Sports Illustrated.* 29 July 2002: 63–79.

Soven, Margot Iris. *Teaching Writing in Middle and Secondary Schools: Theory, Research, and Practice.* Boston: Allyn & Bacon, 1999.

Spandel, Vicki. *Creating Writers through 6-Trait Writing Assessment and Instruction.* 3rd ed. New York: Addison Wesley Longman, 2001.

———. "How to Be a Shark." *WriteTraits 6-Trait Instruction and Assessment 3-Day Workshop Materials.* Salt Lake City, UT. November 5–7, 2001.

Strong, William. *Coaching Writing: The Power of Guided Practice.* Portsmouth, NH: Heinemann, 2001.

Thomson, Ian. "How to Beef Up and Be a Bully." *Sports Illustrated* 99 (27 October 2003): 80.

Tyson, Leigh Ann. *An Interview with Harry the Tarantula.* Washington, DC: National Geographic, 2003.

Weathers, Winston. "The Grammars of Style: New Options in Composition." *Rhetoric and Composition: A Sourcebook for Teachers and Writers.* 3rd ed. Ed. Richard L. Graves. Portsmouth, NH: Boynton/Cook Heinemann, 1990. 200–14.

Weitzman, Jacqueline Preiss. *You Can't Take a Balloon into the Metropolitan Museum.* New York: Dial Books, 1998.

White, Edward M. "Using Scoring Guides to Assess Writing." *A Sourcebook for Responding to Student Writing.* Ed. Richard Straub. Cresskill, NJ: Hampton, 1999. 203–19.

Williams, Vera B., and Jennifer Williams. *Stringbean's Trip to the Shining Sea.* New York: Scholastic, 1988.

Winchester, Simon. *The Meaning of Everything.* New York: Oxford UP, 2003.

———. *The Professor and the Madman.* New York: HarperCollins, 1998.

Wisniewski, David. *The Secret Knowledge of Grown-Ups.* New York: HarperCollins, 2001.

Wright-Frierson, Virginia. *An Island Scrapbook: Dawn to Dusk on a Barrier Island.* New York: Aladdin, 2002.

Yancey, Kathleen Blake. *Reflection in the Writing Classroom.* Logan: Utah State UP, 1998.

Zarnowski, Myra, Richard M. Kerper, and Julie M. Jensen, eds. *The Best in Children's Nonfiction: Reading, Writing, and Teaching Orbis Pictus Award Books.* Urbana, IL: NCTE, 2001.

Index

Author

Deborah Dean, a former junior high and high school teacher, is associate professor of English education at Brigham Young University, where she teaches undergraduate courses in writing and grammar instruction and general language arts teaching methods, along with first-year and advanced writing classes. Since moving to Utah, she has also taught as a volunteer at a local high school. Dean has published articles in *English Journal*, *Voices from the Middle*, *Journal of Adolescent and Adult Literacy*, *English Leadership Quarterly*, and *Syntax in the Schools*.

This book was typeset in Palatino and Helvetica by Electronic Imaging.
The typeface used on the cover was Minstrella.
The book was printed on 50-lb. Williamsburg Offset paper by Versa Press, Inc.